War and Social Theory

Also by Neal Curtis

AGAINST AUTONOMY: Lyotard, Judgement and Action

War and Social Theory

World, Value and Identity

Neal Curtis

First published 2006 by
PALGRAVE MACMILLAN
Houndmills, Basingstoke, Hampshire RG21 6XS and
175 Fifth Avenue, New York, N.Y. 10010
Companies and representatives throughout the world

PALGRAVE MACMILLAN is the global academic imprint of the Palgrave Macmillan division of St. Martin's Press, LLC and of Palgrave Macmillan Ltd. Macmillan® is a registered trademark in the United States, United Kingdom and other countries. Palgrave is a registered trademark in the European Union and other countries.

ISBN 978-1-349-51681-0   ISBN 978-0-230-50197-3 (eBook)
DOI 10.1057/9780230501973

This book is printed on paper suitable for recycling and made from fully managed and sustained forest sources.

A catalogue record for this book is available from the British Library.

Library of Congress Cataloging-in-Publication Data
Curtis, Neal.
    War and social theory : world, value, and identity / Neal Curtis.
        p.   cm.
    Includes bibliographical references and index.

    1. War (Philosophy)   2. Sociology—Philosophy.   I. Title.
    JZ6390.C87 2005
    355.02—dc22   2005051281

10   9   8   7   6   5   4   3   2   1
15   14   13   12   11   10   09   08   07   06

*This book is dedicated to my Grandfather, Henry Curtis,
and to my Great Uncle, Cecil Till,
who had to live having returned without 'Harry'.*

This page intentionally left blank

Contents

Acknowledgements

This book is indebted to a course entitled 'The Images and Rhetoric of Conflict' that I was fortunate enough to teach at Anglia Polytechnic University. The course was devised by Pat Coyle who was determined that students taking a Communications Studies degree should be given the opportunity to reflect upon one of the most intractable problems of human relations. I would also like to thank the students who between the years 2000 and 2004 tried with me to make sense of the 'election' of George W. Bush, '9/11', the announcement of a war against terror, the invasion of Afghanistan, and the invasion and occupation of Iraq. I would also like to acknowledge the support of colleagues who commented on drafts and helped clarify certain issues. In particular, a word of gratitude should go to William Hutson, Matt Connell, Tanya Horeck, Neil Turnbull, Couze Venn, Joss Hands and Constantina Papoulias. Finally and most importantly, I would like to thank my partner Amber. Without her unbelievable support and commitment this book would not have appeared. At a key point in the writing process a little boy called Noah arrived on the scene and in a wonderful way turned our lives upside down.

Introduction

In the wake of the events of 11 September 2001 and the announcement of the war against terror, there was a flurry of publications from within the social sciences and the humanities on the subject of war. The ensuing debates brought to academic attention the great wealth of writings on war in these fields, and yet at the same time this reinvigoration of an interest in war served to show just how marginal an issue it had been. For Hans Joas (2003) the reason for this lies in our conception of modernity. It is as if war is merely an aberration that modernity would correct. Understood as the road away from immaturity, barbarity and the particularities of tribalism, modernity is a beacon of civility and universality; a relatively autonomous intellectual journey of reason towards enlightenment. In this sense modernity is transcendent, lifting itself and its adherents above the violent and aggressive impulses of earlier stages of human development. However, despite modernity's idealization as pacific progress, it is inextricably tied to the violence of political revolution and the wars that issued from it. In addition, warfare in the modern age has been profoundly shaped by two technical revolutions, the gunpowder revolution of the sixteenth century and the industrial revolution of the nineteenth century that have made it evermore destructive. Despite this intimate history between war and modernity, advocates of the modernizing project have always managed to exempt modernity from its implication in outbreaks of violence precisely because violence is the persistence of that which modernity is charged with overcoming. This logic was very much in evidence at the beginning of the twentieth century in the language of a German *Sonderweg*. This construction of an alternative path taken by Germany ensured that the narrative of an evolutionary, rational modernity might be maintained. And yet while we are told that war is anathema to modernity it appears that today, as Michael Hardt and Antonio Negri argue, 'instead of moving forward to peace in fulfilment of this dream we seem to have slipped back in time into the nightmare of a perpetual and indeterminate state of war [which] seems to have seeped back and flooded the entire social field' (2005: 7). War, then, is no longer the exceptional state, but is 'the primary organizing principle of society' (12).

While the significance of warfare is historically specific, the definition of war has remained consistent. Martin Shaw defines war as 'the clash of two organized armed forces that seek to destroy each other's power and especially their will to resist, principally by killing members of the opposing force' (2003: 5). To this, Brian E. Fogarty (2000) would add that war is a social enterprise involving an understanding that killing is legitimate, and an agreement that war is engaged; while Jean Baudrillard (1995), with an eye on the ever-increasing discrepancies of military might, adds that war is also a conflictual situation where the outcome is not predetermined. Without this very important rider war is reduced to a form of police action in which a vastly superior force simply arrests activity that is not in its interest. For a number of commentators, Hardt and Negri being among them, the war against terror epitomizes this challenge to the status of war in which the post-Cold War era is no longer split into bipolar superpowers but governed by one militarily massive hyperpower. While this radical shift in the balance of power as well as potentially revolutionary advances in military technology single out the current era of warfare, it is also noteworthy for the fact that the war against terror claims to be a war in defence of modernity as *a way of life*.[1]

Much of the rhetoric used when speaking of Al'Qaeda deploys the image of a modern us, with modern being used as a synonym for 'civilized', 'advanced' and 'free', against a primitive, that is 'barbaric', 'backward' and 'tyrannical' them. This language is problematic for a number of reasons, two of which I wish to highlight here. The first is the assumption already mentioned that modernity is a singular and necessarily pacific phenomenon, and that its history is coterminous with the development of the West. I will approach this in a little more detail below. The second is the failure to recognize what is modern about Al'Qaeda. It is undoubtedly the case that in some respects the practice of martyrdom does indeed correspond to a pre-modern age in which war and warrior-like behaviour was stitched into the fabric of individual and social identity. In the West, pre-modern texts, such as Greek epic poetry and the Celtic saga, speak to us of a time when partaking in battle was integral to a sense of belonging. In a succinct analysis of Homeric (heroic) society, Alasdair MacIntyre (1985) argues that proving oneself in battle was important because it displayed virtues necessary to sustaining a household and a community. Virtues such as courage and fidelity proved someone to be reliable and trustworthy and were integral to kinship structures. In this regard the moral and the social were homologous. A person's identity, the place they were assigned within a society determined what they owed others and what was in turn owed to them. Most importantly, however, narratives of heroic deeds not only told what happened to men and women but exhibited an exemplary succession of incidents that were to be followed. As MacIntyre notes, 'courage in heroic society is a capacity not just to face particular harms and dangers but to face a particular kind of pattern of harms and dangers, a pattern in which individual lives find their place' (1985: 125). These narratives therefore detailed activities that were to be sought out if a person was to take up their place within a given community. In this sense the practice of martyrdom is a narrative identity in which certain deeds are set before an individual detailing their place and what they owe, in this case to God and to the community of true believers.

Beyond this it is difficult to see what is not modern about Al'Qaeda, unless modernity is tied exclusively to the Western path of secularization, which is increasingly untenable. Al'Qaeda participate in and are made possible by the deregulated flows of capital, images and people across the globe, and as both Paul Berman (2003) and John Gray (2003) have argued, the predecessors of these terrorist cells do not lie in the Muslim tradition but in the very modern European pursuit of a 'new world'.[2] Gray concludes his study of Al'Qaeda and modernity with the claim that it is not the millions of people killed in Nazi death camps, or Soviet and Moaist gulags that is modern. 'It is the belief that as a result of these deaths a new world would be born' (2003: 117). Likewise Berman refers to Islamist leaders from Sayid Qutb and Sati al-Husri to Osama bin Laden as 'hyphenated personalities' (2003: 26), educated in the West with a particular interest in existentialism, German Idealism and Romantic literary fashion, all of which he argues contributed to the European cults of death that plagued late nineteenth and early twentieth-century Europe culminating in Mussolini and Hitler. As Berman writes, after the devastation of the First World War 'these were the years when "vanguards" of self-sacrificing militants tried to lead mankind out of the corruptions and horrors of liberal civilization into a new kind of life' (118).[3]

That war is inextricably tied to modernity and the particular formation of it that achieved hegemony in the seventeenth century is little understood. Stephen Toulmin (1990) is an exception here. He has shown how the very shape of modernity as we have come to understand it was a direct response to a period of protracted and destabilizing conflict in Europe. The effect of the Thirty Years War (1618–1648) was to see the fading of an earlier humanist modernity, epitomized in the writings of Montaigne, and the emergence of a rationalist modernity, or Enlightenment, best represented by the writings of Descartes. 'By 1620', writes

Toulmin, 'people in positions of political power and theological authority in Europe no longer saw Montaigne's pluralism as a viable intellectual option [...]. The humanists' readiness to live with uncertainty, ambiguity, and differences of opinion had done nothing (in their view) to prevent religious conflict from getting out of hand [...]. If scepticism let one down, certainty was more urgent. It might not be obvious what one was supposed to be certain about, but *un*certainty had become *un*acceptable' (1990: 55). Rationalistic modernity, then, is not an inevitable movement of human reason but an urgent response to a devastating war, and if we leap some three hundred years later, yet another war, one that witnessed gas chambers and the atomic bomb, precipitated a commensurate *turning away* from the rationalist project and a reassessment of the embodied, embedded, plural and particularistic philosophy rejected earlier. Observing the European catastrophe that was the Second World War, Theodore Adorno and Max Horkheimer wrote that 'the fully enlightened earth radiates disaster triumphant' (1986: 3). For them totalitarianism was not a departure from enlightened modernity because enlightenment itself behaves as a dictator. It reduces difference to sameness and 'excises the incommensurable' (12). Almost fifty years later the totalitarian spirit of modernity became part of Zygmunt Bauman's post-modern sociology (1989, 1991). For him modernity, where the task of producing order was the archetype of all tasks, signalled 'an era of particularly bitter and relentless war against ambivalence' (1991: 3). In both cases, modernity in its tendency towards abstraction, uniformity and universality, with the concomitant reduction of difference to sameness, was read as inherently violent.

In his study of war and modernity, Joas identifies a number of teleological narratives that encapsulate the modern dream of overcoming war and the violence that undermined progress; and given that it is the avowed intent of the US government to deliver political and economic freedom across the globe it is the republican and utilitarian narratives that are of specific interest in the context of the war against terror. While peace and moderation exemplify the spirit of a republic, for utilitarians these qualities were also carried by free trade. With regard to republicanism Immanuel Kant understood nature in terms of discord, and yet, through an intriguing and eschatological twist, was able to think beyond 'men's inevitable *antagonism*' (1983: 34) only because in the end nature is providential. Through wars man's intentions are over-ridden by nature's objective to bring about new relations and form new bodies from the destruction of older ones. In Kant's essay on perpetual peace, it is the republican aim of international or cosmopolitan right that is believed to contribute to the curtailment of wars. Here peace is understood as the recognition of each person before the law sharing in a common humanity. Kant's belief in a cosmopolitan idea is supported, he argues, by the homage every nation pays to the concept of right, proving that 'there is in man a still greater [...] moral aptitude to master the evil principle in himself [...] and to hope that others will also overcome it' (1983: 116). Recognition, then, of every person as a citizen of the world with inalienable rights becomes the republican vision of democracy and the rule of law.

For utilitarians, war and commerce were contradictory principles. As Michael Howard notes, the utilitarian belief was that no one benefited from wars except for a few contractors and arms manufacturers. War depleted rather than increased wealth. 'Trade should be free, they argued, since economic rivalry was a powerful contributory cause of wars. [...] The laws of nature dictated harmony and co-operation. Providence had linked mankind by a chain of reciprocal needs which made impossible, *a priori*, any clash of economic interests. It was only a misconception of such interests [...] that lead to conflict and war' (1986: 25). Free trade was thus the path to both power and peace. While it is undoubted that international trade has played an important role in intercultural dialogue, setting up new lines of communication where none previously existed, and that the United Nations, the political result of the cosmopolitan spirit, is the most important tool we have to engage in constructive debate rather than destructive confrontation, both the utilitarian and republican traditions have their dark side. For republicanism, the dark side is the failure to see what is particular in its supposedly universal vision of freedom. For utilitarianism, the dark side is the history of colonialism and imperial expansion. In this instance the civilizing aspect of commerce went hand in hand with all manner of barbarous acts, from slavery and genocide, to suppression and persecution. Of course, proponents of utilitarianism would like to distinguish between the economic and the political, that is between, let us say, mercantile exchange or free trade, and the aspirations of state power, but it is very difficult to separate the market, no matter how idealized, from the realism of foreign policy. From the events in Bolivia in 1999 where six people were killed and 175 injured during demonstrations following the US engineering firm Bechtel's acquisition of Bolivian water (Roy, 2002: 136–7), to the genocidal war in the former Yugoslavia that John McMurtry argues resulted from the planned elimination of its socialized economy and its forced entry into the free market (2002: 37–8), the relationship between finance, trade and violence is becoming increasingly hard to mask. Of course, the benefits of trade are evident if one considers the improvement to be made to developing economies if trade regulations were not flagrantly set to the advantage of the already developed world, but again this only highlights how difficult it is to separate issues of trade from issues of power. And  with modernization now being a euphemism for the unfettered expansion of the global market, Western neo-liberal modernity is becoming increasingly embroiled in a value war that recognizes plurality only as a set of differing consumer practices to be administered by the market.

That market forces are seen as the panacea for global problems is wonderfully illustrated by US national security proposals contained in the FutureMAP project. As a weapon in the war against terror, which is a deregulated war against a networked enemy, working within the managed disorder of deterritorialized capital flows, globalized mediascapes, and a transnational criminal economy of money laundering and drug trafficking, the US Department of Defense decided to combat this deregulated risk by fighting fire with fire, proposing that market-based methods of assessment should be deployed to predict future threats:

> FutureMAP will concentrate on market-based techniques for avoiding surprise and predicting future events. Strategic decisions depend upon the accurate assessment of the likelihood of future events. [...] There is potential for application of market-based methods to analyses of interest to the DoD [Department of Defense]. These may include analysis of political stability in regions of the world, prediction of the timing and impact on national security of emerging technologies, analysis of the outcomes of advanced technology programs, or other future events of interest to the DoD. In addition, the rapid reaction of markets to knowledge held by only a few participants may provide an early warning system to avoid surprise.[4]

In a news release of 29 July 2003, after the 'market in death' had been met with incredulity in the international media as well as hostility within the US Senate, DARPA announced their withdrawal from FutureMAP and thereby its cancellation. FutureMAP remains, however, testimony to the mindset of the world's pre-eminent economic and military power, both in terms of their faith in marketized solutions and in their vision of an anonymous foe, and as such it is a defining statement regarding the logic of war and peace at the beginning of the twenty-first century.

The fact that the market is currently seen as the global solution for all social ills reveals an important truth about war that was not included in the brief definitions from Shaw, Fogarty and Baudrillard given above. The claim that terrorists are at war with modernity, understood as political, social and economic freedom demonstrates how wars are as much a matter of interpreting and valuing as they are about fighting. Wars may be physical conflicts, but they are also about ascribing, defending and furthering particular worlds. It is therefore important to recognize that valuations are not separate from the violence of war, rather valuing itself is conflictual and potentially warlike. Joas writes: 'For all the differences, there are in fact parallels or structural homologies between the experience underlying the constitution of values and the experience of violence – whether suffered or perpetuated. The experience of violence is the "perverted twin" of the experience of value commitment' (2003: 18–9). And it is this claim that wars, as interpretation-intensive activities, are as much about preserving and perhaps extending a sense of worldhood that is the main theme of this book. This means that while the physics or logistics of warfare are addressed, my main concern is what might be called the metaphysics or ontology of war, that is the organization of good and evil, order and chaos, self and other, human and inhuman, subject and object, identity and difference, life and death, that are central to the grammar of warfare and central to the making and preserving of worlds. What follows, then, are eight studies of war from within sociology, philosophy and psychoanalysis. Each chapter seeks to give a full account of the theoretical positions being addressed and can be read independently of the rest of the book, but an attempt is also made to draw out those components that might contribute in a preliminary way to this ontology of war. Given that the war against terror is used to legitimize the extension of a very specific set of values across the globe, a consideration of this theme is therefore both apposite and urgent.

This page intentionally left blank

1
Power and *Polemos*

One of the most significant statements concerning the nature of war is to be found in Heraclitus. Fragment 53 reads as follows: 'War [*polemos*] is father of all, and king of all. He renders some gods, others men; he makes some slaves, others free' (Heraclitus, 1987: 37).[1] On face value this fragment proposes that war is the determining principle in the flux of the cosmos; that life is in essence a conflictual struggle. But while history certainly testifies to the centrality of conflict in human affairs, and this chapter assumes that conflict is a central aspect of our being-in-the-world, this fragment will be used to argue against the simple equation that life is a violent struggle between competing forces. For Heraclitus, polemos is father and king; it is generative (father) and governing or ruling (king); it is productive and it is preserving; it brings things into being and maintains them in their being. Taking such a reading, polemos is not simply a violent struggle of becoming between already existing beings, it is the very possibility of one being standing against, alongside and even *with* another. It is the very exposition of beings. It is world-creation, and it is in this sense that this fragment will be important for us.

In a lecture course entitled *An Introduction to Metaphysics*, Martin Heidegger interprets the fragment in the following way:

> The *polemos* named here is a conflict that prevailed prior to everything divine and human, not a war in the human sense. This conflict, as Heraclitus thought it, first caused the realm of being to separate into opposites; it first gave rise to position and order and rank. In such separation cleavages, intervals, distances, and joints opened. In the conflict a world comes into being. (Conflict does not split, much less destroy unity, it is a binding-together, *logos. Polemos* and *logos* are the same). (1959: 62)

In a fascinating study of the importance of polemos in Heidegger's philosophy, Gregory Fried (2000) shows how this reading describes two fundamental aspects of our involvement with the world. First, it reveals the manner in which beings become present, how they come to be and how they pass away, and secondly, and most important for our concerns here, polemos also describes the way in which beings are constantly an issue for us, and nowhere is this more in evidence than in the questions we have concerning our *own* being. Heidegger opens the lecture course by stating that the question of why there are beings rather than nothing is the first of all philosophical questions. Each one of us is touched by this question at some point, he contends, especially at times of despair when 'all meaning becomes obscured' (1959: 1). Our capacity to be touched by the question means that the question can best be answered by interrogating the nature of our own being-in-the-world. Thus in *Being and Time* Heidegger argues that 'to work out the question of being adequately, we must make an entity transparent in its own Being. [...] This entity which each of us is himself and which includes inquiring as one of the possibilities of its Being, we shall denote by the term "*Dasein*" ' (1962: 27). The enquiry into why Being rather than nothing starts with an enquiry into Dasein, that is, our being-there.

The essence of Dasein lies in its existence, its characteristics are not properties but are 'possible ways for it to be' (67). And it is in this important understanding of human being as the creation of possible worlds that the concept of polemos will be important for understanding the nature of war. What is central for human being is that as Dasein it cannot be indifferent to its being, rather its being is an issue for it. It is always *mine* to be in one way or another, that is, Dasein always makes decisions about its own possibility, 'it *can*, in its very Being, "choose" itself and win itself' (68). In this sense Dasein's existence can be said to be hermeneutic; it is a matter of each Dasein interpreting and (possibly) creating the world anew. Human being as Dasein is 'thrown' into a world, into a history and a language, into a world that is never simply given but always given *as* something. Once thrown into the world Dasein projects its own possibilities and potentialities through an interpretation of itself and the other beings with which it is involved. This involvement is an *interpretive confrontation* through which a world becomes meaningful. As Fried notes: 'For Heidegger, the task of this polemos is never merely an academic controversy, the topic of entertainment, or even victory in war, but rather that which is given to us in our historicity as *what matters to us* [...]. This Being-at-issue of the polemos is ultimately what underlies Heidegger's ontological politics' (2000: 31–2). To understand Heidegger's treatment of polemos, and to develop a conception of interpretive confrontation relevant to our context, it is important to work through Heidegger's engagement with Nietzsche. This will provide a means for understanding the persistence of war as well as a possible critique.[2]

Power

Nietzsche's philosophy can only be understood as a response to what he saw as the nihilism pervading Europe in the second half of the nineteenth century. Consequently, in *The Gay Science* he states:

> I welcome all signs that a more virile, warlike age is about to begin, which will restore honor to courage above all. For this age shall prepare the way for the one yet higher, and it shall gather the strength that this higher age will require some day – the age that will carry heroism into the search for knowledge and that will *wage wars* for the sake of ideas and their consequences. To this end we now need many preparatory courageous human beings who cannot very well leap out of nothing, any more than out of the sand and slime of present-day civilization and metropolitanism – human beings who know how to be silent, lonely, resolute, and content and constant in invisible activities; human beings who are bent on seeking in all things for what in them must be *overcome* [...]. For believe me: the secret for harvesting from existence the greatest fruitfulness and the greatest enjoyment is – to *live dangerously*! Build your cities on the slopes of Vesuvius! Send your ships into uncharted seas! Live at war with your peers and yourselves! (1974: 228)

For Nietzsche, the person that epitomizes the virile future and higher age to come is Napoleon, representing neither the 'blooming universal exchange of hearts' (318) promised by the French revolution, nor the pettiness of national movements that were leading Europe into chaos. With Napoleon 'we have entered *the classical age of war* [which] the coming centuries will look back on with envy and awe for its perfection' (318).

Note, however, that Nietzsche does not celebrate war for the sake of war. When war breaks out, he writes, people will rapturously 'throw themselves into the new danger of *death* because the sacrifice for the fatherland seems to them to offer the long desired permission – to *dodge their goal*; war offers a detour to suicide, but a detour with a good conscience' (270). In other words, military heroics is often a way of avoiding the need to be heroic in life, it can too often serve the preservation of the status quo when in fact this is what we should be at war with. The war Nietzsche advocates is not for the homeland, but a war that renders one homeless. He loves neither universalism nor does he support the chauvinisms that counter this universal brotherhood. Those who live dangerously and love adventure 'do not love humanity; but on the other hand we are not nearly "German" enough, in the sense in which the word "German" is constantly used nowadays, to advocate nationalism and race hatred [or] the national scabies of the heart and blood poisoning that now leads the nations of Europe to delimit and barricade themselves against each other as if it were a matter of quarantine. For that we are too openminded [...] too "travelled"' (339). With regard to his homelessness Karl Löwith argues that Nietzsche understood his life in terms of a fateful decision taking place between the old and the new; he was 'a human being at the limit' (1995: 204).

This warlike philosophy, which does not advocate dying for the fatherland or hating one's neighbours, can only be understood in relation to Nietzsche's philosophy of value. The important sentence in the passage quoted from *The Gay Science* regarding the coming virile and warlike age is his call for human beings to seek in everything that which must be overcome. Life, if it is to be meaningful, must be understood as a struggle to practice what is most essential to human beings, namely to give value. In pursuit of this overcoming, Nietzsche does advocate a hardness that many readers and commentators quite rightly find difficult to accept. For example, again in *The Gay Science*, he challenges his readers to seek strength and greatness but to understand they can only do so if they are prepared to inflict great suffering. 'Being able to suffer is the least thing', he argues, 'not to perish of internal distress and uncertainty when one inflicts great suffering and hears the cry of this suffering – that is great, that belongs to greatness (1974: 255). Such statements regarding suffering are often cited as evidence that Nietzsche was immoral, not just amoral in the sense that he may have transcended good and evil, but immoral in the sense that he purposefully turned a deaf ear to the suffering of others in favour of his own will. He does indeed implore us to turn away from suffering in order to affirm joy, and to not get caught up in the pitying discourses of the virtuous and the moralists, that is, to live 'in seclusion so that you can live for yourself' (271), but this is also an argument against becoming involved in the noise of war. Throughout Nietzsche's work there is an ambiguity to war. Warfare is too imbued with the 'religion of pity', or conversely too caught up in the identity of a fatherland, and more often than not it is the work of tyrants, not masters with an understanding of their fateful decision, but men who simply want to breed passivity and extend their domination. If we are to understand the relevance of Nietzsche for an analysis of war, it is necessary to move away from the direct issue of militarized war itself and focus instead on the use of war as an analogy for the struggle to affirm values, or the will to power that is the motor of Nietzsche's overcoming.

In understanding the struggle that was Nietzsche's life and that was so central to his philosophy, the language of conflict is never far away. In *Thus Spoke Zarathustra*, the book published in 1883, a year after *The Gay Science*, and the book in which for the first time he explicitly set out his philosophy of the will to power, he calls on us not to work but to do battle, and to love peace as a means to new wars. 'You should be such men', he announces, 'as are always looking for an enemy – for *your* enemy' (1969: 74). A little later Nietzsche argues that friendship is too often used as a means to hide weakness, as a means to compensate for a lack. We find in others those qualities in which we are most deficient, or we seek in a friend something that confirms our current identity, beliefs and values. Friendship, conventionally understood, is anathema to risk and more closely allied to comfort. For Nietzsche, however, in your friend you should possess your best enemy. Your friend ought to be the locus of the confrontation that will lead each seeker of knowledge onto their *own* path. 'Your heart should feel closest to him when you oppose him' and you should be to him 'an arrow and a longing for the Superman', for 'O my friend, man is something that must be overcome' (83). The enemy like the good warrior is the person that breaks with uniformity and satisfaction, and commends us to this highest of ideas. As Peter Berkowitz has noted, 'Zarathustra believes that loving the friend is identical to loving what is farthest away, because the friend's purpose is precisely to symbolize unachieved freedom and mastery' (1995: 173). To commit oneself to the struggle to overcome and to the conflicts that ensue, this is good, and in a polemical overturning of the logic of the just war Nietzsche mocks those who say it is the good cause that hallows war, when in fact 'it is the good war that hallows every cause!' (1969: 74).

The relationship of struggle is most powerfully expressed in Nietzsche's Foreword to *Ecce Homo*. Here he declares his business to be the over-throw of idols. Nietzsche's philosophy is an undoing of the 'beyond', for him it is the immanent that matters. Thus there is no excuse in the present; there is no *other world* of truth. Man must wrestle for the truth here and now. In the Foreword he states: 'How much truth can a spirit *bare*, how much truth can a spirit *dare*? That became for me more and more the real measure of value. Error [...] is not blindness, error is *cowardice* (1979: 34). Nietzsche's struggle, then, is epitomized by his capacity to suffer and his will to risk all, with the key qualities for an understanding of man and his world shown to be strength and courage. Most notable, however, is Nietzsche's claim that error is not blindness, meaning it is not a question of faulty observation or measurement, it is cowardice. With this one gesture towards the will Nietzsche sums up his entire critique of science as the mode of thought in which truth is to be most fundamentally expressed. For Nietzsche, scientific thinking or what he also refers to as the will to truth is presupposed by an even more fundamental, and one must say primitive, drive to knowledge. Behind every claim to truth is a prior valuing of that truth. A very good example of this is given in Heidegger's essay, 'Nietzsche's word: "God is Dead".' In the essay Heidegger notes how for Nietzsche 'the thought of value is more fundamental than the fundamental thought of certainty in Descartes' metaphysics, since certainty can only count as right if it also counts as the highest value' (2002: 183). Descartes's epistemological reduction failed to recognize the antecedent value given to this search for a secure ground.

In *Beyond Good and Evil*, Nietzsche imagines the many 'strange, wicked, questionable questions' (1990: 33) the will to truth has set before us. Is it any wonder, then, that we should turn impatiently away and ask: What is the value of this will? Consequently, he does not 'believe a "drive to knowledge" to be the father of philosophy, but that another drive [...] has only employed knowledge (and false knowledge!) as a tool' (37). To understand this drive the philosopher needs to examine human instincts, to embark upon a psychology that supposes the moral prejudices and timidities of what has passed as psychology before. Even here the language is of conflict and struggle for each of the human drives practices philosophy, and 'each one of them would be only too glad to present *itself* as the ultimate goal of existence and as the legitimate *master* of all the other drives. For every drive is tyrannical: and it is as such that it tries to philosophize' (37). The tyranny of the will to truth is best seen, Nietzsche argues, when philosophers rapturously claim to have derived their law from nature when in fact these self-deceivers want only to prescribe their morality and their ideal *to* nature. As soon as a philosophy begins to believe in itself, he argues, it 'always creates the world in its own image, it cannot do otherwise;

philosophy is this tyrannical drive itself, the most spiritual will to power, to "creation of the World", to *causa prima'* (1990: 39). This is a hazardous truth, but a truth that only Nietzsche is brave enough to think. Truth is not the objective correspondence between thought and world, but rather the subjective *creation* of a world. Truth is nothing other than an interpreting, evaluating will to power.

The will to power incorporates a constellation of Nietzschean concepts including valuation, revaluation, master and slave, becoming, overcoming and the superman. It is often interpreted as a will to domination, and, as has just been shown, such a reading is not entirely incorrect. The will to power is tyrannical and does seek to create in its own image. It is also an expression of strength, indifferent to suffering and is best conceptualized through analogies of battle, conflict and war. All this lends itself quite easily to a very belligerent reading of Nietzsche's philosophy, and yet to see it purely in terms of power understood as strength or might does greatly reduce its complexity. In this regard I tend to favour Walter Kaufman's (1992) reading of Nietzsche which seeks to draw out the less violent or aggressive aspects of this thinking that are too often forgotten. Kaufman gives the example of a note on Goethe written at the time of *The Gay Science*. It runs as follows: 'The Germans think that *strength* must reveal itself in hardness and cruelty [...] That there is *strength* in mildness and stillness, they do not believe easily. They miss strength in Goethe...!' (in Kaufman, 1992: 92–3). On this reading strength is not domination but creativity. It is having the imagination to invent and the courage to risk all, to see in everything that which must be overcome.

The context or horizon against which Nietzsche's philosophy of the will to power emerges is set out in the parable of the madman in *The Gay Science* who runs into the marketplace shouting incessantly that he seeks God. He then asks the gathering crowd where God has gone, and realizing they do not know he tells them: God is dead and we have killed him! The importance of this statement is contained in its two phrases. The first, God is dead, comments upon the condition of the times whereby, as Heidegger argues in his interpretation, 'the supersensory world has no effective power. It does not bestow life' (2002: 162). The ideal has died. There has been a devaluation of the hitherto highest values and nihilism, to be precise incomplete nihilism stands at the door. The second phrase, stipulating that it is we who have killed him, is the means to complete nihilism, to the realization that it is human beings who create and that we are at the dawn of a new dispensation of values. Complete nihilism is the grasping of this normative phase, an affirmative 'yes' to the new, the seeking out 'of what is most alive' (Heidegger, 2002: 169), whereas incomplete nihilism seeks its escape without any revaluation, seeking refuge in that which is petrified and decomposing. The man speaking of the death of God is mad, of course, because he is ahead of his time.[3]

That valuing is most essential to human beings, or that human beings are no closer to acting according to their essence than when they set values, is the main subject of Zarathustra's discourses. 'A table of values hangs over every people', he declares. 'Behold, it is the table of its overcomings' (1969: 84). Every community has its table of values and every community rewrites it anew. 'Whatever I create', he notes while contemplating self-overcoming, 'and however much I love it – soon I have to oppose it and my love: thus will my will have it' (138). This is not simply a statement about Nietzsche's own propensity to overcome, it is rather a feature of every human culture. Life (and history) tells him, 'I am that which must overcome itself again and again', because 'man is a bridge and not a goal' (215), his evenings are always a way to new dawns.[4] The most pertinent fact for Nietzsche is that no people can live without evaluating. 'Man first implanted values into things to maintain himself – he created the meaning of things, a human meaning! Therefore he calls himself: "Man", that is: the evaluator' (85). What is more, without the creative act of evaluation, 'the nut of existence would be hollow' (85). Nowhere is this made more clear than in the qualification to the observation noted above: 'No people could live without evaluating; *but if it wishes to maintain itself it must not evaluate as its neighbour evaluates*' (84, my italics). Evaluation produces and dispenses both identity and difference. It is world making, world preserving and world changing.

Here is the first reference to valuing as the confrontation between individuals or communities seeking to win their worlds. Too often, however, Nietzsche's references to persons or a people seeking to maintain itself has seen the will to power reduced to a philosophy of self-preservation akin to Darwinism. While the will to power should be understood only as a psychological drive and a condition of the spirit to create and preserve its own world, it is often understood to be a biological drive. This is certainly not helped by Nietzsche's own ambiguous use of language. In *Beyond Good and Evil* for example, he describes evaluations as 'physiological demands for preservation of a certain species of life', and that falseness is not an objection to evaluations, the only question is whether they are 'life-advancing, life-preserving, species-preserving' (1990: 35). However, for evidence that the will to power and the drive to evaluate are not biological we should instead take notice of those moments where Nietzsche states explicitly that self-preservation is only a consequence of the will to power, and that we should 'beware of *superfluous* teleological principles' (1990: 44). In *The Gay Science* he writes:

> The wish to preserve oneself is the symptom of a condition of distress, of a limitation of the really fundamental instinct of life which aims at *the expansion of power* and, wishing for that, frequently risks and even sacrifices self-preservation. It should be considered symptomatic when some philosophers – for example, Spinoza who was consumptive – considered the instinct of self-preservation decisive and *had* to see it that way; for they were individuals in conditions of distress. [...] The whole of English Darwinism breathes something like the musty air of English overpopulation, like the smell of the distress and overcrowding of small people. (1974: 291–2)[5]

In his essay on Nietzsche, Heidegger offers a valuable interpretation of preservation and maintenance as they appear in Nietzsche's philosophy. He refers to aphorism 715 in *The Will to Power*, which reads: 'The standpoint of "value" is the standpoint of conditions of preservation and enhancement for complex forms of relative life-duration within the flux of becoming' (Nietzsche, 1968: 380). In keeping with the quote from *The Gay Science* above, Heidegger argues that for Nietzsche preservation and enhancement mark the fundamental traits of life and that they belong together. 'The desire to grow, increase, is part of the essence of life. To preserve life is to serve the increase of life. Any life that is restricted to mere preservation is already in decline. [...] Increase, however, is only possible where a durable resource has already been preserved' (Heidegger, 2002: 171). For Heidegger, Nietzsche demonstrates that the essence of beings, the being of beings, is the increase of life as will to power and their becoming is characterized by a new dispensation of value which serves as the enduring-preserving realm of future increase. 'Inside of becoming, life, i.e., the living, takes shape as centres of the will to power that are active at particular times. These centres are therefore structures of ruling power. It is as such that Nietzsche understands art, the state, religion, science, society' (172). In this manner, Heidegger continues, so long as Nietzsche understands value as the condition of the preservation and increase of life, and sees life as grounded in becoming, the will to power is revealed as the setting of the necessary conditions for expansion. In other words the growth of life exceeds a biological or physical reduction because the will to power as the esteeming of values 'constitutes the condition of increase and fixes the condition of preservation' (177). The increase in life of animals is set by necessity. An animal's capacity for growth is determined by environmental conditions that it can do little to control. Humans, however, in their freedom have the capacity to determine their conditions for growth and the means for establishing that growth is the will to power, which as Heidegger puts it, is a commanding 'that has at its disposal the possibilities of effective action' (175). This is very much in evidence in Heidegger's critique of technology, but for now we can take from it the notion that the ruling structures of technological power are premised upon the setting of values with regard to nature as mere 'standing-reserve', as a resource open to exploitation, and that such a valuation sets the conditions for our current formation of preservation-increase. This model can also be seen in some of the new writings on empire. Alain Joxe, for example, has argued that the US does not want to conquer the world to ensure order and peace, it would rather 'regulate disorder through norms of behaviour implanted in their allies' (2002: 80). These norms of behaviour express the reading of the will to power given here as the drive to set conditions for the maintenance/expansion of that power. As Nietzsche noted in *The Will to Power*, values and any alteration to them are related to the growth in power of the one who sets values. Preserving this position of command is all important; again, it is the confrontation to win a world.

In this regard Nietzsche remains relevant to our context. If the essence of power is the overpowering of itself, that is the will to an ever-new dispensation of values (increase), together with the will to secure the means to that end (preservation), then Nietzsche's philosophy of the will to power remains a crucial tool in understanding contemporary power struggles and the wars that issue from them. However, Nietzschean philosophy has never simply been a means for making sense of human conflictual becoming, it has often been used to justify and even precipitate such conflict. Domenico Losurdo (2001), in his very interesting study of the ideology of war prevalent in Germany at the turn of the twentieth century, highlights the contribution made by Nietzsche's thought to the *Glaubenskrieg* that was the First World War. Despite Nietzsche's strident criticism of 'national movements' he was successively appropriated by supporters for Germany's war of honour in 1914 and then later by the Third Reich propagandists. We have already noted how much the notion of a fateful decision played in Nietzsche's thinking, and this is especially manifest in his writings on Napoleon, but most significant was the philosophy of an affirmative, overcoming spirit that fought every minute against nihilism. What distinguished the 'ideas of 1914' from the 'ideas of 1789', or what Nietzsche contemptuously called 'modern ideas', was the assertion of a regenerative, creative power against the dulling, levelling down of liberalism and the insipid happiness of 'the last man', all of which were seen to threaten a catastrophic decay. Here Nietzsche is clearly challenging the Hegelian end of history thesis – something we shall discuss in Chapter 3 – as well as the utilitarianism that defined British philosophy in the nineteenth century. The satisfaction of 'universal brotherhood' could only ever produce 'garrulous, weak-willed' people 'who need a *master*' (1990: 173). And this will not be the master that exemplifies the affirmation of life, but quite the contrary, the tyrant that enforces standardization, uniformity and comfort. The lives of the last men are satisfied and trivial. 'They still quarrel, but they soon make up – otherwise indigestion would result' (1969: 47). They are a herd in which everyone is the same, where those who think differently take themselves off to the madhouse.

We may, then, see the persistence of war as the playing out of competing wills to power, a conflict between worlds and the drive to set values. The war against terror epitomizes this struggle between two modes of esteeming that are vying for expansion. Nietzsche's work lends itself to a study of war because he presents us with a globe traversed by competing wills, each trying to complete itself by preserving/expanding its realm. This, however, is only part of the way in which Nietzsche helps us consider the persistence of war. The other way, especially useful when considering the war against terror, which is also a war of fundamentalisms, is the path Nietzsche opens for critique, and for this we need to briefly return to the question of force. If force is present in Nietzsche's work then it surfaces as movement or becoming, because 'man is the animal *whose nature has not yet been fixed*' (1990: 88). Man is thus the site of struggle between reactive, conservative forces, and active, life-affirming forces. It is the struggle between sameness and difference that ought not result in a state of equilibrium. In perhaps the most famous study of Nietzsche's philosophy of force, Gilles Deleuze writes, 'if becoming had an end or final state, it would have already been attained [...] past time being infinite becoming would have attained its final state if it had one' (1983: 47). Indeed, in aphorism 1062 of *The Will to Power* Nietzsche doubts that the universe is capable of 'being' at all, or has one single point of fixity. And this leads to perhaps Nietzsche's greatest insight, an insight that is presented in his very first work, *The Birth of Tragedy*. Given that becoming is the law of the universe, and that becoming necessitates difference, mutability and uncertainty, tragedy registers this condition of indeterminate existence. It registers that existence is to be taken up and fought for over and over again. Unfounded, yet to be affirmed, incomplete existence is the condition of human being. As Deleuze remarks: 'Multiple and pluralist affirmation – this is the essence of the tragic' (1983: 17). Nietzsche's problem, one that Heidegger remained caught up in but later also completely dismantled, was that in the tragic absence of a ground all that remained was the wilful, subjective transvaluation of value; a condition that pitted would-be master against would-be master. It is Nietzsche's failure, then, to overcome the last vestige of metaphysics that permits his work to be appropriated by the belligerent and the violent. Turning to Heidegger it is possible to see how this overcoming of the philosophy of the subject opens up a radical critique of war, and the war against terror in particular.

Polemos

Heidegger's translation of polemos is an example of the change of register from his early existential work epitomized by *Being and Time* to his later work on the history of Being, and yet it is also a sign of the continuity in Heidegger's examination of truth understood as uncon-cealment (*alētheia*). The polemos involved when bringing beings out from their hiddenness was initially translated as *kampf*, signalling Dasein's struggle whereby truth is 'wrested from entities' (1962: 265). Later it is understood in ontological terms when polemos is translated as *Auseinandersetzung*. In German this word has many meanings including to separate, to set out, to explain, to talk and to argue. Heidegger uses it to invoke the positing, placing, exposing, founding or establishing (*setzen*) of differentiated beings (*auseinander*). Polemos is thus the conflictual relation of one with another that is the conflictual separation of the realm of Being itself. For many commentators this shift in Heidegger's questioning of Being represents his break with Nietzsche and the last residues of the metaphysics of the subject. For others, this shift, especially as it is played out around Heidegger's revised translation of polemos in the Heraclitus fragment, represents a political move. In 1933 Heidegger had joined the National Socialist Party and had taken up the position of rector at the University of Freiburg, by 1934 he had resigned. The following years saw an engagement with his affiliation to National Socialism with many people interpreting the disappearance of the word *Kampf* from Heidegger's vocabulary as an attempt to distance himself from its use by the Nazi propagandists with whom he was finding himself increasingly in disagreement. Either way, in philosophical or political terms Heidegger's deployment of polemos is central to the evolution of his thought.[6]

Heidegger was a revolutionary thinker both in the radical way in which he approached philosophy and because the subject of that philosophy invariably involved questions of renewal, overturning and epochal beginnings. In many respects his philosophy could be understood as the systematic destruction of the tradition; a destruction distinct from, yet not wholly alien to Nietzschean transvaluation. In this sense the practice of philosophy itself was exemplary of the radical questioning that faces every authentic Dasein. Along with this distaste for security and comfort Heidegger's philosophy continually warns of the decline in spiritual life through immersion in the talk, habits and involvements of *Das Man*, translated as 'the *anyone*' or 'the *they*'. This is the language of *Being and Time* where Heidegger speaks of Dasein dissolving into the being of others who also become indistinguishable in turn. The neutral anonymity of the *they* is a dictatorship. 'We take pleasure and enjoy ourselves as *they* take pleasure; we read, see, and judge about literature and art as *they* see and judge; [...] we find "shocking" what *they* find shocking' (1962: 164). This 'averageness [...] prescribes what can and may be ventured, it keeps watch over everything exceptional that thrusts itself to the fore' (165). It is 'the "levelling down" of all possibilities of Being' (165). In this sense the *they* disperses the authentic self that has been *taken hold of* in its own way, and unburdens it of its struggle. This language also extends from the immersion in public everydayness to a critique of publicity understood as the creeping bureaucratization and democratization of life during the period of the Weimar Republic. Heidegger, much like Nietzsche, had little time for these universalizing modern ideas. Against the everyday, then, philosophy must do battle in order to keep possibilities, potentialities and the future open. As John Caputo puts it: 'Philosophy is a battle because life is a battle. A being whose being is itself a battle thus demands a philosophizing that knows how to do battle' (1993: 50).[7]

While Heidegger is critical of the everyday, the criteria he uses for an investigation of it in *Being and Time* are not to be taken as expressing a 'negative valuation' (1962: 220), for it remains the realm from which Dasein projects its future, authentically or not. Heidegger calls this projection of a meaning for Dasein resoluteness, and this existential conception of authenticity as standing true is evident in Heidegger's first public treatment of the Heraclitus fragment.[8] In the 1934–5 lecture series on Hölderlin, Heidegger still translated polemos as struggle, declaring that 'Struggle is indeed progenitor, but also ruler. And where struggle as the power of preservation and standing true ceases, there begins standstill, compromise, mediocrity – and harmlessness, atrophy and decline. [...] Through proving true to a test, a being in one way or another first becomes in each case what it is and how it is' (in Fried, 2000: 30). However, as Fried notes, rather than simply plotting a future and holding oneself to a final decision, which could still be little more than a glorified flight from oneself, being resolute means 'constantly holding open the meaning of the future and its possibilities on the basis of an ongoing interpretive reflection on what has been given in the past' (98). This is one early way in which Heidegger differentiated himself from Nietzsche who also understood the weight of history. For Nietzsche, to teach the transvaluation of all values was to teach people to create the future and thereby redeem the past. Zarathustra announces: 'You shall be fugitives from all fatherlands [...] You shall love *your children's land*: let this love be your new nobility – the undiscovered land in the furthest sea!' (Nietzsche 1969: 221). But possibility is never a pure projection of the will. What Nietzsche calls esteeming, and therefore any new dispensation of value, is always based upon Dasein's thrownness, that is the history of its communal, interpretive practices. To resist the virile, even romantic, autonomy of Nietzsche, Heidegger reminds us that '*authentic* existence is not something which floats above falling everydayness; existentially, it is only a modified way in which such everydayness is seized upon' (1962: 224). Dasein, therefore, projects possibilities from within factical life and always as historical being. As Fried notes, Dasein must confront the world, but this confrontation is the 'reinterpretive encounter of Dasein with the world as it has been given, by a history that Dasein can never leap out of and control' (2000: 85).

This discussion of projection also allows us to approach Heidegger's very particular conception of truth as 'Being-uncovering' (1962: 262). He recognizes the radical nature of this rendering, breaking, as it does, with conventional conceptions of truth as agreement between thought and object, and mocks those who worry about 'plunging the "good" old tradition into nullity' (262). For the Greeks, argues Heidegger, if a discourse, as a demonstration or a showing, is to be true, its Being-true is Dasein 'taking entities out of their hiddenness and letting them be seen in their unhiddenness (their uncoveredness)' (262). The world, then, is not something external and permanent but is disclosed only in and through Dasein. There is no split between subject and object, there is no splitting of the phenomenon between human being and a world, rather Dasein *is* the disclosedness of a world. To use another important Heideggerian term, Dasein is the 'clearing', in German *Lichtung*, that sheds light. Only for an entity that is disclosive can things be brought to light or hidden in the dark.[9] In this way Dasein can be said to 'bring its "there" along with it' (171).

This Being-uncovering is a twofold struggle. As has already been noted unconcealment is a wresting of truth from entities. 'Entities get snatched out of their hiddenness. The factical uncoveredness of anything is always, as it were, a kind of *robbery*' (265).[10] However, the struggle is never an unmediated struggle to find some bare truth, it is rather the struggle with the interpretation of entities that is Dasein's 'there'. This means that thrownness is revealed by the fact that in each case Dasein 'is already in a definite world'. Dasein's thrownness is also a 'falling' because 'for the most part Dasein is lost in its "world" [and] is dominated by the way things are publicly interpreted' (1962: 264). Projection is thus Dasein's realization that it can understand *itself* in terms of the world or in relation to its ownmost potentiality. 'The goddess of Truth who guides Parmenides', Heidegger writes, 'puts two pathways before him, one of uncovering, one of hiding [. . .]. The way of uncovering is achieved only in [. . .] distinguishing between these understandingly, and making one's decision for the one rather than the other' (265). The essential task, then, is for Dasein to 'explicitly appropriate what has already been uncovered, defend it *against* semblance and disguise, and assure itself of its uncoveredness again and again' (265). This is a hermeneutic task. Dasein is interpretive, and if it is to win its world, if it is to be authentic, it must address, question and challenge the interpretation of the world as it is publicly set out. The centrality of this interpretive task for Heidegger cannot be denied because it is this ontological questioning concerning what constitutes existence that distinguishes Dasein ontically. Dasein is ontically distinct from other entities in that its being and its world is a question for it (1962: 32).

As was mentioned in the opening of this chapter, the world is not simply given, but always disclosed *as* something. In wresting with entities, they are understood *as* this or *as* that, to be utilized in this manner or in that. That the world is disclosed in this way is the basis of Heidegger's hermeneutical analysis and is the key to understanding Dasein as polemos. As Fried notes: 'Dasein *is* polemos because Dasein's existence it hermeneutic, and all interpretation is polemical' (2000: 52). It is usual to think that interpretation is a process on the way to understanding. For Heidegger it is the other way round; interpretation is the development of a more primordial understanding that characterizes Dasein's being-in-the-world. Only through being-in-the-world, that is, "standing" there, is the world 'disclosed as possible significance' (184) and the totality of our involvements with it revealed. Understanding for Heidegger is therefore an ontological rather than an epistemological problem. Interpretation, likewise, is 'the working-out of possibilities projected in understanding' (189). Through interpretation something is explicitly understood *as* something: 'when something in the world is encountered as such, the thing in question already has an involvement which is disclosed in our understanding of our world, and this involvement gets laid out by the interpretation' (190–1). Fried takes the example of a tree limb lying on a forest floor to show what is at stake in the polemos of interpretation. He explains that the scientist may see decomposing organic material or chemical compounds and processes, but these remove the bough from its involvements with the world where it might 'announce itself to us as [. . .] firewood, as a weapon, as a tool' (54), and to privilege the scientific view is to privilege a particular interpretation of Being. As Heidegger explains: 'Meaning is an *existentiale* of Dasein, not a property attaching to entities' (193). The radical nature of this conception means there is no final thing or substance, no ultimate reality to appeal to. Our world is therefore the privileging of certain interpretations, specific as-structures, over other possibilities that may be projected from within Dasein's understanding. Without an appeal to finality or some ultimate substance interpretation and the creation/projection of a world, the worlding of the world is always polemical. Indeed, it is in the name of these conflicting, competing, contending as-structures that worlds collide. In ontological terms, war is this interpretive confrontation where the worlding of the world is at stake. In ontical terms it is the violent means by which a particular world is preserved/expanded. However, that the ontological confrontation must result in an ontical conflict is by no means a necessity. To understand how the ontological confrontation might indeed undermine the inevitability of an ontical conflict Heidegger's analysis of polemos needs further discussion.

The semester following the first lecture course on Hölderlin, the Heraclitus fragment is revisited, only now Heidegger alters his translation of polemos from *Kampf* to *Auseinandersetzung*. Also, when viewing the two passages together it is evident that much of the existential language which still played a significant role in the lectures on Hölderlin has been replaced by an analysis of the differentiation within the realm of

Being itself. In other words, we can see in this language a move in Heidegger's thinking away from an analysis of the *existentialia* of Dasein to the question pertaining to modes of presencing. This question is undoubtedly active in *Being and Time*, only now it receives significant attention. It is important at this point to remind ourselves that Heidegger was as concerned about nihilism as was Nietzsche and that in many respects his thinking is defined by this concern. In our brief address to Heidegger's thinking with regard to truth, it was noted that truth is *alētheia*, namely unconcealment. The important thing for Heidegger, however, is that no truth, understood as representation or correspondence, is adequate to the hiddenness, or withdrawal, of Being. Each age, or every epoch, has its own manner of disclosing Being, its own world, but in every disclosure Being also withdraws and conceals itself. Being is therefore never fully grasped. The history of metaphysics is the history of the attempt to think Being in terms of beings, assuming that some essential substance or principle lies at the heart of Being, be that Aristotle's *ousia*, the medieval Christian creator, or modernity's claims for reason. All of these principles fall by the wayside, however, before the continual nascency, presencing or bringing-forth of Being.[11]

To return to the question of polemos, the *Auseinandersetzung*, as it is now translated, is the expositing of differentiated beings but also the difference (and conflict) between the two essential powers of Being, that is between withdrawal and unconcealment. In a lecture entitled 'The Origin of the Work of Art', which dates from the same time as the course on metaphysics, Heidegger understands the strife between unconcealment and withdrawal as the conflict between 'earth' and 'world'. 'World and earth are essentially different and yet never separated from one another. World is grounded on earth, and earth rises up through world' (Heidegger, 2002: 26). As Fried points out, world and earth are a 'vocabulary for thinking how structures of sense and meaning happen temporally *for* and *through* Dasein' (2000: 60). In Nietzschean terms, world is the given dispensation of value, for Heidegger it is the dominant as-structure that lays out our possible involvements with other entities. It is the horizon of intelligibility, an order of directives and assignments. It is the governing principle that holds sway, as in the age of technology where nature is treated as standing-reserve, or where the world is regulated according to the rational efficiency of the market, as is now the case under the common sense of neo-liberal economics. Earth, however, can never fully be laid bare because it is what always already informs the fore-structure of Dasein's understanding, and because 'it is what both grants and upends Dasein's historical understanding'

(Fried, 2000: 61). It is, then, on the one hand the deep historicity of Being from which Dasein cannot extricate itself, but it is also the undisclosable, the presencing of Being that is irreducible to what is present. When Heidegger therefore says that world is grounded in earth, it is important to remember that earth is an *Abgrund*, an abyssal, an-archic ground, and for this reason it continually interrupts and dislocates the established certainty of any particular world, it also exceeds the will of any subject. As Heidegger argues in 'The Origin of the Work of Art', earth is disconcerting for it cannot be mastered. 'Earth is not simply the closed but that which rises up as self-closing. World and earth are essentially in conflict, intrinsically belligerent. Only as such do they enter the strife of clearing and concealing' (2002: 31).

Returning to the interpretation offered in *Introduction to Metaphysics* it is this conflict 'that first projects and develops what had hitherto been unheard of, unsaid and unthought', a battle 'sustained by the creators, poets, thinkers and statesmen' (1959: 62). Most importantly, as we have seen, earth and world never fall into a state of empty opposition, they are always involved in a struggle in which 'each opponent carries the other beyond itself. [...] The earth cannot do without the openness of the world [and world] cannot float away from earth if [...] it is to ground itself on something decisive' (Heidegger, 2002: 27). In other words, if Dasein finds nothing to be at issue in its interpretation of Being, it is not living essentially, but inauthentically. This means that where the polemos ceases, where earth and world are no longer set against each other, 'the world turns away' (Heidegger, 1959: 62). There is no more worlding, it is finished, available to all, degenerating into a prototype to be copied, a schema, something exchangeable, inter-changeable, reified and standardized. For Heidegger, the diagnosis is as follows: 'When the creators vanish from the nation [*Volk*], when they are barely tolerated as an irrelevant curiosity, an ornament, as eccentrics having nothing to do with real life; when authentic conflict ceases, converted into mere polemics, into the machinations and intrigues of man within the realm of the given, then the decline has set in. [...] the inherited level of dignity [...] can be maintained only if it is at all times creatively transcended' (63).

It is not hard to see how, with selective reading, it was possible for National Socialism to claim Nietzsche's philosophy as their own. The demand to act decisively, to strive for new beginnings, as well as the call for nobility and mastery were well suited to the virility of National Socialist thinking. However, as I have noted above, such an appropriation of Nietzsche would need to repress his own critique of nationalism and especially racism. It would also need to divest the obedience demanded by the Reich as well as the mass rallies of their herd-like character. Likewise, when considering Heidegger's own affiliation with National Socialism we must remember that his understanding of Being as essentially conflictual did lend itself to supporting the struggle that was the National Socialist project. His belief, like Nietzsche before him, in the importance of thinking and acting decisively, his search for a new beginning, as well as his belief in the destiny of the *Volk* all contributed to his commitment. That he was mistaken, and that National Socialism turned out to be even more nihilistic than the materialism of American capitalism and Soviet Communism, must however, be taken into account. Whilst Heidegger made the most contemptible alliance, it is wrong to reduce his critique of mass movements, technology, biological racism and National Socialist science to the level of the internal squabbles that continually plagued the party, as Lasurdo does. We should note that Heidegger was staunchly anti-democratic, and yet there is little in his thinking that is fascistic as we would understand it today in terms of a denial, repression and extermination of difference, in fact quite the contrary is the case. But it is not the purpose of this chapter to debate the warlike quality of Nietzschean overcoming, or Heideggerian authenticity, it is rather concerned with trying to assess what their philosophy can tell us today about the persistence and onto-logical structure of war. I have sought to show how Nietzsche under-stood human being in its essence as the dispensation of value and how Heidegger understood our being-in-the-world as the interpretive con-frontation to project and win a world. We have also seen from Heidegger's reading of the will to power that power concerns the preser-vation and expansion of itself. In this regard it can be argued that the war against terror is the conflictual expression of the will to power. Rag-ing against each other are two regimes seeking to preserve and expand their own dispensation of value and conception of worldhood.

In keeping with this Nietzshcean vision is Samuel Huntington's thesis of a clash of civilizations. First published in 1993, this argument that the wars of the future will be civilizational, that is, cultural, has become an integral part of the neo-conservative mindset in Washington. Since the attacks of 11 September 2001, it has legitimized the Bush adminis-tration's mantra that the war against terror is a war to defend the values of the West, which Huntington lists as individualism, liberalism, consti-tutionalism, human rights, equality, liberty, the rule of law, democracy, free markets and the separation of church and state (1993: 40). These values do not apparently resonate in the cultures of the other seven civilizations he describes.[12] In Huntington's potted history we have moved from the medieval wars between princes, to the post-revolutionary wars between peoples, to the Cold War between the ideologies of capitalism and communism, to the current cultural wars between civilizations. The absurdity of this argument is twofold. First of all, the idea that, by implication, the other cultures are those of intolerant masses saved from the threat of anarchy only by the desire for hierarchy and domination is profoundly ideological, if not racist, and would seem to fit in well with the 'civilizing' discourse of colonialism. Also, one of the main global conflicts is the destruction of traditional and differentiated ways of being-in-the-world by the practices of neo-liberalism that reduce human being to the aggregated expression of free-market economics. This too is ideological, and it is crass to think otherwise given that capital has no cultural allegiance. Secondly, as Akbar S. Ahmed (2003) has argued, these divisions into civilizations and the expression of 'kin country' syndrome makes no sense in the current situation given that the US is reliant on Turkey, Indonesia, Afghanistan and Pakistan in its current attempts to police the war against terror.

However, the fact that an idea like the 'clash of civilizations' rings true at one level is because the war against terror *is* a war of competing wilful subjects seeking to impose their strength and secure the world as they have interpreted it. The task for us, of course, is to find our way out of this impasse. While Nietzsche's thought helps us strip the moral veil from the clash of civilizations thesis and understand it as one more raw expression of the will to power, it is important to understand how and why Heidegger's conception of polemos as interpretive confrontation challenges this philosophy of violent conflict between competing worldviews. We have already seen how Heidegger moves beyond Nietzsche's subjectivism by thinking Being as the polemos between earth and world. The source for the transvaluation is no longer the autonomous heroic will, but the hiddenness of Being that continually brings-forth new beginnings to which we must respond, a condition that modernity has vainly sought to master. In 'The Age of the World Picture' Heidegger unfolds the essence of modernity as the dual Cartesian moment whereby man becomes subject, the unshakable ground of certainty, and truth becomes the certainty of objective representation. The whole of modern metaphysics, including Nietzsche, he argues, maintains itself with this interpretation of being where '[m]an becomes the referential centre of beings as such' (2002: 67). This is not a shift from the worldview of the Middle Ages to that of modernity because what constitutes the emergence of the age of the world picture is beings being brought before Man as the objective. In the Middle Ages, beings corresponded to the order of creation brought into being by a creator, God, and were never 'placed in the realm of man's information and disposal so that, in this way alone, [were they] in being' (68). The notion of a Greek worldview is even further removed. When the world becomes picture beings are that which Man intends and decides to bring before him. For the (pre-Socratic) Greeks Man is rather the one who is gathered and brought into presencing with *self-opening* beings.[13] In this situation Man is maintained by the openness of beings, 'driven about by their conflict and marked by their dividedness' and to fulfil his essence man must preserve 'the self-opening in its openness; and he must remain exposed to all of its divisive confusion' (68). In stark contrast to this exposure to openness, the fundamental event of modernity is the conquering of the world as picture. This event also involves the interpretation of beings as representing values, value being the compensation for the loss of being that accompanies the shift to representation. This attributing of values, otherwise known as culture, becomes 'the general expression of the highest goals of creation devoted to the self-establishment of man' (77). Striving to promote that which is most valuable, 'man fights for the position in which he can be that being who gives to every being the measure and draws up the guidelines'. Because of this, Heidegger continues, 'the decisive unfolding of the modern relationship to beings becomes a confrontation of world views' (71).

One of the predominant components of enlightened modernity was the distance it took from the pre-modern warrior virtues. What is significant about modern warfare, aside from the scale of the devastation it can bring, is the fact that warfare does not carry its own legitimacy with it, that is, not being a good in itself, the case for war always has to be made. Integral to this is the structuring of identity and difference, self and other, whereby 'we' are always seen to be good, righteous and just, and 'they' are always seen to be bad, ungodly and cruel. Within Heidegger's articulation of the polemos between earth and world we are offered a philosophy that divests itself of the last vestiges of subjectivism and destabilizes the ground of such identities. We are offered instead, what Gianni Vattimo calls 'weak ontology', that is 'the taking leave of metaphysical being and its strong traits' (1988: 86). In Heidegger's opening up of the ground of Being identity becomes increasingly destabilized and unfounded, and such thinking can be used to directly challenge the rhetoric on both sides in the war against terror. Through reading both Nietzsche and Heidegger we can understand human being as interpretive confrontation, and understand just how *uncertain* the world produced through such interpretation actually is. Let us have a war against terror by all means, but that would mean a war against the fundamental certainties that underpin it. The challenge, then, for thinking the polemos of Being is to face the groundlessness of our world while also developing a 'weak' normativity that can save us from the decisionism to which Heidegger succumbed.

2
Life and Death

In 1915 Sigmund Freud published his *Thoughts for the Times on War and Death*, a reflection upon the disillusionment felt by Europeans at the onset of a war more destructive than any other before it. He asked that while people knew that war would never cease as long as nations lived so differently, that is, lived under the guidance of different moral codes, different religions and practised different virtues in the pursuit of different interests, could it not at least be assumed that the great nations had sufficiently comprehended their commonality so that ' "foreigner" and "enemy" could no longer be merged' (Freud, 1991c: 63)? Here Freud paints a picture of civilization very much in keeping with the ideology of modernity as the incremental and progressive movement towards universal peace. Indeed the Kantian echoes are very strong as he describes the unity of civilized peoples that has allowed innumerable men and women to exchange their native home for a 'new and wider fatherland' (63), moving, as cosmopolitanism demands, without 'hindrance or suspicion'. These civilized cosmopolitans did not consider war, but if it were to happen they pictured a 'chivalrous passage of arms' (64) limited to establishing the superiority of one side, while also avoiding excessive suffering and offering full protection to non-combatants. Such war may indeed produce horrors, but nothing that might interrupt 'the development of ethical relations between the collective individuals of mankind' (65). The war that arrived, however, ignored all restrictions of such chivalry. As 'cruel', 'embittered' and 'implacable' as anything that came before: 'It tramples in blind fury on all that comes in its way as though there were no future and no peace among men after it is over' (65). This is a vivid picture of Freud's belief in both civilization, the purpose of which is to extend human relations into ever larger cooperative units, and the immanence of human destructiveness. It is also the

23

reason Freud remains important today; his philosophy of co-present contending forces of life and death refuses the monism that permeates current discourses of war. His persistent demand that we face up to the duality of the human condition disabuses us of the illusion that the forces of death can be clearly and definitively located outside, that the battle is between self-contained units of good versus evil. Freud thus undermines any simple moral topology.

For Freud, the First World War is a conflict in which the state 'confesses shamelessly to its own rapacity and lust for power, which the private individual has then to sanction in the name of patriotism' (66). This relaxation of morality by the state is also reflected in the action of individuals because when 'the community no longer raises objections, there is an end, too, to the suppression of evil passions' (67). Such evil cannot, according to Freud, be eradicated, because 'our conscience is not the inflexible judge that ethical teachers declare it' (66). Evil passions always remain our potential, existing in the form of primitive instinctual impulses just beneath the surface of even the most civilized of people. The conscience, once established, is not a permanent regulator of action towards the good, but rather a reflection of the community in which each individual lives, and is prone to the 'ambivalence of feeling' that splits every subject. This chapter, then, is the story of this 'ambivalence'. It works through Freud's development of the instinctual opposites of life and death that turn humans at once towards the beauty and order of civilization (*Kultur*) as well as the chaos and destruction of war. It is an account that allows us one consolation, which Freud wryly notes: an understanding of the instinctual impulses serves to indicate that '[i]n reality our fellow-citizens have not sunk so low as we feared, because they had never risen so high as we believed' (72). In other words, in living a civilized life, seemingly holding our evil passions at bay, we are psychologically speaking, living beyond our means.

While these meditations on the darker aspects of human existence have found favour with many thinkers, the second part of the chapter will turn to Herbert Marcuse whose interpretation of the life instinct manages to recover the progressive path that Freud finally lost sight of. In *Eros and Civilization*, Marcuse seeks to rejuvenate the, albeit limited, optimism still evident in Freud's 1915 meditations. There, while representing civilization as being inherently hypocritical, Freud can still hold on to 'the prospect of paving the way in each new generation for a more far-reaching transformation of instinct which shall be the vehicle of a better civilization' (1991c: 72). For Marcuse, however, it is not transformation of instincts but, on the contrary, their *release* that can assist civilization. It was his contention that Eros could do much more work in support of civilization than Freud had dared to think, and that civilization, therefore, need not be so repressive. Reading Freud in conjunction with Marx he argued for a reconception of our mode of being-in-the-world by questioning and confronting the competitive and possessive individualism that reproduced the social relations of the prevalent mode of production.[1] Where Freud offered us a psychoanalytical and even cosmological explanation for our violent world, Marcuse gives us the socio-political tools to challenge it.

Death

War is the abiding theme of Freud's work. Not only did he regularly reflect upon the violence of warfare, and later in his life flee the violent advance of German National Socialism, he continually saw himself at war with the mysteries of the psyche, and was committed to breaking their cover. What is more, his work is also dedicated to the internal war in which every self is engaged, the conflict between competing psychical forces that determines the actions of every individual, positions them as a potential threat to the culture that binds them, and places every particular cultural unit in potential conflict with the broadening of civilization. This 'conquistador of thought' (Elshtain, 1989: 49) repeatedly sought an account of, and a possible treatment for, the destructive capacity of humans, something he would refer to in his later work as the death drive. In the opening pages of *The Future of an Illusion*, Freud offers a succinct view of the ambiguous relationship between civilization and aggression. Civilization is both the capacity to control nature and the means through which human beings regulate and adjust their relations to one another. However, such protection and accommodation is secured only through the renunciation of certain primitive drives for satisfaction that might be more readily, albeit fleetingly, secured through the instrumental, aggressive use of others. In this sense the individual is the enemy of civilization and civilization must be defended against the individual. In order to understand this tension lying at the heart of human culture, it is necessary to trace Freud's investigation of the instincts that lead to his conclusion in *Civilization and its Discontents* that the death drive is 'an original, self-subsisting instinctual disposition' to aggressiveness 'and the greatest impediment to civilization' (1991c: 313).

That the death drive is difficult to approach let alone conceptually pin down is evident in Jean Laplanche's complaint that it is a 'virtual monster', a chimera 'constructed out of the most heterogeneous body parts' (1976: 108). However, if we are to give an account of the death drive, it is perhaps expedient to work towards the decisive turn in Freud's thinking that announced an inclination to aggression as a distinct instinct ultimately compelling us towards death. The 1920 essay 'Beyond the Pleasure Principle' marked a dramatic departure in Freud's thinking and overturned much of his earlier thought in relation to pleasure as the guiding thread to psychical processes. Although the shift towards an independent aggressive impulse can be seen to be developing in essays predating 'Beyond the Pleasure Principle', the instincts in the period up to 1920 are generally understood in terms of a conflict between the sexual and ego instincts governed by the pleasure and reality principles.

Freud defines the instincts in relation to stimuli which operate as singular and periodic events that can be dealt with by requisite action. Instincts, on the other hand, rather than being momentary excitations are a 'constant force' (1991b: 115) whose essence is the 'exercising of pressure' (118). What is more, because the instincts are internal compulsions and not external stimulations, they cannot be avoided. Relief from this pressure can be momentarily attained through the satisfaction of the instinct's aim, but this satisfaction is never complete and the aim resurfaces and exerts further pressure almost immediately. This constant pressure, for Freud, is regulated by the search for pleasure and the avoidance of unpleasure. The drive for satisfaction and the lack of immediate gratification creates an unpleasant tension in the primary psychical processes, with action being determined by the need to lower tension. This is what Freud in his metapsychology called the 'economic' factor in psychical processes producing a positive, pleasurable 'yield'.[2] In *Civilization and its Discontents*, Freud declares that the efficacy of the pleasure principle cannot be doubted and yet it is 'at loggerheads with the whole world', in fact 'all the regulations of the universe run counter to it' (1991c: 263), prompting him to note that one might be inclined to believe that man's happiness was not included in the plan of Creation. While happiness remains a remote aim, the possibilities for our unhappiness stem from three directions: 'from our own body, which is doomed to decay and dissolution and which cannot even do without pain and anxiety as warning signals; from the external world, which may rage against us with overwhelming and merciless forces of destruction; and finally from our relations to other men. The suffering which comes from this last source is perhaps more painful to us than any other' (265).

While the pleasure principle is primary, this is only the first of the two principles governing mental functioning. In the 1911 essay on these two principles bearing this title, Freud offers the reality principle as a mode of mental functioning that modifies the pleasure-ego's wishfulness with the reality-ego's usefulness. In this the pleasure principle is not deposed, but is rather safeguarded; a momentary and uncertain pleasure is given up 'only to gain along a new path an assured pleasure at a later time' (1991b: 41). The reality principle is not only the key to the securing of more permanent, if less intense, pleasure, it is also central to the functioning of civilization. When in 1920 Freud reviews this earlier division between pleasure and reality he offers a very clear assessment of the relation between these two principles. The pursuit of pleasure is not only difficult to achieve, but can actually be highly dangerous. With regard to the ego instincts, violence and aggression are employed to further life and satisfy immediate demand through the destruction of objects for consumption, while also setting in place a competitive struggle between individuals in pursuit of scarce resources, an issue that will be of importance for Marcuse's historicizing of the reality principle. This in turn requires the exercise of aggression in the pursuit of satisfaction. It may even require a struggle to the death. Similarly, while the sexual instinct provides the germ of civilization, in that it turns one person towards another in an erotic rather than destructive relationship, it is evident how the sexual instincts also run counter to civilization in that love is between two and does not require a third party. Love is often insular and exclusive, it does not lead to a broader sociality in itself. It finds (temporary) satisfaction or pleasure in the closed unit of two people. But this is not all, for it hardly needs to be mentioned that such coupling is also the focus of aggression and violent expression.

Both of these instincts, then, while evidently committed to preserving both individual and species, can also undermine that survival. The blind consumption in pursuit of an immediate goal can also become life threatening. Consequently, in the pursuit of self-preservation the ego readily submits to 'the postponement of satisfaction, the abandonment of a number of possibilities of gaining satisfaction and the temporary toleration of unpleasure on the long indirect road to pleasure' (1991b: 278); and likewise immediate and exclusive erotic satisfaction must also be converted into, what Freud calls, 'aim-inhibited love'. Genital love leads to the founding of a family, which in turn brings about 'positive feelings' between parents and children as well as between siblings. This non-genital, aim-inhibited love is more readily termed affection and extends beyond the family, creating 'new bonds with people who before were strangers' (1991c: 292), affording friend-ships that are beneficial from a cultural point of view. These two analyses of deferred gratification and aim-inhibited love therefore also suggest that while pleasure is proper to the primary workings of the mental apparatus, it cannot be said to dominate. The experiences of both defer-ment and aim-inhibition contradict the notion that each and every mental process is accompanied by pleasure. Instead Freud develops his position to argue that it is preferable to posit a *tendency* away from unpleasure. The aim of the mental apparatus might then be said to keep the excitation of external stimuli and the tension of internal instinctual pressure 'as low as possible or at least to keep it constant' (1991b: 277). This dynamic between wish and reality Freud calls the constancy prin-ciple which is, as we shall see, central to his analysis of the death drive.

That repression is thus central to the development of culture is evident from Freud's equation of civilization with non-satisfaction, or the renunciation of instinct; and if we return briefly to the analysis of aim-inhibited love the reason that Freud placed such importance on the function of repression becomes clear. The primary, familial form of aim-inhibited love, while possibly opening us up to the stranger does not guarantee civilization for, as Freud warns, the family does not readily give up the individual. 'The more closely the members of a family are attached to one another, the more often do they tend to cut themselves off from others, and the more difficult is it for them to enter into the wider circle of life. The mode of life which is phylogenetically the older, and which is the only one that exists in childhood, will not let itself be superseded by the cultural mode of life which has been acquired later' (292). This persistence of the mode that is phylogenetically older, that is older to the development of the species, is a continuing threat to the extension of civilization and the broadening of culture. The more primitive state of psychical development, those instincts that direct the individual towards immediate gratification, cannot be eradicated.

In *Beyond the Pleasure Principle*, Freud claims that protection against stimuli is almost more important than the reception of stimuli. He spec-ulates that some element of the system we call 'consciousness' must form a protective shield against overexposure to stimuli that could cause a potentially life threatening tension. Indeed, he describes trauma as any stimulus that is strong enough to break through this protective shield. However, the system is also affected from within, and while the protective shield lessens the level and intensity of excitation coming from without, there can be no such shield against excitations coming from within. This means that a particular way of dealing with these internal excitations is developed: 'there is a tendency to treat them as though they were acting, not from the inside, but from the outside, so that it may be possible to bring the shield against stimuli into operation as a means of defence against them. This is the origin of *projection* which is destined to play such a large part in the causation of pathological processes' (301). The study of this pathological turn is perhaps best expressed in the study entitled 'Instincts and their Vicissitudes' where projection is said to be governed by the three polarities of subject–object, pleasure–unpleasure and activity–passivity. Every individual is governed by pleasure in relation to both itself and the external world. With regard to external stimuli it is passive, while in relation to its instinctual impulses it is active. In early life the subject (ego) is self-cathected and autoerotic, that is to say narcissistic. At this point subject, pleasure and activity are harmoniously joined, and flow unhindered. At a later stage of development the subject is turned towards the external world and those objects that are the source of pleasure are introjected, while feelings of unpleasure brought about by objects are expelled. If the object brings about pleasurable feelings it becomes the site of attraction, if those feelings are unpleasurable the object becomes the site of repulsion. This internal feeling of unpleasure which interrupts the flow of instinctual activity is projected outwards and the object that is the cause of this unpleasure becomes the object of hate. This also enables the free flow of instinctual activity to be re-engaged as the object is now the focus of the desire for destruction. We have noted above that the aim-inhibited erotic ties of the family, despite appearing to transcend the desire for gratification that singles out the individual, do not guarantee such transcendence, and that the family unit, and by extension a clan, tribe or community can still be so tightly identified as to operate as an individual. In this respect the sociological aspect of Freud's analysis is fully revealed and this model of repression/projection becomes the model for inter-group, and even inter-nation hostilities.[3]

It might be said that Freud's model of repression/projection explains how the individual maintains itself against the threat of excessive tension from external stimuli as well as offering a model of how the individual maintains its instinctual activity, but it does not give us much help with regard to the kind of repression or renunciation of instinctual impulse that is required by civilization. In fact what this model of repression offers, especially with regard to internal stimuli, is exactly the opposite, an explanation of and justification for the inclination towards aggression that is the greatest threat to cultural expansion. How then is this primitive mode of phylogenetic life itself repressed and restrained? For Freud the prerequisite for cultural expansion and advancement to higher stages of civilization is the 'mastering or binding' (1991b: 307) of these instinctual excitations. Initially this might be achieved through external coercion, but such disciplinary force is itself at odds with the ideals of human civilization, founded as it is on the rule of reason and the autonomy of rational agents. The course of human development is therefore marked by the internalization of a disciplinary authority in the guise of the super-ego, something we might also refer to as ethics, morality, or the law of the community. This internalization is the moment of world-creation for Freud and absolutely central to the normative expansion of civilization.

In Freud's analysis of the evolution of the law in 'Totem and Taboo', the plot moves from the 'brute force' of the primal father to the 'right' of the sons. The dawn of civilization takes place when the sons murder the primal father, who up until that point ruled by force and had a monopoly over sexual relations and material goods. The sons who wish to have a stake in the spoils beyond those distributed by the arbitrary will of the father murder him and set in place the first moral community. This first community sets in place the primitive law that is to organize the decisive step towards civilization. This early totemic culture is therefore based on restrictions that will maintain the distribution of sexual relations (the taboo on incest) and the taboo on murder, which if not followed will simply throw the nascent community into a cycle of violence and arbitrary will that they had sought to leave behind. The law, and therefore the course of civilization, is the extension of these prescriptions to an ever broader community whose members include those who are able to renounce their instincts and enter the world of the sons. The murder of the primal father, however, is not the end of his rule for the external threat of force has become introjected aggression in the shape of the super-ego and the feeling of guilt. One key difference between the two forms of authority, aside from one being internal and the other external, is that in relation to external authority one might be 'quits' following the renunciation of aggression. With the super-ego, however, instinctual renunciation is not enough. Because the aggressive instinct is a permanent force, every aggressive desire demands greater instinctual renunciation, and every renunciation increases the super-ego's strength. We have, then, a situation in which the introjected law, as conscience and guilt, is ambivalent in that is ensures the future inviolability of the law, but it also creates an 'economic' disadvantage in that '[i]nstinctual renunciation no longer has a completely liberating effect' (1991c: 320). In this model one can only anticipate periodic explosions of aggression that release this growing tension, but given that any such projection of aggression will be used by the super-ego against the ego, some legitimate outlet for this tension *must* be found if it is not to threaten the psychical life of the individual itself.

In the early essay on war, Freud intimates a legitimate outlet for this tension. The chivalrous, heroic conception of war had previously been understood as the establishment of the superior civilization, that is, the establishment of the superior law and the world it brought into being. In the war against terror, this rhetoric of war as a chivalrous passage returns, and it is the triumph of the superior civilization that permits the release of tension. The war against terror is a war of good versus evil and it is this language of the maintenance of the world versus the world's dissolution that *tempers* the tyranny of the super-ego and allows the explosive release or 'yield' that the economy of the psyche requires. Only if the other is represented as a threat to the law itself can the ever increasing strength of self-directed aggression be rescinded; only if the other is seen as an agent of world-destruction can aggression be legitimately expelled. The war against terror in this scenario becomes, in metapsychological terms, a necessary war where each side represents the other as transgressing the law and thus threatening to reintroduce rule by arbitrary force. For each side the other threatens (and must be represented as threatening) the bond of culture and the very tissue of civilized humanity. This mobilization also requires additional support from cultural ideals that bind the instincts and help mask any inequalities within a culture. The satisfaction promoted by the cultural ideal is shared by the privileged as well as the suppressed classes 'since the right to despise the people outside [a culture] compensates them for the wrongs they suffer within their own unit. No doubt one is a wretched plebeian, harassed by debts and military service; but, to make up for it, one is a Roman citizen, one has one's share in the task of ruling other nations and dictating their laws' (Freud, 1991c: 192–3). This is a sado-masochistic relation in which the plebeian bows his head to authority while releasing tension through dominion over the non-Roman.

With regard to the war against terror, the most important ideal proclaimed by the US is that of *the patriot*. In the language of the Bush administration, the ideal of the patriot has functioned in the same manner as the ideal of the Roman citizen above. It is an ideal that seeks to bridge division in its call for belonging and national commitment. Although the broad consensus after the Second World War that America was a global force for good has been put to the test by a succession of morally and legally questionable military interventions, capped by the recent invasion of Iraq, the ideal of the American patriot remains a powerful binding force given that it incorporates, and is increasingly used to define freedom. In the main, this ideal works because patriots are defenders of the law. The etymology of the word patriot gives us 'belonging to one's father' (*pátrios*) and 'fellow countryman' (*patriótes*). The patriot is a son and a member of the cultural community borne of the primal patricide; the son is therefore both representative and defender of the law; guardian against the chaos of arbitrary will. On the other side of the war against terror, it is possible to see how the martyr functions in a similar way, binding a community of witnesses to the law. In this way Freud's conception of civilization allows us to comprehend the legitimation of explosive killing in the name of freedom and goodness, and violence in the name of peace and order. It is also the point where Freud's analysis becomes ontological. War is a defence of the law by the sons: it is righteous destruction, it is the preservation/ expansion of a world. Of course, it must be noted that despite the pronouncements of the Bush administration, America is not a monoculture and against the current rhetoric of war, there is an alternative vision of civilization borne by those American sons and daughters who do not identify with the Bush doctrine of militarism and belligerence; and it is with their law that hope for the future lies.

Towards the end of Freud's life, hope had become a precious and very rare commodity. In his 1933 dialogue with Albert Einstein, he concluded that the only hope for civilization, if it is to transcend the local cultures of nations and produce a truly universal culture, is for the education of 'an upper stratum of men with independent minds, not open to intimidation and eager in the pursuit of truth, whose business it would be to give direction to the dependent masses' (1991c: 359). This ideal community would consist of those 'who had subordinated their instinctual life to the dictatorship of reason' (359). These 'pacifists' who have substituted science for necessity could be the Platonic philosopher-kings of the twentieth century, but Freud did not believe there was sufficient time for this community of men to save us from ourselves.[4] Because of Freud's belief in the persistence of the earliest stage of phylogenetic development, each time he accounted for the increase and expansion of culture, this primitive and ever-forceful desire was able to find expression; between individuals, tribes, nations and civilizations the satisfaction of instinctual impulse remains the prime mover. Who, in the face of experience and history, he writes, will have the courage to dispute the assertion: '*Homo homini lupus* ['Man is a wolf to man']'? (1991c: 302).

At this point in Freud's intellectual journey, he had come to the conclusion that human aggression demanded a refiguring of instinctual impulse, that it should no longer be understood as operating through the dyad of egoistic and sexual instincts, but through the opposition of life and death instincts, that is between what expands and unites and what divides and destroys; and as I mentioned at the beginning of this chapter, this shift in focus was announced in the seminal 1920 essay 'Beyond the Pleasure Principle'. This shift, however, was not a sudden and radical departure. It was, rather, preceded by developments, both clinical and metapsychological, that necessitated the revision. The 1914 study 'On Narcissism' as well as the clinical studies of war neuroses contributed to this change in outlook. What is important about the 1914 study is, as Freud later summarizes in 'Civilization and its Discontents', 'that the ego is itself cathected with libido, that the ego, indeed, is the libido's original home, and remains to some extent its head-quarters' (309). In this regard the division between egoistic and sexual instincts becomes clouded and even unworkable. In addition to this, Freud's analysis of war neuroses was equally troubling. In studying the compulsion to repeat traumatic events in the minds of shell-shocked soldiers, Freud came close to making a claim for a death drive. This, however, was only announced in 1920 in the essay that took his thinking regarding tension and constancy to its logical conclusions and surmised that every individual, governed as they are by the need to minimize tension, instinctually seeks that moment when there was the least tension, that is, that time before birth, the time prior to any disturbance whatsoever. In 1920 Freud made the startling claim that according to the constancy principle one must assume that the aim of all life is death.

That Freud needed to go beyond the pleasure principle in 1920 is due to his gradual realization that the active appropriation of unpleasure was key to the relief of tension. According to the earlier studies of repression, the protective shield should guard against the resurfacing of trauma, but in the case of sufferers of shell shock the mind seemed to actively appropriate unpleasure in order to push the individual towards collapse as evidenced by the prevalence of catatonia in those returning from the front. One aspect of the earlier instinctual analysis that remains relevant, however, is the conservative nature of the instincts. Both the egoistic and sexual instincts were conservative in that they aimed at maintenance of the individual and the species, but what the constancy principle now exposes is that this conservative impulse does not have life as its aim, but death. The constancy principle now leads us to an instinct that is *'an urge inherent in organic life to restore an earlier state of things'* (1991b: 308). A little further on Freud continues: 'It would be in contradiction with the conservative nature of the instincts if the goal of life were a state of things which had never yet been attained. On the contrary it must be an *old* state of things, an initial state from which the living entity has at one time or other departed and to which it is striving to return by the circuitous paths along which its development leads' (310). The primary instinct thus becomes 'the instinct to return to the inanimate state' (311); and life is an evermore complicated detour from that inanimate state. What is most remarkable about this theory, however, is not the death instinct itself, which I do not believe is as counter-intuitive as it at first appears, but the conclusion Freud reaches to account for the fact that the human race has not already destroyed itself in one catastrophic conflict or mass-suicide. With a perverse Aristotelian logic he proposes that the preservative instincts are now to be understood as 'component instincts whose function it is to assure that the organism shall follow its own path to death, and to ward off any possible ways of returning to inorganic existence other than those which are immanent in the organism itself' (311). Following Freud's tendency to re-apply this insight at the level of culture and society, we might say that cultures clash in order to preserve their own routes to death and their own mode of world-destruction. In line with Marcuse's analysis, to whom we must now turn, the route to death that the West is trying to preserve might be rendered as the narcosis and anaesthesia of the spectacle, as promoted by the culture industry, or the one-dimensionality of an ever-expanding realm of consumption. The West's route to death might therefore be read as the commodification of the world; and in this scenario, it must annihilate and dispose of anything that blocks this aim.

Life

Herbert Marcuse's philosophy, like that of Freud's, was profoundly shaped by the traumatic experience of war and its aftermath. As the first volume of his collected papers clearly shows, Marcuse's thinking is inextricably linked to the Second World War. Not only did he experience exile, but, like so many European intellectuals of that time, he was required to think in response to the human devastation (material, intellectual and spiritual) that resulted from the Holocaust. What is more, this thinking took place within an environment of developing Cold War suspicion that threatened to repeat in the 1950s the persecution and exile forced upon him in the 1930s. During these two decades

Marcuse was forced to flee the ascendancy of National Socialism in Germany, leaving his position at the Institute for Social Research in Frankfurt to work in Geneva in 1933. In the following year, he emigrated to America where he was initially invited to work at Columbia University; and while it is well known that in America he would find his own philosophical voice and become a guru for both the civil rights and anti-war movements, becoming at the same time an irritant if not an enemy of the state, what is less well known is that from 1942 to 1951, when a position at an American university became increasingly difficult to secure, Marcuse was actually employed by the state in both the Office of War Information and then in the Office of Strategic Services. In this role he worked on intelligence projects with the specific objectives of analysing the best way to appeal to the German people via counter-propaganda and also how to contribute to the denazification of Germany at the close of the war.

In early essays entitled 'The New German Mentality' and 'State and Individual Under National Socialism', Marcuse is explicit about the break with civilization and even the break with the former German *Kultur* (1998b: 141) evidenced by the rise of National Socialism.[5] It represents the hatred and distrust of the ideas of Christian civilization in favour of a brutal pragmatism where 'only the most ruthless and most efficient competitor can get along in this world' (73). While the two essays on National Socialism share similar concerns, as one might expect, they address in turn the ideology and the institutions of governance. In 'The New German Mentality' Marcuse offers an interpretation of National Socialist ideology based on a split between the rational and the irrational, the administrative and the mythological. Its prime mover is the technical efficiency required to respond to scarcity and competition. This rationality is the fixation of all things within an operational system, and yet this 'presupposes a "supra-technical" language community from which it draws its force and appeal' (149). This total ordering of the German mentality represents a 'ruthless utilization of all available means for getting a bigger share in the distribution of power' (158), and a situation in which all aggression is directed outwards against the weak, the alien and the intellectual, whose ideas might hamper the efficient use of those means by and for the German people. The new German mentality under National Socialism was the belief that 'all standards and values, all patterns of thought and behaviour are dictated by the need for the incessant functioning of the machinery of production, destruction and domination' (161), and where men and women are forced to think and feel 'in terms of things and functions which pertain exclusively to this machinery' (164), in order that the mythical Aryan community will rise as master.

At an institutional level Marcuse argues that National Socialism is defined by the abolition of the separation between state and society. The Third Reich is not the totalization of the state, but the totalization of the National Socialist movement, part of which is the subordination of all individuals to the functioning of the technical apparatus. A further component is the situation whereby the state does not rule as such but rather coordinates self-government by 'prevailing social groups' (70). National Socialist governance is the 'threefold sovereignty of industry, party and army which have divided up among themselves the former monopoly of coercive power' (76). Harmony within this tripartite division is maintained through the sharing of pre-existing interests as symbolized by the *Führer*.[6] Marcuse offers an excerpt from a speech delivered to the *Industry Club* in 1932 in which Hitler articulates these interests in terms of the (global) over-production threatening the German economy, something that could be resolved only through expansion.[7] Marcuse argues that the commitment Hitler gave in that address explains the coincidence and harmony of industry, party and army integral to the National Socialist movement. To assist the economy, which can no longer function through its own forces, 'Hitler promises that the new state shall become the executive agent of the economy, that it shall organize and coordinate the entire nation for unhampered economic expansion, that it shall make German industry the winner in the international competition. And he furthermore promises that he will furnish the weapon which alone will enable German industry to run down its competitor and to open up the required markets, namely the most formidable army in the world' (74). This harmony between the imperial forces is underpinned by the productivity of a *Volk*, unified by 'the most primitive self-interest and bare instinct of self-preservation' (80), their destructive capacity socialized through the 'correct performance of required operational functions' (164).

This analysis of German National Socialism did not remain an historical element of Marcuse's academic biography, instead it became a living framework through which he was to criticize the emergent neo-fascism in the US and the wider capitalist world. Reading 'State and Individual under National Socialism' in 2005 one cannot help but be struck by the resonances this analysis has with contemporary formations of power and empire. However, in 1955, the year that Marcuse published *Eros and Civilization*, America's own flirtation with overt totalitarianism, in the form of the McCarthy witch-hunts, suggested to Marcuse that fascism was not a local, historical issue, but a permanent threat to liberty. But what made possible the continuation of work started in the 1940s was not simply the persecution of those on the Left. A whole range of social, economic and political conditions seemed to echo the ideology and practices of National Socialism. In the introduction to the first edition of *Eros and Civilization*, Marcuse considers a world free from National Socialism but sees domination everywhere, domination that is 'growing in scope and efficiency' (1998a: 4). He continues, very much in line with the wider Frankfurt School critique, by arguing that concentration camps and atom bombs 'are no relapse into barbarism, but the unrepressed implementation of the achievements of modern science, technology and domination'. In the 'Political Preface' to the 1966 edition, his analysis of the continued threat of fascism has become much more refined. 'Scientific management of instinctual needs', he writes, 'has long since become a vital factor in the reproduction of the system: merchandise which has to be bought and used is made into objects of the libido; and the national Enemy who has to be fought and hated is distorted and inflated to such an extent that he can activate and satisfy aggressiveness in the depth dimension of the unconscious' (2001: 99). Here Marcuse is tracking the social control endemic to fascism in the emerging consumer culture of the 'affluent society', where productive energy, rather than being used for truly liberatory freedom, is channelled by capitalism towards the consumption of commodities. By 1972 in an essay entitled 'The Historical Fate of Bourgeois Democracy' (written, as Doug Kellner notes, after Richard Nixon's defeat of the liberal, anti-war candidate George McGovern) he is no longer articulating the continued threat of fascism within Western civilization, he is readily announcing its return:

The spectacle of the reelection of Nixon stands as the nightmarish epitome of the period in which the self-transformation of bourgeois democracy into neofascism [has] taken place [binding] the people, beyond the persisting class conflicts, in new ways to the established system.

In new ways: because the interplay between production and destruction, liberty and repression, power and submission (i.e., the unity of opposites which permeates the entire capitalist society today) has, with the help of technological means not previously available, created, among the underlying populations, a mental structure which responds to, and reflects the requirements of the system. In this mental structure are the deep individual, instinctual roots of the identification of the conformist majority with the institutionalized brutality and aggression. An instinctual, nay, libidinal affinity binds, beneath all rational justification, the subjects to the rulers. (2001: 170)

In 1972 at the height of the Vietnam War, Marcuse saw in the US the social domination, libidinal sublimation, violence against the other, aesthetics of the spectacle,[8] technical efficiency and mythological identification that had defined National Socialism as a movement in 1942. At this time, his analysis of how to create a more liberated and open society as set out in *Eros and Civilization* remained pertinent if not central to his concerted critique of technology and his identification with both the anti-war and civil rights movements. At the heart of his philosophical enquiry into Freud lay a reassessment of two key notions central to both fascism and contemporary capitalism, namely scarcity and repression. Marcuse agreed with Freud that culture equalled repression. However, his contribution to the debate pertaining to the instincts was to historicize both scarcity and repression and argue that technological advances, if coupled with new social relations, could eradicate scarcity, and thereby undermine, or show existing repressive apparatuses to be excessive, hence his historicizing of repression as 'surplus-repression'. It is important therefore to work with Marcuse's reading of Freud in a little more detail in order to show why he believed that human destructive capacities need not be catastrophic and how eros may yet subdue its violent twin.

In a world in which the domination of man by man was becoming increasingly rationalized and institutionalized and war was becoming evermore destructive, Marcuse proposed that the only pertinent question is whether or not 'a state of civilization can be reasonably envisaged in which human needs are fulfilled in such a manner and to such an extent that surplus-repression can be eliminated' (1998a: 151). In his introduction he briefly outlines Freud's position that the 'methodical sacrifice of libido' (3) and its ordering into socially useful activities *is* culture. However, if we are to ask whether or not a non-repressive or less repressive civilization is possible, it is important to reveal the 'sociological' element of Freud's thought. In other words, Marcuse asks if the interrelation between freedom and repression is the unchanging and necessary principle of civilization (and therefore always exists in some form), or if this interrelation only results from a specific organization of human existence. This then raises the possibility that repressive civilization is not a given, but can be challenged through 'a fundamentally different experience of being' (5), and in this call for a reconception of our being-in-the-world it is possible to hear the echo of the confrontation with nihilism demanded by Marcuse's teacher, Martin Heidegger. Marcuse's task, then, is twofold. He seeks to recapture, as he says, the 'historical substance' (34) of Freud's work on civilization in order to, first, challenge the centrality of scarcity in Freud's analysis of the egoistic drives, and thereby challenge capitalism as the best answer to the ruthless competition that ensues; and secondly, to demonstrate the full, civilizing potential of a liberated eros.

While Marcuse would not deny that some element of instinctual repression is necessary for civilization to persist his argument challenges the naturalization of repression that prevents us from seeing beyond it. A central component in the naturalization of repression is its connection to competition for scarce resources, but this is a falsehood in that it assumes scarcity to be a brute fact when scarcity and the existential response to it is actually *organized* (36). At a time when technological advances are producing an abundance of consumer goods, and contributing to the 'affluent society', the need for repression is not so much determined by scarcity *per se*, but a very specific *distribution* of scarcity. Scarcity thus becomes a component in social engineering rather than a necessary, biological given, and capitalism perpetuates the myth in order to perpetuate its hierarchy of domination. In order, therefore, to expose what Marcuse calls the socio-historical vicissitudes of the instincts, Freud's framework must be qualified with terms that draw out this socio-historical component. To this extent Marcuse offers the concepts of surplus-repression, which is composed of restrictions necessary for social domination, and the performance principle. This is the stratification of an acquisitive and antagonistic society according to the competitive performances of its individual members and is the 'prevailing historical form of the *reality principle*' (35). These two combine because each form of civilization, or mode of domination, has its own reality principle which becomes embodied in the institutions, laws and values of any given society. The reality principle therefore encapsulates the social relations of the prevalent mode of production, with the performance principle of possessive individualism signifying the surplus-repression in its current form. In this sense, Marcuse's critique of the performance principle not only socializes but also ontologizes Freud's theory of the instincts and becomes the site of his own interpretive confrontation with the prevalent as-structure of the capitalist world.

It was noted above that Marcuse saw in the performance principle of post-war capitalism certain features comparable to the elements of the reality principle regulating National Socialist society. There remained the rational efficiency of a system that bound humans to machines producing what he referred to as 'objective personality', a phrase borrowed from Lewis Mumford; there was the violence inflicted on dissenters and those who did not comply; as well as the identification with leaders via the aesthetics of the spectacle. This is not to say there is a direct congruence, or that the US, despite McCarthyism, was at any time a totalitarian regime of the order established by Adolf Hitler. In fact the opposite is the case. The affluent society was not only one in which the struggle over nature had largely been completed, meaning that scarcity, the prime mover of violence and hence the primary justification for repression, had potentially been overcome, but there existed a democratic system of government bequeathed by a series of rebellions and revolutions that had opened society in ways unimaginable even at the beginning of the twentieth century. In order to explain this co-presence of liberty and an evermore systemized surplus-repression, Marcuse not only recaptured the socio-historical element of the reality principle, but also drew out the dialectical relationship between freedom and violence, to show how the progress of civilization, which by definition is the repression of aggressive instinctual drives, actually increases destructive forces.

In order to understand this, we need to return to Freud's analysis of guilt and the development of the super-ego. We saw in *Totem and Taboo* how civilization first appeared through the primal act of patricide and the implementation of the law of the sons, immediately outlawing the liberatory act they had carried out. In Marcuse's reading, their objective of lasting satisfaction can only be secured through a new form of domination. In this we have the continuing struggle between liberation and domination, whereby '[t]he crime against the reality principle is redeemed by the crime against the pleasure principle' (68); liberation is both achieved and cancelled out. As Marcuse notes, from the slave revolts to socialist revolutions every struggle by the oppressed, every victory has resulted in a better system of control and domination. We now have a culture in which the individual has a whole gamut of rights that protect them from the arbitrary will of a dictator and yet the individual is also never left alone. She is constantly informed and instructed regarding how she is to live, what to value and how to judge. Leisure has been so tied into the commodity form, for example, that there is little external to the system of functions and operations demanded by the performance principle. Marcuse, then, recounts Freud's cycle of 'domination-rebellion-domination', but points out that each mode of domination is progress in the methods of domination. In other words,

'Civilization has to defend itself against the spectre of a world which could be free' (93). The model for Marcuse here is the crucified Christ.

> The message of the Son was liberation: the overthrow of the Law (which is domination) by Agape [chaity/love] (which is Eros). This would fit in with the heretical image of Jesus as the Redeemer in the flesh, the Messiah who came to save man here on earth. The subsequent transubstantiation of the Messiah, the deification of the Son beside the Father, would be the betrayal of his message by his own disciples – the denial of the liberation of the flesh, the revenge on the redeemer. (70)

In Freud's analysis of the law he noted how at a key stage in civilization the law became internalized as the super-ego which forces the ego to regulate instinctual desire through sublimation and projection, and which controls the recurring desire for a liberation not quite secured through the feeling of guilt. It is this guilt, combined with the satisfaction of basic needs within the affluent society, that ensures each individual represses the desire for liberation and submits to the administered society whose laws, values and division of labour are believed to guarantee the maximum satisfaction permissible; and to this end there is a 'total mobilization against the return of the repressed' (71), and in particular against the dissenter who symbolizes this return. In *An Essay on Liberation*, Marcuse claims that freedom and liberty will always be defined in terms that privilege and support the status quo. 'One of the most effective rights of the Sovereign', he argues, 'is the right to establish enforceable definitions of words' (1969: 73); words that not only define the enemy, but also create the enemy 'in order to perform his function for the Establishment' (74); and words that relegate revolutionary ideas about freedom 'to the no-man's land of utopia' (1998a: 150). Thus the desire for transcendence of the given is anathema to society, and the person desiring transcendence the (unpatriotic) pariah.

As in Freud's analysis, however, guilt cannot completely control aggression. The tension caused by the continuing desire for liberation (a repeat of the original patricide) still troubles the individual, or group, who must secure a release of tension and thereby the constancy that the balance of psychological processes aims at. However, in the affluent society where the individual is materially better off than ever before, the aggressive impulse 'plunges into a void – or rather the hate encounters smiling colleagues, busy competitors, obedient officials, helpful social workers who are all doing their duty and who are all innocent victims' (99). What is more, 'with his consciousness co-ordinated, his privacy abolished, his emotions integrated into conformity, the individual has no longer enough "mental space" for developing himself *against* his sense of guilt, for living with a conscience of his own' (99). In this analysis the accumulated aggression has nowhere to go. A physical challenge to the system could lead to material impoverishment, if not destitution, as well as criminalization; and an intellectual challenge is cut-off through constant exposure to a culture industry offering passification via a diet of pre-digested baby food (Adorno, 1991: 58). In this situation the accumulated aggression is projected outside. 'It turns against those who do not belong to the whole, whose existence is its denial. This foe appears as the archenemy and Antichrist himself: he is everywhere at all times; he represents hidden and sinister forces, and his omnipresence requires total mobilization' (1998a: 101). The result is regression to the sadomasochistic phase, outlined earlier in Freud's deployment of the Roman plebeian. Importantly, however, 'the impulses of this phase are reactivated in a new, "civilized" manner'. For Marcuse, *the* expression of 'civilized' sadism at the time was the war in Vietnam.

> Almost unadulterated sadism reigns in the American massacres in Vietnam, in the Saigon dictatorship, but also in the crimes which pervade the metropole, in the police, prisons and mental institutions, in the insane construction of ever more wasteful buildings, in sports, etc. With a larger masochistic component, sadomasochism is rampant in the rock concerts where the massive audience suffers joyfully and orgiastically the gratuitous violence of the noise [...]. And sadomasochistic is the tolerance of the people – the 'free people': tolerance of the crooks and maniacs who govern them.
>
> [...] This confluence makes the psychological category into a political one. Sadomasochistic is always an individual and not a society, but where the individual syndrome is displayed by the behavior of the larger society, it becomes a social syndrome. This society is delivered over to the *Death Instinct* in one of its most brutal forms. (2001: 171)

Today, more than ever, we remain libidinally tied to the spectacle of an expanding consumer culture and the 'civilizing' project of the 'warfare state' (165).

According to Marcuse, the path beyond the sadomasochism of the affluent society does not lie in further repression of aggressiveness but in the full liberation of eros. The pleasure principle has its own cultural effect and the erotic aim has its own civilizing project. It seeks 'the abolition of toil, the amelioration of the environment, the conquest of disease and decay, the creation of luxury' (1998a: 212). These activities flow from the pleasure principle, constituting work that binds individuals into greater unities. What is more, these erotic aims will produce greater cultural ties if work exists as part of a subject's self-realization, that is, if work is part of an autonomous project. While Freud was adamant that aggressiveness could not be reduced by the redistribution of wealth or the abolition of private property (1991c: 189 and 304), Marcuse argues that the civilizing capacity of the pleasure principle can be developed through non-alienated labour, the humanizing and democratic use of technology, and an alternative relationship to nature, that is, a different reality principle and a different mode of being. Contrary to the widely held belief that Marcuse was anti-technology, it needs to be noted that he was only critical of the particular technological formation he experienced. In *An Essay on Liberation*, for example, he writes that it is not technology, nor is it machines that are the engines of repression, but 'the masters who determine their number, their life span, their power, their place in life' (1969: 12). Rather than an externally enforced division of labour the liberated expression of work would be creative cooperation. Because labour has been organized with the utility of the established productive apparatus in mind, rather than the needs of individuals, 'productivity [has] tended to contradict the pleasure principle and [...] become an end-in-itself' (1998a: 155). While work will always force a modification in the pleasure principle in the direction of the governing reality as well as a concomitant sublimation of eros, the introduction of a new reality principle based on autonomy, cooperation, creativity, empowerment and public ownership would equate to 'the liberation of Eros [creating] new and durable work relations' (155). In other words, in an age when scarcity has been overcome, or should have been and only exists because its deliberate distribution supports the structure of social dominance, a liberated Eros can do much of the work normally given over to repression. Under a different reality principle, that would include the transvaluation of the capitalist mode of social organization, productivity would break out of the dehumanizing division of labour and pacified consumption demanded by utility, and open up new horizons of human potential, a movement that would also lead away from the frustrations feeding the appetite for destruction and affirm creation instead.[9] Such a society, born of a new sensibility, would develop people with 'an instinctual barrier against cruelty, brutality, ugliness' (1969: 21).

In such a society, where technology already has the means to deliver mankind from scarcity, play becomes the vehicle of liberation. According to Marcuse, the mark of a truly civilized existence is the dominance of play over toil and display over need and anxiety; indeed display becomes 'the free manifestation of [human] potentialities' (1998a: 190), and society becomes a work of art.[10] In a like manner, this principle of play and potential demands a transformation of sexual relations from those of genital supremacy as demanded by the performance principle, as well as the eroticization 'of the entire personality' and a 'reactivation of all erotogenic zones' (201). For Marcuse, the focusing of the infant's polymorphously perverse capacity for an eros of the whole body into the form of genital sexuality that Freud celebrated as maturity actually marks a repression of eros into a socially functional but problematically limited form. This reactivation Marcuse refers to as the self-sublimation of sexuality; and with 'this restoration of the primary structure of sexuality [the] organism in its entirety becomes the substratum of sexuality [...] Thus enlarged, the field and objective of the instinct becomes the life of the organism itself. This process almost naturally, by its inner logic, suggests the conceptual transformation of sexuality into Eros' (205). In this way, so Marcuse concludes in *Eros and Civilization*, the removal of surplus-repression equates to a strengthening of eros, which in turn brings us closer to the aim of all psychic life which is gratification through the lessening of tension, and in this way eros is able to 'absorb the objective of the death instinct' (235).

One might be forgiven, therefore, for thinking that Marcuse's message was 'make love not war'! This, however, would be a misrepresentation for he noted how the lifting of sexual taboos does not necessarily have a liberating effect. In fact the lifting of sexual taboos was a key component of the National Socialist movement, and even the sexual liberalization of the 1960s had little political impact given that, as a new marketing opportunity, it became subsumed by the performance principle. In fact Marcuse's message is more strident, and it is not the voice of the hippies that he takes as emblematic of the required resistance, but the ghetto population and the black activists, for it is nothing less than a different mode of being that Marcuse is calling for, and in this interpretive confrontation over the nature of our world we see the last vestige of the destructive instinct in Marcuse's vision. The fight against domination and suppression does not require pacifism but the counter-activation of aggression: 'The world cannot be changed by love  [...] but it can be changed by love that has turned into hatred and will return to love when the struggle has been won' (2001: 173). Even here the alloy of death and life determine the course of action.

3
Master and Slave

In the 'Philosophical Interlude' separating parts one and two of *Eros and Civilization*, Marcuse notes how Freud's analysis of the instincts is very much in keeping with the scientific rationality of Western civilization. Integral to this rationality is a metaphysics of subject *against* object, self *against* other. In this '*a priori* antagonistic experience', Marcuse writes, objective nature is ' "given" to the ego as something that had to be fought, conquered, and even violated – such was the precondition for self-preservation and self-development' (1998a: 109–10). The issue of self-preservation has been considered in relation to the destructive instincts and their repression. In this chapter the issue of self-development, explicitly the relation between self and other, is considered as a key component in the ontology of war. According to Marcuse the antagonistic experience that is central to this self-development receives its greatest treatment in Hegel's *Phenomenology of Spirit* which seeks to unfold the antagonism between subject and object, self and other, and seek a path to their overcoming in Spirit. For Marcuse the central argument in the *Phenomenology* is that reason 'develops through the developing self-consciousness of man who conquers the natural and historical world and makes it the material of his self-realization. [The ego] can become conscious of itself only through satisfying itself in and by an "other". But such satisfaction involves the "negation" of the other, for the ego has to prove itself by truly "being-for-itself" *against* all "otherness" ' (113). The implications of this conflictual definition of humanity, in which negation becomes the prime mover of self, history and world, will be explored here. It will also be important to examine how, if at all, this concept of negation might offer us a position from which to critique war. If, in this antagonistic metaphysics of world-creation, the ego must prove itself by being against all otherness, is it not this egoistic philosophy itself that needs to be challenged if violence is to be lessened?

The quote from Marcuse above is of course a brief summation of the famous dialectic between master and slave set out in the *Phenomenology*. Given that self-consciousness exists 'only in being acknowledged' (Hegel, 1977: 111), the conflictual dialectic between master and slave becomes the motor for history seen as successive struggles in an ongoing quest for recognition. Published in 1807, the *Phenomenology* was written at a key moment in German history. The Prussian State was defeated by Napoleon at Jena the year before, and it is said that Hegel wrote this work to the accompaniment of Napoleon's cannons in the distance. In a letter to Friedrich Niethammer, Hegel recounted how on the eve of that battle he ' "saw the Emperor – this world-soul – riding out of the city on reconnaissance. It is indeed a wonderful sensation to see such an individual, who, concentrated here at a single point, astride a horse, reaches out over the world and masters it" ' (in Franco, 1999: 121). We saw in Chapter 1 how Napoleon was also the epitome of the Nietzschean superman, and the discussion of the Hegelian dialectic here will provide a little more content for both the Nietzschean concept of transvaluation and the Heideggerian polemos.

To relate Hegel's work to our current context, this chapter considers the master and slave dialectic as it has influenced two other theorists, each of whom, in very different ways, can contribute to our understanding of war. First, continuing the psychoanalytic approach, the chapter explores Jacques Lacan's appropriation of Hegel and his deployment of the struggle for recognition as a key moment in the formation of subjectivity and the key to explaining human aggression. Secondly, and seemingly something of a departure, the chapter considers how the dialectic of master and slave has been used by Francis Fukuyama in his explanation for war and the dramatic claim that we are living at the end of history.[1] While Fukuyama's work introduces us to the rhetoric that is very much part of the neo-conservative ascendancy in Washington, Lacan's analysis of subject formation offers the means to challenge the very conceptions of self and other as they appear in that rhetoric. The connection between these two writers is not only Hegel, but the particular reading of the dialectic offered by Alexandre Kojève. Lacan is known to have attended Kojève's lectures on Hegel delivered at the École des Hautes Études between 1933 and 1939, while Fukuyama would have been introduced to Kojève when studying Leo Strauss. I will begin, then, by giving a brief overview of Kojève's reading of Hegel before going on to see how Lacan and then Fukuyama might help us understand the logic of war.

Kojève

Kojève opens his *Introduction to the Reading of Hegel* in the following way: 'Man is Self-Consciousness. He is conscious of himself, conscious of his human reality and dignity; and it is in this that he is essentially different from animals, which do not go beyond the level of simple Sentiment of self' (1980: 3). Man is self-consciousness and this 'I' that produces itself is accomplished by revealing itself to others as intentional becoming. Hegel informs us that 'the living Substance is being which is in truth *Subject*, or, what is the same, is in truth actual only in so far as it is the movement of positing itself, or is the mediation of its self-othering with itself. This substance is, as Subject, pure, *simple negativity*' (Hegel, 1977: 10). Negation, or negativity, then, is the historical movement of human becoming. For Kojève this can be rendered in the following simple equation: Man=Negativity=Action.[2] 'In short', he writes, 'to describe Man as a *dialectical* entity is to describe him as a negating *Action* that negates the given within which it is born, and as a *Product* created by that very negation, on the basis of the given which was negated. And on the "phenomenological" level this means that human existence "appears" in the World as a continuous series of *fights* and *works* integrated by *memory* – that is, as *History* in the course of which Man freely creates himself' (1980: 234). Because Man as pure negativity must be empty of positive content, what gives Man positivity are the products of fighting and work, the production through destruction, that are representative of the struggle against given-being. In this sense there can be no starker declaration of how important war and conflict are for human progress.

For Kojève, desire is the negation or transformation of the objective world that in turn transforms Man. It is in this movement that Man, in radical opposition to the objective world, begins to be formed through a 'series of successive "conversions"' (224). What is more, this movement, this becoming is a tendency in self-consciousness to perpetually '*extend* itself, to *expand*, to spread through the *whole* domain of the reality given to man and in man' (82). One might say that the ego is therefore inherently imperial, always seeking to overcome its current limitations. Desire in itself, however, does not contribute to human progress. Desiring objects, for example, is still animal in that it is brought about by such instinctual impulses as the need for food or the need to reproduce. In short they are the concern of the drive for preservation, discussed in the previous chapter. Also, as recurrent needs they can never be completely satisfied and continually recall Man into the world of the animal. What is required to be truly human is a form of desire 'higher' than need, and one that can be maintained over and above its incessance. This is the desire for recognition that makes humanity's realization twofold. First of all, anthropogenetic desire, as Kojève calls it, is defined as desiring the desire of the other. This is the desire to substitute oneself for the value of the other's desire. However, for this to acquire objectivity the second stage of completion in recognition is required. In this second moment, self-consciousness progresses to the knowledge of self-certainty because its subjectivity is revealed by another as an objective reality. Kojève, after Hegel, names this 'the doubling of self-consciousness', existing '*in* and *for* itself in and by the fact that it exists [...] for another self-consciousness' (9). The first stage of anthropogenetic desire, the desire for the other's desire, places the subject outside of itself. At this point the subject is vulnerable, a vulnerability that is only overcome if the subject is returned to itself through recognition. For Kojève, of course, vulnerability is the path to war, because vulnerability means the subject must impose itself and overcome its 'other-being'. This can be achieved by the pre-political destruction of the other, or as humanity progresses we may secure the pacific route of universal recognition that is the cornerstone of liberal politics.

In the *Phenomenology* the path towards the liberal polity is the path of history. It is the end point of successive bloody battles for the prestige of recognition. For Kojève it is freedom before death that in the end is the test of humanity, for 'no animal risks its life to capture or recapture a flag, to win officer's stripes, or to be decorated' (226). Only the subject who can liberate itself from Being – defined in terms of nature or what is given – by risking his life, can realize freedom. 'Death and Freedom', he writes, 'are but two ("phenomenological") aspects of the same thing, so that to say "mortal" is to say "free"' (247). Clearly though, death is not ideal for either combatant, as whoever wins must have a vanquished opponent to do the recognizing. While one is prepared to risk all in the name of freedom, the other must succumb to natural necessity, and out of sheer terror submit. One becomes master, the other slave. The difficulty, of course, is that while the master has proved his humanity to himself he still lacks any objective certainty as the person doing the recognizing has been reduced to the level of animality by preserving itself; its validity as another self-consciousness is thus void.

The master can never win; his lot is a tragic one. Somewhat ironically, the result of the struggle is that the slave is the one who realizes himself objectively as man. Through his work he modifies his natural conditions and does so to satisfy an instinct that is not his own (but that of the master), thereby acting in relation to a non-biological need. The food he prepares he does not eat, the wine he does not drink and so on. In becoming conscious of this, the slave realizes his autonomy and his potential freedom. For Hegel, the slave cannot free himself by becoming a master, for this would merely repeat the tragedy. Instead both master and slave must be dialectically overcome and a new synthetic man must appear; a man subject to the law, but a law to which he has given his authority. This man is the citizen of the French Revolution. The Declaration of 1789 secured the recognition, and therefore the satisfaction, of all 'men' through the implementation of what Kojève called the universal and homogenous state. As 'human reality is nothing but the fact of the *recognition* of the one man by *another* man' (p. 41), the founding of modern democratic institutions and the normative utterance 'We the people' saw the end of the struggle.[3] For Hegel, the Declaration and the later defeat of the Prussian state by Napoleon ushered in the end of history, that is, the end of the historical movement marked by the struggle for recognition, and the dawn of the age of the Wise, or the Last Man. Kojève notes, however, Hegel's insistence that only the 'germ' of the perfect state existed in 1806; so while history had come to an end, this meant an age had arrived in which human existence 'reveals itself to be actively realizing its own possibilities' (45).

Before continuing to think through the annihilative moment in Kojève's reading, and how this might help us think about the persistence of war in human society, I wish to briefly offer an alternative reading of Hegel in order to do some justice to the complexity of his thought and introduce some material that will be useful in relation to Fukuyama's position. Robert R. Williams argues that the 'significance of recognition for Hegel's philosophy as a whole may be stated thus: the threshold of the ethical is reached when the other comes to count' (1997: 6).[4] Such significance is missed in Kojève's reading, according to Williams, which 'truncates and distorts' (4) the concept of recognition and lends itself to an overly violent reading of intersubjectivity. He argues that for Hegel autonomy or freedom is achieved only in relation and in community. Genuine autonomy is, then, 'mediated autonomy' (6). In this sense freedom can be actual only in and as community – the 'I' that is the 'We' of spirit – and cannot be represented as self-realization which falls foul of the individualism that Hegel's critique targets. In this way the pattern of mutual recognition differs from the pattern of desire which is over-extended in Kojève's account. Instead of the simple self-coincidence achieved through negation, recognition is a 'mediated self-coincidence made possible by and conditioned on allowing the other to be what it is, a letting the other go free [*Freigabe*]' (57). Recognition, then, is a concept of intersubjectivity wider than the struggle between master and slave. Williams argues that the master and slave dialectic is only the first unequal phase that *must* be transcended. This means that Kojève's reading is 'a gross interpretive error' (10).

In Kojève's anthropology human agency is central and any mediation of recognition becomes impossible according to Williams, overplaying as Kojève does the desire that is the struggle between master and slave, while also omitting to note that this struggle is recovered from its relentless negativity in Hegel's later work.[5] But the *persistence of desire* in Kojève is precisely what is important for both Lacan and Fukuyama, for it is not clear how self-overcoming must in the end obliterate desire. Williams writes that desire is 'a preethical, prerational condition of individual consciousness that must be sublimated if recognition is to occur' (49), but, as was noted in the previous chapter, does repression not also occur in the moment of sublimation meaning that desire persists, only now removed to another scene? Also, if we turn from a focus on individuals to a focus on relations between nations, a matter that is of central importance to the subject of war, is it not evident that this pre-ethical, pre-political desire returns with catastrophic effects? While the state may form a sovereign 'We' in mutual recognition, there is no international or interstate 'We', as Williams freely admits. At this level the battle, the first phase, recommences. History is thus fundamentally tragic. In Hegel, however, international or interstate violence is not simply the reappearance, or persistence of desire, it is also esteemed because it wards off the threat to the state from the priority given to individual, private pursuits during peacetime. 'In peacetime, individuals come to be entrenched in their individuality and regard the material needs and interests as the ultimate perspective from which everything, including the state, ought to be measured' (343). War, on the other hand, 'relativizes the life and property of individuals in favour of the higher need of the state to secure itself collectively, even if that means that individuals must be sacrificed. War shifts attention from individuals as their own ultimate ends to sovereignty as the ideality of individuals and their property in relation to the end of the whole' (344). It seems strange, then, to down-play the annihilating, battling desire only for it to resurface on the international scene. In fact, for Hegel, it is a tragic but necessary component of ethical health (Hegel, 1967: 210). It would seem, therefore, that Kojève was right to talk of a negativity that continually seeks to extend itself, and according to

Williams's account must extend itself if only for the political and ontological security of state sovereignty.

Lacan

This issue of ontological security is central to Jacques Lacan's use of Kojève. In a translation of the negating activity of the desire for the other's desire that forms the basis of the struggle for recognition, Lacan developed a formative function in the process of subjective development called 'the mirror stage' and claimed that 'it is an experience that leads us to oppose any philosophy directly issuing from the *Cogito*' (Lacan, 1977a: 1). It is an experience that also prevents us from anticipating the completion of the subject because the mirror stage is a process of *misrecognition* ensuring the Lacanian subject is forever removed from itself in a state of dereliction brought on by its desire for union with an ideal other. Whatever else Lacan took from Kojève, he categorically refused the perfect, Wise Man. It is through Lacanian psychoanalysis that the illusion of this ideal, and, as we shall see, its emergence as the dark side of Fukuyama's daring hero can be more readily understood as the tragic condition of the subject that wants-to-be. And while the concept of negativity may still provide an impetus for human history, it is through the psychoanalytic implications of the split subject that one can better understand the destructiveness and aggression implicit in the goal of an ideal union, as well as open up a possible critique of egocentric thinking (and fighting!). It is also very useful for studying the rhetoric of war in which the ontological insecurity produced by this incompletion is deployed as a tool of mobilization every bit as important as the military's weapons systems. In order to open up these issues, it is necessary to explore the articulation of the subject through its Imaginary identifications in the mirror stage, to its entry into the Symbolic order of language, where it assumes its social role and takes up its place in the world.

It was Kojève's reading of the master and slave dialectic and the dependency of self-consciousness on another person that inspired Lacan's formulation of the 'mirror-stage' in psychical development. This moment of Imaginary identification with a specular image begins the process of subject formation. From about the age of four to six months, the child's gaze rebounds from a mirror (actual or metaphorical) in a dialectical cycle of (mis)recognition. The child, in viewing the reflection, brings back an image which it 'jubilantly' affirms as itself: the specular image thus becomes the well-spring of selfhood. However, bearing in mind the child's experience is one of limited motility and absolute dependence, the genesis of the subject, the ego, is therefore an introjected other; a desired, complete and autonomous form, an 'Ideal-I'. The nature of the gaze thus acts as an initial form of estrangement. The subject conceives itself as (a lost) object, and otherness is its condition of possibility. For Lacan, then, the foundation of self-consciousness is the immediate alienation of the subject from itself, and this remains the condition that haunts its every future move.[6] The contradiction that exists between the image of the unified body, sometimes referred to as the Gestalt, and the experience of the fragmentary, dependent body in which the subject actually resides is the source of a permanent tension, even paranoia. The perfect specular image is, then, both an ideal to be attained and a rival threatening annihilation. Ultimately the perception and introjection of the Gestalt situates the agency of the ego 'in a fictional direction', and as Lacan is at pains to stress, this fiction will not be overcome no matter how successful 'the dialectical syntheses by which he must resolve as *I* his discordance with his own reality' (1977a: 2).

In this phase, as with Hegel's conception of the master and slave dialectic, the subject is vulnerable. It is taken outside of itself in its wanting-to-be. While the negativity outlined by Hegel in the *Phenomenology* is strongly evident in Lacan he refuses the Hegelian end of this movement through the gradual attainment of Spirit. As Edward S. Casey and J. Melvin Woody have pointed out in their study of the dialectic of desire, 'Hegel too naively assumed that the self finds complete and transparent expression in the language and culture it produces and can attain full satisfaction and freedom by recognizing itself therein' (1983: 97), a point I would refer back to Williams's argument for the sublimation of desire. The subject is cut in the mirror stage, severed from any adequation with itself, a splintering that is irredeemable no matter how 'great' the historical stage, and it is this cut that is to have such a profound affect on the subject's future actions. As with the master and slave dialectic, Lacan situates the subject's misrecognition in a 'temporal dialectic'. On the one hand the mirror-stage is an anticipation, a projection of pure potentiality, but it is at the same time a retroactive experience in that the subject realizes for the first time what it was – but, of course, still is – namely incomplete, a body 'in bits and pieces', which Lacan playfully calls *l'homlette*. The initial euphoria of recognition is doomed to an immediate fear of slipping back into the chaos from which it mistakenly believes to have just delivered itself. This brings me back to my response to Williams's presentation (and separation) of desire and

recognition, for in the future perfect of Hegelian temporality the satisfied subject would always be looking over its shoulder, threatened by its
'preethical, prerational condition' (Williams, 1997: 49). Assuming what
it will have been, the ideal is the projection that fills the subject anew
with a dreadful recollection of where it was. It is also the source of the
ego's primordial jealousy.

> It is in this erotic relation, in which the human individual fixes upon
> himself an image that alienates him from himself, that are to be
> found the energy and the form on which the organizations of the
> passions that he will call his ego are based.
>   This form will crystallize in the subject's internal conflictual
> tension, which determines the awakening of his desire for the object
> of the other's desire: here the primordial coming together is precipi-
> tated into aggressive competitiveness (1977a: 19).

The Gestalt, then, represents for the subject the still-to-be-realized
possibilities of its being.[7] It offers the promise of self-mastery and the
overcoming of its dependence. For Lacan, however, this is a paradox,
for to 'master' the self, in all truthfulness, would be to understand and
accept the fact that ' "I" is another'.

Spurred on by the spectre of the fragmented body and the threat of
annihilation that continually haunts the subject's phantasy of unity,
the subject may strike out, or affirm its own activity, in order to redress
any perceived imbalance of power. As the subject is founded upon an
irresolvable crisis, projection can only have temporary success, and the
narcissistic fear of damage is a recurring theme of unconscious activity.
In the vain attempt to bridge the abyss of its own bipolarity, the ego
projects all of the hostility issuing from its own lack onto the other, or
identifies with another who seems to enjoy a more complete satisfaction: someone who seems to be more perfect and might compensate for
these unrelenting psychic ghosts. In such narcissistic identifications the
subject will lose itself in the other and in order to see itself as subject again;
that is as ego, as its own potentiality, the subject requires the disappearance or the death of the other. The ego seeks to force open the doors of
its potentiality by impressing its narcissistic self-image onto others.
Lacan suggests that this struggle manifests in a vertiginous domination
of space. Subjects enter their own battle (of pure prestige) in order to
eradicate any undermining of their fragile position. Speaking of the ego,
Lacan concludes his paper on 'Aggressivity in Psychoanalysis' with the
following, rather fatalistic lines: 'It is this pitiful victim, this escaped

outlaw, who is condemning modern man to the most formidable social hell, whom we meet when he comes to us; it is our daily task to open up to this being of nothingness the way of his meaning in a discreet fraternity – a task for which we are always too inadequate' (1977a: 29).

The normalization of the subject in its entry into the Symbolic, where it is socialized and given a specific identity, does not rescue it from its original cut by making it adequate to itself. Instead this entry into language is a further process of alienation. The entry into the Symbolic is the moment where the desire for union with the (m)other is substituted by more limited and legitimate aims permitted by the Symbolic order. With the entry into language the subject appears, suspended beneath the signifiers of the Symbolic; the subject as being, thought as essence, presence and truth, disappears under the subject as meaning, a process Lacan refers to as *aphanisis* (1977b). The slippage of the subject along this chain of signification is only brought to an end by one signifier pretending to be the signified, a role played by the phallus/law, which stabilizes the subject in relation to a specific identity.

My concerns with the politics of recognition are, therefore, twofold. First, negating desire is said to be overcome in the mutual reciprocity of recognition, but such thinking forgets that negating desire is always present. Secondly, dialogue will be reasonable, reciprocal and mutual as long as the subject is faced with what Michael Shapiro (1995) calls an 'imitative other' who reinforces the security the subject has found in the Symbolic. The subject is thus thrown into crisis when it is met by non-imitative others, who challenge this security and trigger the paranoia of the earlier Imaginary identifications. Whereas those who promote a politics of recognition believe radical difference between subjects, individual or communal, may be negotiated reasonably between mutually recognizing citizens, Lacanian psychoanalysis suggests how the appearance of non-imitative others that threaten the subject's assumed stability within the Symbolic bring into play the unconscious and the irrational phantoms of its negating desire, and the non-imitative other is met with an aggressive or hostile response.

A good example of this dynamic is Shapiro's discussion of the distinction between state-based, strategic warfare and tribal, pre-state, ontological warfare. His analysis contends that beneath the strategic, rational discourse of warfare through which the modern state presents war as peace, there lies a primitive desire to violently constitute and reinforce a sense of identity that is central to our interpretive confrontation to win a world. To explore this he considers societies in which warfare plays a prominent and continuing role in the every day organization of social identity. In pre-state societies, he argues, warfare is 'explicitly recognized as intimately constitutive of the body politic' (1995: 109). In this situation, warfare is not a matter of policy but an existential feature of life and world-creation, affirming notions of inside and outside, kin and alien, order and disorder. At this point Shapiro refers to Peter Huber's work on the Anggor of New Guinea who see their village as an autonomous cosmos of order delimited by very clearly defined boundaries. Evidently, in such an environment the external disorder always threatens to contaminate, invade or relativize the inside; and under these circumstances the outside represents both a constant threat of dissolution as well as the otherness constitutive of the tribe's identity. For Shapiro, this dynamic is best explained, and receives the most sustained theoretical attention in Lacan's appropriation of Hegel set out above. The fragility evoked by the non-imitative other causes the subject, as a matter of necessary self-defence, to project the fragility founded in misrecognition outwards in the form of aggression. The success of the projection is only a temporary satisfaction, for disorder remains a constant threat. As Shapiro notes, because the debt to otherness is unrecognized the incoherence within the coherence of the subject is never dealt with: 'What the subject represents as a hostile object of an aggressive aim is a stand-in for an inward aim, a drive toward the production of an inner coherence that would reconcile those elements of the self that defy this coherence' (1995: 112). This interpretation also allows us to escape the prejudice that locates such a dynamic in pre-state societies alone, and understand how this primitive need for the other to support our sense of self and our mode of esteeming is at the heart of all modern conflict. This is not to reduce strategic, ontical warfare to the dimension of ontological conflict, it is rather to say that all strategic warfare has its ontological component, and in many respects the ontological component is what justifies the call for sacrifice and death.

To illustrate his point Shapiro notes how during the Cold War the cosmos for the US was 'the free world', functioning much in the same way as the village functioned for the Anggor. It was the boundary of the civilized world, of morality and right. The Soviet Union was the 'Evil Empire' that helped define the boundary between the inside and outside, the difference that allowed the formation of identity. This dependency on an outside, however, is also a threat to the coherence of the cosmos as it does not reinforce the security assumed in the Symbolic. This conjures up the lack of satisfaction that marks Lacan's mirror-stage. The unrequited desire for completion in and through the other then appears at the level of the Imaginary in the guise of aggressive impulses. And where that aggression did not manifest itself physically, it emerged in demonizing rhetoric where the pre-ethical aggression is framed by a 'rationalized' discourse at the level of the Symbolic. The preethical aggression is displaced, as Shapiro points out, 'through a complex chain of signifiers' pertaining to freedom versus oppression, democracy versus totalitarianism, liberty versus conformity, open versus closed and so on (with a few changes to some key signifiers this logic would have been the same, of course, within the Soviet Union).[8] For Shapiro, therefore, Lacan's use of the master and slave dialectic proves to be a useful diagnostic tool, allowing us to comprehend the deep ontological issues that accompany warfare, and shape every confrontation with an enemy.

This relationship between the ontological and the strategic is best illustrated in the reversal of affiliations that mark both Gulf War I and the wider war against terror. While both have their origins in the climate of the Cold War, it is the war against terror and the invasion of Afghanistan that are most closely connected to the stand-off between the Soviet Union and the US. On 24 December 1979 the Soviet Union invaded Afghanistan (or, depending on your point of view, came to the aid of an Afghan government struggling to defend itself against Islamist terror). Over the following ten years the US spent in the region $2 billion to support an anti-Soviet resistance army from more than twenty Muslim countries. These Mujahideen were very important for the United States' strategic conflict with the Soviet Union, and in support of this strategy the ontological component of warfare was deployed to indicate how these 'freedom fighters' were very much part of the US cosmos, indeed in 1985 Ronald Reagan proclaimed they were 'the moral equivalent of America's founding fathers', thus representing them as imitative others. Of course, once the strategic requirements of the US changed, so too did the ontological warfare. By 1998, when President Clinton ordered missile strikes against 'terrorists' in Afghanistan and in particular the most infamous of those former 'founding fathers', Osama bin Laden, they were represented as non-imitative and as the absolute threat to the ordered cosmos of the US.

The same fate awaited Saddam Hussein. The regime change of 2003–4 was the second practised by the US in Iraq. The first, in February 1963, under the stewardship of President Kennedy and with British and Israeli backing, saw the removal of Abdel Karim Kassen once tolerated to counter Nasser in Egypt, and the installation of the anti-Communist Baath Party (Morris, 2003). By the time Saddam Hussein had risen to power, the US, while not liking the regime, were happy to use the Baathist government as a bulwark against the Islamic revolution in Iran (itself a response to the US/British sponsored regime change in that country in 1954). While France in the 1970s and Britain in the 1980s gave material, that is nuclear and chemical, support to the Baathist regime, in the light of the arguments used by the US in 2003 that Saddam Hussein's chemical weapons programmes were a threat to world peace, it is particularly interesting to note their material contribution to these programmes at this time. Donald Rumsfeld's visit to Iraq and meeting with Saddam Hussein in 1983 was seen as a means of opening the way for US companies to sell biological and chemical weapons to the Iraqi regime (Reid, 2002). In terms of the ontological warfare, it is important to note that as the relationship was covert there was little reason to represent Saddam as either an Arab 'founding father' or the absolute threat of disorder that he was portrayed to be from 1990 onwards. In fact, when Saddam Hussein killed 6000 Kurds in 1988, an event perpetually cited as a justification for war in 2003, the US sought to exonerate their man and blame the Iranians (Hiltermann, 2003). However, once Iraq and Saddam Hussein in particular had become the greater strategic threat, the full force of an ontological war was needed to convince an uncertain American public to give their support to military intervention. In 1990 the spectre of disintegration and dissolution was raised and a new world order was deemed the solution; in 2003 it was an 'Axis of Evil' that not only threatened the ontological heart of America, but actively hated it.

This deployment of non-imitative others in the rhetoric of the war against terror has a long history in the discourse of 'Orientalism'. As Edward Said has argued, the Orient is a fiction that provides some of the oldest, most profound, and regularly recurring images of the other. Orientalism is a way of both describing *and* ruling. It is not a set of representations of something that already exists, but the creation or production of an object ('the Orient') via literary, aesthetic, anthropological and psychological discourses, that is, the Orient is a vast interpretive task. And, as Said remarks, the Orient was Orientalized not because it was discovered to be exotic, but because a specific colonial power relation permitted it to be made exotic. The Orient is produced within a network of different kinds of power: political, intellectual, cultural, moral and economic, and, an example of projection, it says more about us than it does about those people who live 'in the East'.

That the Oriental is sensual, cruel and despotic has always permitted the West to define itself in terms of reason, civility and democratic government, something that in turn legitimized the 'civilizing' effect of the former colonies. Today our imagination is replete with Orientalist images that lend themselves to the current demonization of the Arab world as a non-imitative other; its intractable and threatening difference giving legitimacy to a new phase of Western hegemony.[9] As Said noted in the new preface to *Orientalism*, without the belief that these people did not like us and did not appreciate us, there would have been no war in Iraq. As for our new venture to civilize the Arab hoards:

> What our leaders and their intellectual lackeys seem incapable of understanding is that history cannot be swept clean like a blackboard, clean so that we might inscribe our own future there and impose our own forms of life for these lesser people to follow. [...] But this has often happened with the 'Orient', that semi-mythical construct which since Napoleon's invasion of Egypt in the late nineteenth century has been made and re-made countless times by power acting through an expedient form of knowledge to assert that this is the Orient's nature, and we must deal with it accordingly. (2003: xiii)[10]

The genealogy of imitative and non-imitative others thus becomes a very useful means for mapping the interpretive confrontation that is the preservation/expansion of conflicting worlds.

From this perspective it is possible to see the colonial residue in the war against terror. It is a situation in which Arabs are discursively ordered as either the embodiment of evil if they do not affirm the values of the West, or are considered good only when they adopt the legitimate difference afforded them by the West's increasingly formal understanding of democracy and its credo of economic deregulation. In other words, it is possible to understand the resentment in the Arab world caused by the refusal to recognise this world in-itself. We can also see how the radical difference of the Arab world is in turn deployed to give legitimacy to its overcoming by military means. There can be no doubt there was a strategic need for the US to defend itself after the events of 11 September 2001, but there existed numerous ways of doing this, and without the Taliban and then Saddam Hussein being mobilized as the absolute threat of disorder and disintegration it is unlikely that the Bush administration would have received popular support for its chosen course of action. In the light of this it will now be useful to see how the master and slave dialectic has been used by an important neo-conservative ideologue to support the claim that the United Sates' cosmos, that is, its definition of the good society, has been vindicated as *the* world at the end of history.

Fukuyama

Fukuyama opens *The End of History and The Last Man* by assuring us that there is a notable and general shift towards liberal democratic ideals throughout the world. His figures are meant to show how the struggle for recognition is being fought on a global basis and that more countries are reaching the conclusion that the best method of satisfying disputes and securing stability is to recognize the autonomy of the members of its divergent communities, that is, make them citizens with particular rights. The recognition of individuals as citizens is justified in Fukuyama, as it is in Kojève, through Man's negating freedom. This means that humans have the capacity to radically alter their environment through the use of science and technology, and it is scientific method that initially allows Fukuyama to conceive of a directionality to history. For Fukuyama one way in which natural science produces this directionality is through military competition: 'Modern natural science confers a decisive military advantage on those societies that can develop, produce, and deploy technology the most effectively' (1992: 73). He continues by arguing that the threat of war compels states to develop social systems most conducive to such technological development. This conception of directionality in history, however, while positing conflict at its heart, remains too deterministic a view for Fukuyama; where is the moral and ethical valuation of this directionality?

For Fukuyama it is the struggle for recognition, the transhistorical standard and definition of man as *man* that gives an ethical dimension to the series of historical progressions. He argues that there exists something essentially human behind the struggle; a desire to live meaningful lives and it is this that needs to be understood. At this point it should be noted that Fukuyama's use of Kojève is radically different from Lacan's. First, for Fukuyama Kojève is used simply as a means of justifying the liberal state as the purpose of history. This possibility, according to Fukuyama, was proposed by Kojève who made 'the startling assertion that Hegel had been essentially right, and that world history, for all the twists and turns it had taken in subsequent years, had effectively ended in the year 1806 [...] that the principle of liberty and equality that emerged from the French revolution, [...] represented the end point of human ideological evolution beyond which it was impossible to progress further' (66–7). Secondly, Fukuyama tries to overcome the ambiguity of the negating force that lies at the heart of Hegel's conception of human becoming by turning to Plato's interpretation of *thymos* found in *The Republic*. According to Fukuyama, thymos is an innate sense of self-worth, which, when not recognised, or when people are valued less than they believe themselves to be worth, causes anger and indignation. Although it is Plato that apparently resolves the ambiguities of Hegeliam negation, Fukuyama nevertheless gives Plato a significantly Kojèvian spin. Thymos thus becomes:

> a *desire for a desire*, that is, a desire that that person who evaluated us too low should change his opinion and recognize us according to our own estimate of our worth. Plato's *thymos* is therefore nothing other than the psychological seat of Hegel's desire for recognition: for the aristocratic master in the bloody battle is driven by the desire that other people evaluate him at his own sense of self-worth. Indeed, he is driven into a bloody rage when that sense of self-worth is denigrated. *Thymos* and the 'desire for recognition' differ somewhat insofar as the former refers to a part of the soul that invests objects with value, whereas the latter is an activity of *thymos* that demands that another consciousness share the same valuation. (1992: 165)

For Fukuyama, thymos is 'the psychological seat of all the noble virtues like selflessness, idealism, morality, self-sacrifice, courage and honorability' (171), and when a person's freedom is recognized it is precisely this source of human struggle that is valued.

Interpreted predominantly in Fukuyama as 'restlessness', thymos is of special interest since it is not reducible to desire or reason.[11] We are told by Fukuyama that culture comes from the thymotic part of the soul; it is thymos that encourages expression in the arts, as well as the powerful passions of religion and national identity. But not everyone can compose the sublime, sculpt devotion out of marble, or inspire sacrifice. The discrepancies between people's different levels of identification and drive come from the fact that thymos is more well developed in some than in others. The consequences of this are a paradox for democracy. While equality for all citizens is the *raison d'être* of any democracy worthy of the name, the equality is meant to ensure that those with a highly developed thymotic aspect are afforded greatest opportunity to realize their potential in positions of power, influence and favour.[12] It therefore supports hierarchy and upward mobility in order to supplant any socialist egalitarianism present in Kojève's writing.

This dialogue between Hegel and Socrates hosted by Fukuyama adds a level of sophistication to our understanding of the difficulties inherent in the struggle for recognition. What transpired in the earlier 'bloody battle' was universal recognition of the equality of all citizens as human beings by the state. But the interest of Fukuyama's thesis lies in a subject seeking recognition beyond that offered by the state, or a subject wanting to be *better* than, rather than equal to. The analysis of Plato's discussion of thymos allows Fukuyama to approach these questions by sub-dividing thymos into two distinct yet related components: *isothymos*, the struggle for equal recognition, while *megalothymos* is reserved for anything in excess of that.[13] While Kojève does not make the distinction between differing modes of struggle, enveloping all in a general desire, it can be assumed that the indefinite restlessness that is an aspect of Fukuyama's writing was inspired by Kojève's later, more ironic work. It is known that through an ongoing correspondence with Leo Strauss, and a series of reflections on the mundanity of life when desire is satisfied, Kojève shifted his position from one of militant Marxism, where because history was the product of human action our responsibility was to realize the universal state of freedom, to a position where the end of history would actually be the death of philosophy (Roth, 1985). For Kojève, the US was the perfect example of a post-historical State where universal recognition had made it languid. If human history had been a series of struggles moving towards universal recognition, once history ended with the recognition of citizens in a Bill of Rights, there proceeded from this moment on to be a vacuum at the heart of human negation and action. There was no longer a cause. Thymos we are told, deliberately searches for struggle and sacrifice. It is what drives the self to 'prove' that it is 'better and higher' than a fearful animal conditioned by instinct. It is what cannot be satisfied by sharing a value that acts as a common denominator for all human beings, it is not anonymous, and is something he likens to Nietzsche's will to power. Fukuyama tells us that Nietzsche's work 'is a celebration of Hegel's aristocratic master and his struggle to the death for pure prestige, and a thunderous condemnation of a modernity that had so fully accepted the morality of the slave that it was not even aware such a choice had been made' (1992: 189). Fukuyama goes on to argue that Nietzsche was 'absolutely correct' to believe that a certain degree of megalothymia was necessary for civilization, suggesting that without the wish to be better than others there would be little art, literature, music or intellectual life.

It is in this regard that Fukuyama makes his claims for liberal democracy. In spite of the marriage of civilization to a certain spirited and heroic aspect of the soul, Fukuyama is well aware that thymos has its 'dark side'. It is not only the source of artistic creativity but also the source of fanaticism, hatred, brutality and war. The establishment of a just political order, therefore, requires the taming as well as the cultivation of thymos. Initially it is evident that democratic government formally satisfies isothymos through the granting and protecting of rights, and due to its commitment to a notion of pluralism maintains a modicum of differentiation. The institutional structure of a democratic state, that is the opposition of different electable parties and the composition of the legislative body into two houses, ensures that (Fukuyama after Madison) 'constitutional government was explicitly established as a way of using ambition "to counteract ambition" ' (1992: 187). Despite its founding being a commitment to equality, it is the perfect vehicle for the expression of megalothymia. A life in politics can satisfy the desire for power and prestige while guarding against any violent conflict that might normally arise from such a condition, while in tandem with capitalism, megalothymia might also be satisfied on the board of a multi-national corporation.

For Fukuyama, liberal democracy in conjunction with capitalism satisfies the desire for objects and the desire for the desire of the other. 'The best regime' according to Fukuyama 'had to satisfy the whole of man simultaneously, his reason, desire and *thymos* [...]. By this standard, when compared to the historical alternatives available to us, it would seem that liberal democracy gives fullest scope to all three' (337). But while Fukuyama's discussion of megalothymia is a thinly disguised apology for the modern corporate master, it does also prevent us from bringing down the curtain on history. Indeed Fukuyama suggests that such talk is premature, proposing that the coming years will see a growth in authoritarian capitalism. Fukuyama, of course, is right to point out that the logic of capital does not require a plural democracy and the equivalence of isothymos, but the development of differentiated markets is one reason why pluralism makes democracy and capitalism good bed-fellows. However, to maximize its potential for growth, capital requires 'sweat shops', not organized trade unions, and the demand for swift economic revolutions driven by the will of megalothymotic individuals across the globe can only encourage such economic despotism.

The drift towards democratic capitalism remains inevitable, but megalothymia will still throw up some 'first men' capable of restarting the bloody battle even within systems in which recognition is universal.

> There will be plenty of metaphorical wars – corporate lawyers specializing in hostile takeovers who will think of themselves as sharks or gunslingers, and bond traders who imagine [...] that they are 'masters of the universe'. [...] But as they sink into the soft leather of their BMWs, they will know somewhere in the back of their minds that there have been real gunslingers and masters in the world, who would feel contempt for the petty virtues required to become rich or famous in modern America. How long *megalothymia* will be satisfied with metaphorical wars and symbolic victories is an open question. One suspects that some people will not be satisfied until they prove themselves by that very act that constituted their humanness at the beginning of history: they will want to risk their lives in a violent battle, and thereby prove beyond any shadow of a doubt to themselves and to their fellows that they are free. (328–9)

For Fukuyama, then, the reasoning behind the promotion of a continuing thymos is not to provide a philosophical excuse for the ego-maniac, as politician or tycoon, which, curiously, it does very well, but to maintain the very possibility of the freedom that would cease to exist if history drew to a close. In his *Introduction*, Kojève returns on numerous occasions to the importance, albeit the eventual impotence, of the master. It is the absolute dread experienced in the struggle to the death that is, as has been said, the catalyst of self-consciousness. Without an awareness of one's mortality one can never become. It is because we know death, because we can stare it in the face, because the subject, as Spirit, 'endures it and maintains itself in it' (Hegel, 1977: 19) that our freedom is assured. Hegel understood that without war and sacrifice 'men would grow soft and self-absorbed; society would degenerate into a morass of selfish hedonism and community would ultimately dissolve' (Fukuyama, 1992: 329). Death was a force like no other that reminded individuals of their shared ideals. For Fukuyama, once the people who fought Ceaucescu's Securitate had overcome this terror and achieved a representative state, their struggle ceased to be necessary and 'the possibility of their ever again being as free and as human as in their revolutionary struggle had been abolished' (312). Indeed, mega-lothymia is such a powerful part of the soul that even if the just cause is won, men may begin to struggle *against* the just cause simply for the sake of struggle (330). This is one of the reasons why for Plato the irrationality of thymos must be tempered and trained, ruled by reason to serve the common good.

The End of History and the Last Man, then, is an attempt to be faithful to both the Spirit of Hegel and the spirit of Socrates. It plots the unceasing and necessary movement of negation towards universal recognition, while also presenting an innate human restlessness that will not be satisfied with equality.[14] However, despite this incoherence there is one certainty that '[t]he ultimate ground of war among states is [...] thymos rather than self-preservation' (255), and that liberal democratic capitalism is the socio-economic system best able to lessen the chance of war and satisfy the whole of man. At the close of Fukuyama's book, then, there is no ambiguity as to the directionality of history. We are told that the nations of the world are gravitating towards a society best adapted to accommodate thymos. This society is a very peculiar brand of liberal democracy, one that is prepared to permit megalothymia even if it runs counter to the principle of equality, but this is the direction. The only difficulty is the differing speeds and differing routes taken by individual nations. Fukuyama's analogy of the state of world affairs is 'a long wagon train strung out along a road'. He writes:

> Some wagons will be pulling into town sharply and crisply, while others will be bivouacked back in the desert, or else stuck in ruts in the final pass over the mountains. Several wagons, attacked by Indians, will have been set aflame and abandoned along the way. There will be a few wagoneers who stunned by the battle, will have lost their sense of direction and are temporarily heading in the wrong direction, while one or two wagons will get tired of the journey and decide to set up permanent camps at particular points back along the road. Others will have found alternative routes to the main road, though they will discover that to get through the final mountain range they must all use the same path. (339)

It is difficult to assess whether this analogy displays crass insensitivity towards the annihilation of indigenous peoples by settling Europeans, or if the analogy was chosen precisely because of the supposedly necessary violence it recalls. Either way, this tells us a lot about the mindset of Fukuyama, while also giving us an insight into the neo-conservative worldview of which he is part. First, it is interesting to note that despite Fukuyama's ambiguity regarding the precise nature of the socio-economic system history is moving towards, that is, it is liberal but not plural, democratic but not egalitarian, we can be certain of two things;

there is only one path, and that path leads to one town: Fukuyama's town. Secondly, the fact that Fukuyama's imagination is still dominated by the Hollywood image of how the West was won, and that such an image allows him to unproblematically portray the 'Indians' as 'the bad guys' – so bad indeed that they have not even *attempted* to get on the path – tells us a great deal about how important ontological warfare is to Fukuyama and his desire to negate otherness. Fukuyama, may fantasize that he is the sheriff of this town, satisfying his thymos by sending out posses to kill the Indians, or discipline the dissenters who have set up permanent camp outside the town, but to continue the Hollywood theme, it is also possible to picture this hostility and aggressiveness towards non-imitative others as the activities of Lacan's 'escaped outlaw', negating that which does not reinforce his world.

The continuing relevance of the Hegelian model of international relations was clearly demonstrated in the invasion of Iraq in 2003. It was noted above how the struggle for recognition between individual subjects is repeated at the level of nation states. We are told in §331 of the *Philosophy of Right* that an unrecognized state has as little actuality as an individual 'without *rapport* with other persons' (1967: 212). In other words a state, while having attained internal sovereignty achieves its final legitimation through external sovereignty, that is recognition by other states. While this recognition is a mutual recognition of sovereignty and forms the basis of international law, states remain in a state of nature in relation to each other mediating their relations through treaties; with international law as a supranational power remaining at the level of the 'ought-to-be, since its actuality depends on different wills each of which is sovereign' (212). In other words, the dependency of international law on particular sovereigns wills means it remains 'infected with contingency' (214); open to the unilateral designs of the powerful. In Fukuyama's language, we might say that the ideal isothymia of the UN is dominated by the realist megalothymia of national sovereigns, as demonstrated by the stance of the US and Britain over Iraq.

This stance is justified in the literature published by the *Project for the New American Century* (PNAC), most notably by Robert Kagan (2002) who writes:

> Most Europeans believe in what might be called principled multilateralism. In this view, gaining UN Security Council approval is not a means to an end but an end in itself [. . .]. Even if the United States were absolutely right about Iraq, even if the dangers were exactly as

the Bush administration presents them, Europeans believe the United States would be wrong to invade without formal approval. If the Security Council says no, the answer is no. Not many Americans would agree. Most Americans are not principled multilateralists. They are instrumental multilateralists. Yes, they want to win international support. They like allies, and they like approval for their actions. But the core of the American multilateralist argument is pragmatic.

Multilateralism, then, 'is a cost-benefit analysis, not a principled commitment to multilateral action'. It is, he declares, 'multilateralism, American style'.

This stance is certainly thymotic, if not megalothymotic, and there is no better testament to the continuing relevance of Hegel's analysis of international relations. However, as Williams argues, despite Hegel's equation of war with the ethical health of a community, Hegel was no apologist for militarism, he rather sought to portray the tragedy implicit in the struggle for recognition where 'the conditions for [an individual's] well-being are at the same time the conditions of opposition and possible conflict with others' (Williams, 1997: 360). This tragedy is most clearly stated by Hegel in the *Philosophy of Right* when he writes: 'Perpetual peace is often advocated as an ideal towards which humanity should strive. With that end in view, Kant proposed a league of monarchs to adjust differences between states [...]. But the state is an individual, and individuality essentially implies negation. Hence even if a number of states make themselves into a family, this group as an individual must engender an opposite and create an enemy' (1967: 295). In the light of the analysis of recognition presented in this chapter, however, it is Lacan's diagnosis that gives us a much greater understanding of this tragedy than Fukuyama's ennobling of violence. In one important respect, both Kojève and Fukuyama miss the radical possibilities of Hegel's philosophy as a critique of war. Instead of thinking through the full implications of the dependency of the self on the other, they highlight the journey of the self for whom the other is only a vehicle in the subject's world-creation. Lacan, however, in the simple statement that 'I is another', offers us a theory of *misrecognition*, and with it the means to interrogate and challenge the subject in its relentless, violent search for completion.

4
Community and Sacrifice

The relationship between the risking of life and the movement of Spirit, which is such a central motif in the rhetoric of warfare, was nowhere more striking (and tragic) than in the enthusiasm that met the outbreak of the First World War, an enthusiasm noted not only for its intensity, but for the near universality of the sentiment. As Roland N. Stromberg demonstrated in his fascinating account of the intellectual currents of the time, the 'ideas of 1914' anticipated an experience that held 'archetypal echoes of the oldest tribal solidarity' (1982: 7). The idea of solidarity, of course, is not novel in the arena of warfare. What was significant in 1914 was its expression as a reaction to the perceived anonymity, instrumentality and alienation of modernity, which understood itself as the mode of deliverance from such irrational fervour. In our own time, the galvanizing effect of a war on the identity of a people cannot be underestimated. Admittedly we should not be so naïve as to think that the identity politics saturating the war against terror is the pure, unmediated expression of national belonging, but at the same time to dismiss the sentiments of unity and strength that underlie the rhetoric of George W. Bush's administration as nothing but manipulative propaganda is to miss important insights into the role of both community and sacrifice in war.

The enthusiasm of 1914, which to us now seems absurd if not perverse, must not be dismissed as some unthinking aberration for some of the greatest minds of the time, including Georg Simmel, Henri Bergson, André Gide, Henry James, Thomas Mann, Rudyard Kipling, Igor Stravinsky, to name only a few, all had positive and supportive statements to make about the imminent struggle for the soul of each and every nation – and, indeed, of Europe as a whole – that was about to be joined. The centrality of the notion of community as well as its sacred aspect is encapsulated in a passage from Max Scheler's *Genius des Krieges*: 'In this hour', he writes, 'it was generally felt that a special national destiny reached into everyone's hearts, the greatest and smallest alike, and decided what each of us is and is worth... We were no longer what we had been – alone! The sundered living contact between the series individual-people-nation-world-God was restored in an instant' (in Stromberg, 1982: 85). And it is this transcendence of limited, bounded and finite existence that will be the guiding theme here.

With regard to the link between war, community and transcendence one of the greatest theoretical exponents is George Bataille, another person to have attended Kojève's seminars. Like Émile Durkheim before him, Bataille understood the sacred character of the social. He also understood how integral sacred violence, both physical and symbolic, was to the life of a particular community, and how it 'elevates the victim above the humdrum world where men live out their calculated existence' (2001: 82). Echoing the sentiments of 1914, albeit written over forty years later, this statement encapsulates Bataille's critique of instrumentality and his virile celebration of violence. While his writings submit to no disciplinary boundary, ranging instead across sociology, philosophy, anthropology, economics and poetry, there remains a consistency in subject matter, namely the human desire to transcend or exceed the limits of singular, individual existence. This, he argued, is due to an awareness, no matter how opaque, that each individual is part of a larger whole. As was the case in the work of Durkheim, this awareness, in the first instance, gives a sacred character to the social and the community on whom we depend. It can also take on cosmological dimensions through an understanding of the fact that it was from undifferentiated non-being that we appeared and into which we will disappear. Of course, this cosmological connectedness is part of Durkheim's analysis of totemic structures (1995), but Bataille's analysis of the human desire for connectedness is much more radical. Where Durkheim's analysis of the totem establishes the position of the tribe in relation to the earth, the plants, the animals and the heavens, Bataille's pursuit of connectedness is a *loss* of self. This is another reason for discussing Bataille's work in relation to the ideas of 1914, because, as Scheler commented above, the war that was soon to arrive would cancel out the isolation of individuals, which modernity with its division of labour, bureaucratization and industrialization had only accentuated. In 1914 the war would restore the 'sundered living contact' between man, world and God; war would lift individuals out of their isolation and reconnect them with the infinite. In relation to the current

situation and the war against terror, we do not need to say too much about how the infinite is pursued. We need only recall that the response to the attacks on 11 September 2001 was originally given the name 'Operation Infinite Justice' until it was pointed out that such absolution was the provision of God alone. The name was changed, but the intention was clear, the war against terror was a war of the good infinite, as François Flahaut's (2003) refers to it, the community of Truth and Order, against the bad infinite and the agents of Chaos.

1914

While there are innumerable examples of the sentiment that greeted the First World War, none can surpass Rupert Brooke's language of regeneration, when in the 1914 sonnets he compared young men called to fight with 'swimmers into cleanness leaping'. He describes half-men alienated from themselves, each other and their heritage, woken by God from the dullness of sleep and gifted the honour they seek. The war will reconnect heaven, earth and man. This thinking is very much part of the first of the two intellectual currents feeding into the ideas of 1914 that Stromberg identifies. The war will bring about a restoration of the communication destroyed by the deracinating trends of modern life. This tension is most succinctly expressed in Friedrich Tönnies's articulation of the split between *Gemeinschaft* and *Gesellschaft*, where *Gesellschaft* is the alienating, anonymous and administered society that erodes the vital, organic connections of *Gemeinschaft*. The second current feeding into these ideas was the *Lebensphilosophie* that sought to articulate the spontaneously evolving cultural forms that were manifestations of the vitality of life itself. This was a continuation of the German vitalism that stemmed from Goethe, and was developed via Nietzsche's Dionysian philosophy and Willhelm Dilthey's insistence on the centrality of *Erlebnis*. A significant figure in France who was to have a profound influence on this thinking in the first few years of the twentieth century was Henri Bergson, whose philosophy of creative evolution and the *élan vtal* made him one of the most popular intellectuals of his day. According to Stromberg, Rudolf Euken, a noted proponent of *Lebensphilosophie* claimed: ' "Life is too rich and colored too mobile and variable, to be reduced to the forms and formulae of Thought. The stream of life breaks through the dam which was meant to enclose it, and flows into the open and the boundless" ' (in Stromberg, 1982: 12). In an age dominated by positivism and the demise of religion, Bergson's philosophy was liberation from the confines of strict determinism, materialism and mechanical thought. It satisfied a renewed interest in intuition, creativity, spontaneity and movement.

As Patrick Watier (1991) has pointed out, with regards to the social theory of the early twentieth century, the First World War arrived at a time when the abiding concern for the emerging discipline of sociology was the 'constitution, consolidation' and perpetuation of the social bond' (220), within which the relationship between individual and community was crucial. This was a time when, as Stromberg notes, the majority of intellectuals would have agreed with the sentiments of the Bohemians who in defiance of bourgeois society 'made art or energy or revolution an end in itself' (Stromberg, 1982: 15). Having inherited the Romanitcs desire for authenticity, intimacy and organic unity, the Bohemians' rage against the philistinism of an ever-expanding bureaucratic and capitalist society became the stock judgement on almost everyone's lips. The subjective, in its fully sublimated sense of the spirit or the soul, was that aspect of human life most in need of protection as the order of things, the order of capitalist and bureaucratic reification threatened to devour the world. The twentieth century begins with novels of 'adolescent revolt' and 'testimony of a profound malaise' (Stromberg, 1982: 18) evidenced in the increased standardization, massification and democratization of society. Heroism, a long favoured pursuit of Romanitcs and Bohemians alike became the popular demand in the face of bourgeois vulgarity and the 'new barbarism' of money. In the light of this the violent patriotism that stirred in the years just before the outbreak of war became the antidote to the advancing selfishness of an increasingly materialist world. In keeping with Durkheim's claims regarding society setting itself up as a God, Stromberg comments how 'nationalism was a substitute religion, involving a quasi-religious veneration for the symbolized figure of the Nation, sometimes visualized as the very soil or earth' (32). Again the metaphor of organic connectedness is all pervasive. Exaltation, spiritual awakening, transformation, regeneration, salvation and deliverance from rootlessness and pettiness, these, as Stromberg remarks, were the watchwords at a time when slaughter would become a 'purifying or cleansing fire' (40).

What is curious about the ideas of 1914 is that everyone seems to agree on the enemy, it was a confrontation with the bureaucratic, mechanistic, anonymous, calculating and deracinating world of modernity, but the war itself arises from a determination to attribute blame to certain national characteristics. Werner Sombart, for example, argues that the cancer of British utilitarianism was wasting away the idealism of Germany. In *Helden und Händler* published in 1915 he declares: ' "Frequently, we really imagine that we are fighting against a department store" ' (in Joas, 2003: 60). It could also have been French rationalism that was contaminating the German spirit; Cartesian dualism versus Goethe's unity. Alternatively, the French could equally set Bergon's *élan* against the mechanical and 'bureaucratic monster' of Germany. This first, fully industrial war was also, then, a *Glaubenskrieg*, a war of ideas in which the victor would determine the path of this interpretive confrontation and set the course for a new, or renewed way of being.[1] In the central chapter of Stromberg's account, he quotes Italy's most influential philosopher of the time, Benedetto Croce, solemnly announcing how the gravity of the war has lead to the rediscovery of unity: ' "we all seek the same goal in the same form" ', Croce declares (in Stromberg 1982: 86). Herbert Read likewise spoke of how the war overcame distinctions of class, rank and education: ' "we did not call it love; we did not acknowledge its existence; it was sacramental and therefore sacred" ' (87). Amidst the atomization of human relations the war bridged the gulf between reality and consciousness, experience and desire. As Stromberg notes, the nineteenth century had been a century in which human communities of all kinds, and 'the forms of human association inherited from an immemorial past' (90), had been taken apart by the forces of urbanization; once separated from the communal bond the individual was set on a path of decay. All in all the war was a response to the society of strangers and the anonymity of money that had replaced an earlier sense of intimacy and belonging.

With regard to the work of Georg Simmel, for whom the dominance of money was indeed a sign of decay, the war represented a possible renewal of culture and with it the re-establishment of the ultimate aim which was the 'perfection of man' (Simmel, 1976: 245). While Simmel described the event as an 'absolute situation', this should not be taken as evidence that Simmel was a cheerleader for war. In fact, as Watier claims, it is more the case that the crisis of culture was the absolute situation and the war was the possible means of transforming and giving a new form to it. Simmel, therefore, 'allowed himself to be totally overcome by the War [...] as the only conflict to take hold of everything in order to submit all to its uniquely sovereign task of transforming [...] a life which needed direction' (Watier, 1991: 226). The war is thus charged with a twofold task. From the perspective of the individual soul the war might renew culture, which is 'a unique adaptation and teleological interweaving of subject and object' (Simmel, 1976: 246). It might, therefore, unify the division that threatens the development of each and every person. From the social perspective the war might give a form to the chaos of life's fragmentary activities 'which, only to a very limited extent, have, or can be seen to have, any common direction' (Simmel, 1997a: 91). In this sense, Simmel's writing is very much in keeping with the central theme here, namely the transcendence of the limited, the bounded and the distinct in favour of the complete, the unified and the perfect.

In *The Meaning of Culture*, Simmel argues that cultivation is the development towards perfection of a predetermined potential within any given entity. His example is a fruit tree that is cultivated to improve the quality of its fruit. This drive towards perfection, however, is a peculiarly human trait. Perfection is what man demands of nature through cultivation, but his own development which is the 'a priori demand for perfection [...] inherent in the human soul' (1976: 245) is called culture. Cultivation is the admixture of the human demand for perfection to nature, whereas culture is the inherent expression of, or vehicle for the perfection that is a predetermined state of human beings. Perfection, however, cannot be achieved internally, but can only come about through the purposive use of the world of objects, and objects are judged purposive only if they contribute to subjective advancement. The totality or unity that culture aims at is thus a balancing of multiplicity; the giving of coherence, or what Simmel called 'a common style' (1997b: 102), to the plurality of objects and the many aspects of our subjectivity. If objects do not contribute to such a totality they cannot be considered cultural. The crisis, as stated in 'The Future of Culture' is that objective and subjective culture have become independent of each other, which in turn 'robs the individual of any consistent inner relationship to culture as a whole' (102).

In the essay 'The Crisis of Culture', first published in the *Frankfurter Zeitung* in 1916, the problem is understood in terms of means and ends, with the crisis definable as the immense, almost incalculable series of means that make up the objective world being taken as ends in themselves. For Simmel, the economic sphere best represents the superimposition of means upon ends, where money has become the supreme end and possession of it is the ultimate goal. One very important consequence of the war, he notes, is that people have been asked to economize with food, meaning that people's attention has been drawn to these commodities and away from the currency used to purchase them. People had been made to realize that one cannot eat money. Thus, 'a blow has been dealt to the absolute status of money [which is] a profound psychological gain' (97). Similarly with regard to the subjective world, sacrifice for the preservation of the nation is the antidote to the

egoism that places the individual as the ultimate end. The individual in war is reduced to the means to pursue the higher end, which is the community, without which the individual is nothing. Simmel writes: 'The malaise of our culture, the elevation of everything that is relative and provisional into ultimate values, will not come about quite so easily in a generation which has seen for itself that it is possible even for self-preservation, usually the most autonomous of ultimate ends, to become a mere means to an end' (98). Peace causes men to attach significance to secondary aspects of life, but these men 'will be immune for a while to that squandering of end-status on what is relatively insignificant and peripheral' (98). The war machine, therefore, is more vital than the factory machine because it proves directly the values of strength, courage, skill and stamina. As a consequence, soldiers may think more resolutely about 'the connection between the work they do for the means of life and the ultimate values of personal life [and] will have been given a sense [...] of some meaningful relationship between the part and the whole, the *thing* and the *person*, – even if this is no more than a pause for breath before fresh strife and alienation' (93).

It is not only the economic sphere and its distortion of means and ends that has brought about the crisis it is also the inadequacy of intellectual life. Simmel notes how great philosophical concepts that ought to bring unity to the chaos of life are merely a set of antinomies that permit no ultimate solution. The war 'would not have had such a shattering effect had it not encountered cultural forms that were already so eroded and lacking in self-assurance'. In the war 'we can perhaps already discern the quest for a universal interpretation of life' (96).[2] The war, then, is not simply the chance to resolve the tension between subject and object, individual and community, it is a battle for the sake of the infinite itself. Born of chaos it may yet offer a glimpse of the form that will harmonize culture and permit man to realize his predetermination towards perfection. Of objective culture Simmel writes: 'Countless forms which had begun to harden and become immune to creative dynamism have been drawn back into the stream of life' (99). The objective elements of culture will be reintegrated, they will 'break out of that rigidity and insularity which had turned our culture into a chaos of individual elements devoid of any common style' (100). The tragedy of culture is that its objective element does not necessarily work towards subjective perfection; infact quite the opposite is the case. Through war, and the 'absolute situation' marked by *this* war in particular, the source of life 'reimposes unity on that objectivity which is alien to life and which estranges life from itself'

(101). The war represents life rising 'in revolt' (101) against the chaos of the times. In the end the war is a confrontation between the two infinities of perfection and perversion. On the one hand is the infinity of order, creation and unity, on the other, the infinity of chaos, destruction and differentiation, and in this way the crisis that is the war must be understood as the crisis of our own soul.

Economy (general versus restricted)

In 1939, the year that the persistent ideology of community, spirit and destiny erupted once more onto the world stage, Roger Caillois, the co-founder with George Bataille of the Collège de Sociologie, published *Man and the Sacred*. In this book he likened war to the primitive festival, which 'purifies and rejuvenates society' (Caillois, 2001: 166). Like the festival, war, which Caillois called a 'black festival' (179), is the only modern phenomenon that compares in its function with regard to collective life. As in the festival, war 'assembles, arranges, aligns and welds [people] together, body and soul' (166). While Caillois recognizes that the intelligence must condemn war the heart, he remarks, can only respect it, for it appears as 'the very norm of the universe', 'the essential mechanism of the cosmos' and 'the most beautiful flower of civilization' (171). It thus has a religious or sacred significance. For Caillois, war is creative in contrast to peace which 'causes everything to perish through engulfment and erosion' (171). Like Simmel there is a struggle here between a creative order and a chaotic entropy, but while Simmel only speculated regarding what the benefits of war might be, speculations he reviewed afterwards, Caillois remained convinced that wars 'are necessary to regenerate societies and save them from death, to preserve them from the effects of irretrievable time', which is why 'the quality of the fountain of youth is lent to these blood baths' (171). But while Caillois conceives of war in relation to the centrality of transgression and the expenditure of energy, his analysis is rather limited. A more stimulating and challenging address to the importance of these excessive practices, as well as the community and communion that is their aim, is to be found in the work of Bataille.

To approach the subjects of community, violence and the sacred in the work of Bataille it is helpful to start with the first of the three volumes that comprise *The Accursed Share* in which Bataille sets out his own interpretive confrontation with our mode of being-in-the-world and proposes a conception of economic thinking that surpasses the calculating concerns of individuals and nation-states in favour of an economy in keeping with the boundlessness and continuity of the cosmos as a whole. The first volume opens with what Bataille calls a basic fact that the living organism 'receives more energy than is necessary for maintaining life; the excess energy (wealth) can be used for the growth of a system (e.g. an organism); if the system can no longer grow [...] it must necessarily be lost without profit; it must be spent, willingly or not, gloriously or catastrophically' (1988: 21). The question for the living organism is therefore always posed 'in terms of extravagance' (23). This general movement of waste, being a necessity, is also something that man cannot stop. Paradoxically it is also tied to his freedom, or what Bataille calls sovereignty. Being (at) the summit of living matter, Bataille argues that man is identified with this movement and this excess. What is more, 'it destines him, in a privileged way, to that glorious operation, to useless consumption' (23). Failing to understand this does not affect the outcome, which is as inevitable, he claims, as a river flowing into the sea. 'We can ignore or forget the fact that the ground we live on is little other than a field of multiple destructions. Our ignorance only has this incontestable effect: It causes us to *undergo* what we could *bring about* in our own way [...]. For if we do not have the force to destroy the surplus energy ourselves [...] it is this energy that destroys us; it is we who pay the price of the inevitable explosion' (23–4).

The price was paid in 1914 and again in 1939 with the outbreak of wars, the scale and destructive force of which could not have previously been imagined. It is Bataille's contention that economic growth in the hundred years preceding the outbreak of the First World War could soak up the excess of the system only temporarily. Increases in resources, production and population that were key features of the age of the industrial revolution all contributed to the use of surplus energy until that expenditure was impossible to sustain. This 'industrial plethora' (25) was at the origin of both wars. To avoid such a future catastrophe, we must learn to divert the surplus into further industrial growth, or we must direct it into 'unproductive works' (Bataille, 1988: 25) that dissipate the excess. Given that Bataille only truly prescribes the latter, it is odd that he should offer these two alternatives. What he regards to be truly necessary is an 'overturning of economic principles' (25), which is also an overturning or transvaluation of ethics. The problem with economic science and the temporary solution of further industrial growth is that such a conception is based on the traditional *restricted* conception of economic activity and the limited ends of economic man. It does not consider 'a play of energy that no particular end limits: the play of *living matter in general*' (23). The solution of unproductive works and glorious expenditure is part of a *general* economy that recognizes how life 'aspires in manifold ways to an impossible growth'; the exuberance of 'a movement always bordering on an explosion' (30). Bataille thus states that this analysis of general economy takes the problem of war as its 'first priority' (40).

With this in mind, if part of our wealth is doomed, or ought to be doomed to destruction without profit, 'it is logical, even *inescapable*, to surrender commodities without return' (25) and subordinate growth to the act of giving. One example of such general economic practices was the Marshall Plan that sought to reconstruct Europe at the end of the Second World War. The situation that could 'hardly be better for an awakening of the mind' (171) was the onset of the Cold War between the US and the USSR, which Bataille described as an 'absolute schism', where 'what prevents one from believing war to be inevitable is the idea that under the present conditions "the economy", to alter Clausewitz's phrase, might "continue it by other means"' (171). While the US economy, as in Germany in the 1930s, remained an explosive threat due to its overaccumulation and need for exudation, Bataille saw in the Marshall Plan an inkling of a war that need not result in military conflict. He writes:

> While it is true that it is hard to imagine the United States prospering for long without the aid of a hecatomb of riches, in the form of airplanes, bombs and other military equipment, one can conceive of an equivalent hecatomb devoted to nonlethal works. In other words, if war is necessary to the American economy, it does not follow that war has to hold the traditional form. Indeed, one easily imagines, coming from across the Atlantic, a resolute movement refusing to follow the routine: A conflict is not necessarily military; one can envisage a vast economic competition, which for the competitor with the initiative, would cost sacrifices comparable to those of war, and which, from a budget of the same scale as war budgets, would involve expenditures that would not be compensated by any hope of capitalist profit. (172)

Did the Marshall Plan indicate that a revolution in economic thinking was taking place, as claimed at the time by the French economist François Perroux; a revolution where the rules of the capitalist world were suspended and goods could be delivered without payment; and where the product of labour could be given away? For Perroux, the revolution lay in the fact that the Marshall Plan proceeded not from the isolated calculations of one nation on which classical economics are based, but proceeded instead from the *general* perspective and was ' "an investment in the world's interest" ' (Bataille, 1988: 177). But while the Plan did indeed contest the economics of isolation, it was not as revolutionary for Bataille as Perroux had thought, for while it operates from the general perspective as an unsecured investment, it nevertheless remains a component of restricted economy by defending capital against the advances of communism in Europe. However, what the Marshall Plan did indicate was that as long as there was a tension between the US and the USSR, as long as there was a threat of war, the war would be continued by economic means and the US would continue to think from the general perspective. But, as Bataille wryly notes, 'if this tension were to fail, a feeling of calm would be completely unwarranted; there would be more reason than ever to be afraid' (188).

That the current US administration is isolationist and militarist is testament to Bataille's fears of a world with only one hyperpower, a situation in which the economic experiment that was the Marshall Plan no longer has a place. While the Plan never did match the exuberance of living matter as a whole, gift-giving today, in the form of international aid, is absolutely tied to a restricted economy of utility, calculation, strategy and return. Aid is the antithesis of a gift. As Michael Mann has noted in 2003, despite George W. Bush's announcement of an increase in the US aid budget, aiming, by 2005, at $18 billion dollars, a 50 per cent increase over 2001 levels, this still only represents 0.2 per cent of GDP, a level that will still rank the US as the meanest of the 22 wealthiest nations (2003: 53). What is more, over a quarter of this money is military assistance and training programmes, with a further quarter going as 'security aid', that is, the provision of weapons. The instrumentality rather than beneficence of aid is further exposed, as Mann points out, when one examines who actually gets it. 'A third goes to one of the 20 richest countries in the world – Israel. A fifth goes to Egypt, which is effectively being paid not to attack Israel. Tiny Jordan, also paid not to attack Israel, rivals massive India and Russia as the next largest recipient. So over half the total aid program goes to prop up the small state of Israel, which contains one-thousandth of the world's population! [...] In fact strategic rather than development needs dominate most aid' (53–4).[3]

The very possibility and indeed necessity of Bataille's gift economy rests on a complete rejection of the founding principle of traditional economics, namely the notion of scarcity. For Bataille, scarcity was little more than a myth, and a dangerous one, from the beginning. Understanding the world in terms of scarcity is an error based on the perspective of an individual and not society, or indeed, the cosmos as a whole. In truth there is 'an excess of resources over needs' (Bataille, 1988: 45). The problem arises because, as noted above, the current economy proceeds from judgements made from the particular rather than the general point of view. 'As a rule, *particular* existence always risks succumbing for lack of resources. It contrasts with *general* existence whose resources are in excess and for which death has no meaning. From the *particular* point of view, the problems are posed *in the first instance* by a deficiency of resources. They are posed *in the first instance* by an excess of resources if one starts from the *general* point of view' (39). According to Bataille, then, the restricted economy is based on a 'miserable conception' (1985: 117) of life. It reduces the world to utility, conservation, calculation, rationality and useful activity. Pleasure and play become subsidiary, diversionary concessions where bourgeois society, maintaining 'sterility in regard to expenditure [...] has only managed to develop a universal meanness' (125). In the light of this, classical economics, argues Bataille, has always misunderstood primitive exchange by reducing it to the restricted world of barter. Against this, Bataille notes how Marcel Mauss discovered that primitive forms of exchange also included the need to destroy and expend as evidenced in a practice known as *potlatch*, which 'excludes all bargaining and, in general, it is constituted by a considerable gift of riches, offered openly and with the goal of humiliating, defying and *obligating* a rival. The exchange value of the gift results from the fact that the donee, in order to efface the humiliation and respond to the challenge, must [...] respond with interest' (121). Connected with festivals on the occasion of marriages, funerals and initiations, it is a manifestation of wealth very different from what we understand from the perspective of our restricted economy. It is not about avarice, greed is not good, and wealth is not determined by a capacity for the expanding accumulation of money. On the contrary, wealth is determined by the capacity to lose, and only through loss can the donee acquire honour. Expenditure is a risk in which man stakes his whole being. It brings unproductive glory, which is the ability 'to grasp what eludes him, to combine the limitless movements of the universe with the limit that belongs to him' (70).

To return briefly to the Cold War that was, as Bataille correctly pointed out, a war between economic methods, it is possible to see the space race as a form of agonistic *potlatch* between capitalist and communist rivals, where one expedition into the heavens would obligate the other to not only match the expenditure, but match it with interest. While space exploration is undoubtedly part of the calculations of restricted economy, developed with a view to the procurement of new resources, the invention of new technologies and the domination of a realm increasingly important for national security, the intensity of the space race and the fact that NASA's budget was so dramatically cut after 1989 suggests that the space race was as much a symbolic gesture as it was the cold calculation of an economic prospector. Throughout the 1960s, 1970s and 1980s vast sums of productive surplus were sacrificed in these extravagant gestures of excess, and while it is reductive to tie the Soviet collapse to the effects of this *potlatch*, it was certainly a contributing factor in its demise. The result for the victor was the bestowal of *rank* with the near sacred capacity of declaring a close to the course of history.

Sacrifice

Despite the first priority of Bataille's essay on general economy being the avoidance of the catastrophic expenditure that is war, it is not entirely alien to the analysis. In the first volume of *The Accursed Share* he addresses the festive character of 'primitive war' via a study of the Aztecs who he argues were dedicated to consumption not conquest. Aztec wars were justified in order to capture prisoners destined to be sacrificed to the sun, which, having been born from a sacrifice by fire would cease to give light without this constant supply of human, sacrificial gifts. Unlike the Egyptians and the Romans that used slaves for production, Aztec slaves were purely the objects of extravagant consumption. Although the Aztecs were warriors and were known for the extreme violence and cruelty of their culture, they were not, according to Bataille, a military society, but a religious one. 'The reasoned organization of war and conquest', he writes, 'was unknown to them. A truly *military* society is a venture society, for which war means a development of power, an orderly progression of empire. [Military society] is a relatively mild society; it makes a custom of the rational principles of enterprise, whose purpose is given in the future, and it excludes the madness of sacrifice. There is nothing more contrary to military organization than these squanderings of wealth represented by hecatombs of slaves' (1988: 54–5).

What Bataille reveals in these anthropological examples is not simply an alternative justification for violence and warfare, but the practices of an economy otherwise to the utilitarianism and instrumentalism that he believes condemns mankind to catastrophic destruction. Where archaic religious society took slaves for the purpose of extravagant consumption in the form of sacrifice, the instrumental and utilitarian military order converts slaves into labour and 'makes conquest a methodical operation for the growth of an empire' (1989: 66). This is an order in which all entities are stripped of their intimacy and arranged as functional components regulated by rational operations. It is an order of servility in which all entities are reduced to the order of *things*, or what Bataille also refers to as the order of the *real*. In relation to the order of the real, empire is not some external agent that benefits from this methodical operation, but is the effectuation of the operation itself. In empire, 'Every presence around it is ordered relative to it in a project of conquest. In this way it loses the simple individualized character of the limited community. It is not a thing in the sense in which things fit into the order that belongs to them; it is itself the order of things and it is a universal thing' (66–7).

In contrast, religious societies, according to Bataille, use violence in keeping with the cosmological principle of a superabundance of energy. Captives gained during exchanges (violent or otherwise) with other communities are not deployed in pursuit of further gains or conquests but are expended in extravagant festivities that put the community itself at risk. This is an internal violence wholly at odds with the external violence of the ever-expanding, instrumental empire. Also, aside from these festivals being in keeping with the cosmological principle of unprofitable waste, the sacrificial festival 'restores to the sacred world that which servile use has degraded' (1988: 55). In other words, it restores the subjectivity and the 'intimate participation' (56) with other entities that the instrumentality of the restricted economy and the order of things destroys. The intimacy of primitive warfare is also illustrated in Jacqueline Rose's essay 'Why War?' in which she refers to the work of Geza Roheim who recorded how the blood avenger of the Ngatatara tribe of Central Australia was required to take his victim in his arms lest he dies himself. Identifying with the victim, the avenger is believed to be susceptible to his own violence which only an embrace can save him from. Likewise, the hero of the Papago Indians of North America when returning victorious from war is put into isolation 'as if he was inflicted with a terrible disease' (Rose, 1993: 21). As was noted above, this quest for intimacy amid the anonymity of calculation was a sentiment shared by the numerous intellectuals that contributed to the ideas of 1914.

As the superabundance of energy provides Bataille with a cosmological explanation for the violence of wasteful destruction, so this concept of intimacy provides the anthropological and ontological reason for the place of violence in human society. For Bataille the order of the real is in stark contrast to the immediacy of animality. 'The animal', he writes, 'is in the world like water in water' (1989: 24). This is true of humans too, even if our industrialized world has blinded us to this primary mode of being. The lifting of individual objects out of immediacy is ascribed to the invention of technology because, according to Bataille, it is through the use of tools that entities are first comprehended as objects and reduced to things in the service of a seemingly infinite chain of particular ends.[4] This is an order of servility and subjugation, for as the order of the real subjugates nature, so it ties man to this subjugated nature which then becomes his property and 'ceases to be immanent to him' (41). From this ordering of the real, immediacy, in its contrast to the world of things, took on a new significance and 'offered man all the fascination of the sacred world' (35), a fascination at once attractive and vertiginous. Thus the real world, the profane world of tools, objects and things is a 'fallen world' (41) that gives birth to a consciousness of the divine. In spite of the instrumentality of the real, there remains a feeling for immediacy and intimacy, a desire for community and communication in the sense of a profound fellowship of being. The restricted economy, however, 'rejects the affirmation of intimate life' (46), it reduces all beings to things and the servitude of productive work in which each entity is exchangeable and dispensable. Against such an order the true end of man is the fullness of being, which has no end other than itself. It is this sovereignty rather than servility that is man's primordial condition. 'Sovereignty comes first' (1991: 285).

This awareness and experience of intimacy is, finally, what is at stake for Bataille, for it is the attainment of this sovereignty that is most important for comprehending man's place in the cosmos and ensuring the glorious expenditure that avoids the catastrophe of world war. The truth of the matter, as far as Bataille is concerned, is that there remains within man 'an undercurrent of violence', which reason 'cannot bring to heel' (1988: 40). Contemplating the simple joy one might experience on a beautiful spring day, Bataille notes how 'something cruelly rises up in him that is comparable to a bird of prey that tears open the throat of a smaller bird in an apparently peaceful and clear blue sky' (1985: 235). There is thus a movement in man that always exceeds the boundaries set for it by the order of reason and the restricted economy. In his Heraclitean meditation he declares: 'I MYSELF AM WAR' (239). This is recognition of his negating, annihilating becoming, something that can only be appeased by a war against limits, a war that 'implies intervention in public affairs, certainly; but first of all and more profoundly, what it aims at is consciousness' (1988: 41). Such sovereign consciousness involves the sacrilizing of actual and symbolic violence in a face-to-face encounter with death. Death alone, he writes, can reveal the *'invisible brilliance of life that is not a thing'* (1989: 47). Death dissolves the real order. Sovereign practices thus include the risking of the life of the community through the extravagant exchange of potlatch; the ecstasy of the mystic who seeks communion in an agonizing ecstasy; the poetry that seeks to dramatize the disappearance of the object (Lala, 1995), and the eroticism through which we might be able 'to bear a negation that carries us to the farthest bounds of possibility' (Bataille, 2001: 24). Eroticism is especially important to Bataille because it is related to the sexual reproduction that generates discontinuous beings, that is, the distinct individuals that appear from the intimacy and continuity of being and are posited and then socialized as independent selves. Eroticism, which exceeds the instrumentality of reproduction affords a glimpse of continuity, and is the best way to face death without dying: 'Continuity is what we are after, but generally only if that continuity which the death of discontinuous beings can alone establish is not the victor in the long run. What we desire is to bring into a world founded on discontinuity all the continuity such a world can sustain' (2001: 19).

Sacrifice is of course the exception for this does require the physical death of an entity. And it is here in the practice of sacrifice that the cosmological excess, the anthropological violence and the sociological transgression are crystalized in one sovereign event. The taboo on murder is the most central taboo of any society, but duels, feuds and war break the taboo according to set rules. Society permits, within certain formal parameters, the overturning of the taboo established to maintain it. The reason for this is that human society is founded through prohibition. Humanity is thus defined not by its reason but by interdiction, and it is interdiction that separates us from and raises us above animals. Interdiction thus founds the world of discontinuous beings and taboos form the basis of the human society through which man can escape the necessities of his animality; but as the immediacy of animality remains something we crave, transgression becomes the means to approach its intimacy. Sacrifice, thus plays a key role in the attainment of the ultimate inner experience because through sacrifice, as the suspension of the primary law of discontinuous being, the individual 'identifies with the victim in the sudden movement that restores it to immanence (to intimacy)' (1989: 51). Because sacrifice gives us access to the immediacy of being, it must be understood as 'the religious act above all others' (2001: 81). Sacrifice, by opening life to death opens it to the infinite. 'A violent death disrupts the creature's discontinuity; what remains, what the tense onlookers experience in the succeeding silence, is the continuity of all existence with which the victim is now one. Only a spectacular killing, carried out as the solemn and collective nature of religion dictates, has the power to reveal what normally escapes notice' (22).[5]

These sovereign practices that prevent the war against limits exploding into a catastrophic conflagration are part of, and are maintained by, what Bataille refers to as heterogeneous society. In contrast to the homogenous society where human relations are based on a fixed identity and commensurability of all social components, heterogeneous society is marked by its recognition of elements that are 'impossible to assimilate' (1985: 140). Homogenous society, like the restricted economy of which it is part, is productive society. In terms of world-creation, the useless is excluded and the useful is defined by the common denominator we know as money. Everything in the homogenous society must comply with the productivity of monetary exchange. In this way, as Michael Richardson notes, the restricted economy of capitalism reduces people to their socio-economic function and denies them the 'communal effusion to be discovered in [...] heterogeneous activity' (1994: 34). Within homogenous society, everything heterogeneous 'is subjected to a *de facto* censorship' (Bataille, 1985: 141) and operates at the level of a social unconscious. The heterogeneous is the excessive: waste matter, parts of the body, the erotic, dreams, mobs, warriors, the aristocratic and the impoverished, as well as all manner of people 'who refuse the rule' (142). Again, in terms of world-creation, heterogeneous society is allied to the force of affective value rather than the abstract and neutral moral order of homogeneity. This means that a heterogeneous society is open to the creative process of organic institutions that proceed from the immanent activity of social cooperation and interaction. In contrast, homogenous society is the imposition of a transcendent and inflexible law that cannot match the movement and dynamics of affective relations. The result, notes Richardson, is social disintegration because only a heterogeneous society, which opens itself to the margins and to the forbidden, can accommodate the cosmological and anthropological need for transgressive intimacy.

To return to the 'ideas of 1914' with which this chapter opened we find that the compulsion for intimacy and solidarity manifested itself catastrophically. We saw how Tönnies's distinction between *Gesellschaft* and *Gemeinschaft* was crucial to an understanding of the enthusiasm that greeted the First World War. This distinction also motivates Bataille's division between homogenous and heterogeneous societies, but his point is that the desire for community within a restricted economy, which has no place for excessive practices, can only result in its own explosive destruction. Again, as Richardson notes, under capitalism it is impossible for individuals to reproduce themselves as anything but isolated individuals meaning that the deep need for social solidarity takes on reactionary forms of social hierarchy as people seek to lose themselves through an identification with a charismatic leader, a Party, a nation or a *Volk*. In the case of the First World War the identification took the form of a desire to return to the lost, organic and authentic community obliterated by the anonymous forces of modernity. In the ensuing bloodbath, sacrifice lost its heterogeneous element. It no longer functioned as an integral moment of general economy but was reduced to the logic of utility as the deaths of hundreds of thousands of men were either rendered necessary through the perverse calculations of military logistics, or were recuperated for the reproduction of society and donated to the care of a transcendent God. Having failed to satisfy the profound need for intimacy, and with capitalism still tying all social productivity to the restricted realm of utility, this same feeling would reappear only twenty years later in a second wave of reactionary identifications. In a society where intimacy is prohibited through the division of labour and the ideology of possessive individualism, or it is separated from the immediacy of social relations as a transcendent, universal and absolute moral category, fascism steps in as 'a meaningful experience of the sacred' (Richardson, 1994: 93).[6]

In the context of the war against terror the sacred becomes reified as an object within the order of the real. To say it is within the order of the real, however, is slightly problematic given that the sacred is in fact the object guaranteeing, or underwriting the world of objects. The war against terror is a confrontation between two worlds claiming completion and absolute right through their proximity, even ownership of the sacred. Rather than the sacred exceeding the order of property it becomes what is most proper to each of the opposing communities. Rather than the sacred operating as an outside that cannot be assimilated, an exteriority that posits otherness and an 'opening on to the unknown' (Bataille, 2001: 91), the sacred becomes a test of a community's identity (signified by the wearing of a totemic pin), compelling it to destroy that which stands against it. This is what we see in a US president with Appollonian pretensions and a British prime minister with messianic delusions. This is not to suggest that Bataille's vision is one of peace, love and tolerance, for it remains a world of violence and cruelty. Only violence, he argues, can bring everything to the state of flux required to touch discontinuity. But Bataille at least is honest. He seeks to understand the human need for violence and seeks ways and means to localize the ritual expression of violence and war 'that brings modern man back to what is at stake' (1991: 346).[7]

Of course, Bataille fails to give sufficient account of the ritualized violence that takes place on a modern battlefield. He fails to address how individuals and groups can partake in violence of the kind he would argue satisfies the human desire to touch limitlessness. Writers such as Paul Fussell (1975) have given wonderful accounts of the transformative, renewing and ecstatic experiences that take place in war, experiences which themselves blur Bataille's distinction between the practices of a restricted and a general economy. In the end, however, we are left with two economies of violence. Bataille's account places violence centre stage in order to limit its expression through the periodic transgression of limits. On the other we have the supposed pacific, utilitarian vision of the restricted economy that preaches non-violence and yet practices expansive, unlimited violence in an infinite war. While Bataille could, in truth, only localize violence because he underplayed the warlike capacity of, say, the Aztecs, and could not really challenge the destructive path of war because he remained locked within a virile metaphysics he inherited from Nietzsche and later from Kojève, his identification of our desire to touch if not actually claim limitlessness remains integral for understanding the human capacity for destruction.

The good and the bad infinite

While Bataille's work is important for thinking the excess that compels us to transgress the limits of discontinuous being he remained blind to the need to challenge the virility of the struggle he inherited from Kojève, which was central to his conception of death and communication. Without this element of self-critique his thinking sailed much closer to the catastrophic than he would care to admit, a problem that is exposed in François Flahaut's book *Malice*. Flahaut's account of our relationship with limitlessness opens with a discussion of the creation narratives that posit the formation process emanating from an omnipotent power understood as chaos or the abyss. Differentiated beings rise out of non-being and in turn set limits to this limitlessness through the categorical ordering of knowledge, be that mythic, narrative knowledge or scientific reasoning. In this manner, human beings assume a sense of control, but *'it is only non-being that exists absolutely or infinitely'* (2003: 22). Early creation myths conceived of this limitlessness ambiguously, that is, it was destructive because it was not limited, it exceeded every boundary and category, but at the same time it was the source of differentiation, it was the source from which the ordered world of discontinuous beings sprung. This ambiguity, or *duality* as Flahaut refers to it, becomes the *dualism* of Christian and later Enlightenment thought. In the former, ambivalence is represented as the division between good and evil, the Devil and God, and 'the fount of limitlessness is, so to speak, dismantled. The infinite toned down and idealized, becomes God's, while destructiveness and confusion become Satan's' (25). The morality stemming from the earlier conception of duality, he argues, suggests that we ought to make the most of our incompleteness. There is an element of resignation here that prevents us from, either epistemologically or ontologically, claiming completion and authority. By contrast the later dualism (Christian and Enlightenment) constructs morality as the pursuit of self-fulfilment in relation to the good infinite in a battle against forces of the bad infinite. Infinity only remains a challenge for me, or a questioning of me, if I stray from the path of the good. In this scenario the self, once attuned to the good infinite, is on a gradual path towards completion given the requisite tuition, influence and guidance.

In truth, however, the self with a name and a particular place in society will always be locked in a confrontation with a 'non-bounded, non-differentiated proto-subjectivity' that persists through every aspect of socialization and remains an opening to the chaos of limitlessness that predates the establishment of authority. Our relationship to this persistent limitlessness is 'the frontier separating the construction of the world from its destruction' (45). Crossing it, as we do in our conjuring of monsters (Flahaut's example is that of *Frankenstein*), is something we are compelled, if not 'ordered', to do. It becomes something of a test. In the context of warfare, Flahaut refers to the stories of barbarity and cruelty practiced by Native Americans. These stories, he notes, were based partly in fact, but were also fantasies of an absolute malevolence that white people were to pit themselves against. The projection of violence onto the other is not simply a means of rendering one's own action legitimate and necessary, it is also a means by which we are permitted an encounter with limitlessness and the bad infinite in order to conquer it. Flahaut describes this sequence as follows: 'I perceive myself as good [...]; I am conscious that someone with whom I have dealings is carrying out an act of aggression towards me; I project my fantasy of all-powerfulness (of all-malignity) on to him; since the other is all, I am going to be annihilated; to defend myself against this annihilation, I myself must be all – a whole, undivided, total being. Thus I shall abandon myself to the pleasure of all-powerfulness' (50). This projection of violence functions as a confrontation with absolute evil that supports our own desire for what Flahaut calls *'self-begetting in completeness'* (58), a narcissistic fantasy in which the self is all. As love requires sacrifice, reciprocity and a certain abdication of self, it is only hate that permits the securing of the narcissistic fantasy. Only by hating can I affirm myself 'absolutely and unconditionally' (71), and the conjuring of monsters and the threat of destructive limitlessness permits the expression of hate. Hating produces 'an immediate extra-being' (126–7) similar to the bond of individuals during war who create a moment of self-expansion through their solidarity and through the destruction of the boundaries that others 'set up against the expansion of one's being' (126).

To illustrate his argument Flahaut also uses the example of Aztec sacrifice, but Flahaut's treatment leads to starker conclusions than Bataille's and helps us visualize the dangers involved in our own encounters with unbounded and absolute evil. Rather than sacrifice acting as a satisfying release of energy in which the members of the Aztec community expend their surplus in keeping with the sun's expenditure, Flahaut understands the consuming god to be a devouring god. It is not excessively productive, but infinitely destructive. Yes, sacrifice is a means of renewing the sun's energy against the threat of darkness, but what is most important in Flahaut's analysis, and something that Bataille certainly underplays, is the fact that the Aztecs *struggled against Chaos by plunging into it.*

> It was not the sun [...] that the Aztecs [...] were really dealing with, but their own infinitude. To ward it off, to limit its pressure, they paid it a tribute. Whatever benefit one might find in living in material and psychic worlds that are differentiated, ordered and bounded, one never entirely renounces limitlessness and the desire for omnipotence. Moreover, [...] the need to struggle against Chaos, far from being expressed in the building of some fundamental barrier capable of resisting it, is presented as the need to confront it, to enter into a relation with it in order to counter it with a remedy comparable with the evil, a means of pacification which responds to its voracity. And since only the infinite can be measured against the infinite, the remedy ultimately fosters the evil. (132)

The urgency of this reconceptualization of the Aztec's consuming god, and of violent sacrifice more generally, is that through the violence that was deemed essential for the maintenance of an ordered and habitable world the Aztecs, as Flahaut notes, *'imitated the predator from which they sought to protect themselves'* (131, my italics); and it is this imitation that is currently at play in our engagement with evil today. At the end of Stromberg's account of the ideas of 1914, he permits himself this last apology: 'The war had psychic explanations, but these are not of the order of hidden springs of malevolence; they involve, rather, a powerful thirst for identity, community, purpose – positive and, in themselves, worthy goals, perverted and misdirected but not poisoned at the springs' (1982: 191). However, this sublimation of violent completeness into visions of idyllic completeness is always possible after the fact. We noted how Georg Simmel, a man committed to the Good and to human perfection, pitted the source of all life, the good infinite, against a disintegrating, fracturing and destructive chaos, the bad infinite. In the end, his search for the continuity of community and the creative intimacy of life called forth the forces that annihilated it, and if we refuse to face up to the dangers of our flirtations with limitlessness in the war against terror we will also continue to write apologies for the most brutal practices imaginable.

5
Injuring and Mourning

Not only does war *produce* countless deaths, it is also, according to Sara Ruddick, the *product* of an obsession with death in Western thought. In *Maternal Thinking*, Ruddick argues that one of the chief contributing factors to the persistence of war is the philosophical privileging of death over life, something that has been clearly illustrated in the preceding three chapters. For Ruddick, Western philosophy has consistently relegated life to a supporting role in relation to death, which is the true motor or goal of human existence. Although such an interpretation of the Western tradition must bracket out vitalist, or life philosophies, it is difficult to play down the significance of death within the Western, predominantly male, canon.[1] Curiously, however, when it comes to warfare and the official rhetoric of a military campaign, death largely disappears. Victories are not noted or recorded by body counts. We tend not to report or show the mounting dead preferring to perform the disappearance of injured and mutilated bodies in the name of 'decency'. When death is recorded, however, it is invariably a key moment in the sublimation of violence as heroic sacrifice. Central to Ruddick's argument, then, is that a reconsideration of life, or more specifically, a celebration of birth and birthing labour would be a valuable contribution to anti-militarism: 'women tend to know', she comments, 'in a way and to a degree that men do not, both the history and the cost of human flesh' (1989: 186). In the light of this, Ruddick's philosophical revaluation will be used to open a consideration of the function of both injuring and mourning in war and how a reconception of the place of mourning and the role of the mourner might help us question militarism.

Birth

This reconsideration of birth, Ruddick argues, is a means to 'honor reason differently' (9) and develop criteria for our understanding of the world that arise out of the specific practice of 'mothering'. The difficulty with this revaluation of birth and birthing labour is the position it occupies within a society that is still patriarchal, where common sense passes a suspicious gaze over the reproductive, female body: 'Regarded ungenerously, a woman's birthing body – bloody, swollen out of shape, exposed in its pain, its otherwise concealed parts broken open – is repellent. It is disturbing in itself and because it forces on any onlooker the intimate knowledge of his or her own fleshy beginnings' (190). Pregnancy and birth also undermine the individuation of bodies so important to the classification of the world. Further to this, the lack of individuation and voluntary regulation resonates with responsibility and privileges the dependencies that question the autonomy central to enlightened thought in which men accept no rule aside from those they have given to themselves, and accept 'no presuppositions but those they stipulate' (192).[2] Ruddick argues that such invention is the rational usurpation of the creativity of female birthing labour, and is exemplified in one of the defining texts of the Western tradition. In *The Symposium* where Plato differentiates between those who desire physical creation, and hence have recourse to women, and those 'whose creative desire is of the soul' and 'who long to beget spiritually' (1951: 90), he repeats the departure from the physical, and specifically the feminine, that is central to his metaphor of the cave, or 'the original matrix/ womb' (Irigaray: 1985, 244) in *The Republic*. True knowledge recognizes that the shadows flickering on the walls of the cave/womb are exactly that, and that enlightenment lies outside the cave/womb in the light of the sun. For Ruddick, these two passages epitomize the rejection of female sexuality and the maternal that is endemic in Western philosophy. The allegory of the cave is thus an allegory of the detachment and separation required of reason. Reason is the taking of distance from the affective bonds and particular passions associated with birth. Socratic maieutics, with the philosopher as midwife, delivers every body from the excessive physicality of the feminine and gives it over to the discipline and order of male truth.

Reason's body, abstracted from the concrete peculiarities, dependencies, irregularities and frailties of actual bodies, regularly lends itself to the conception of the military body, or rather the military non-body. In the first instance the disciplined and regular body of reason, designed to become the vehicle transporting the mind to higher purposes also becomes the controlled and hardened instrument of war. For Ruddick, the basic training that raw recruits must endure, with its punishments and its humiliations, 'is the epitome of [the] effort to mold flesh in authority's image. The military body must be obedient to the soldier's will, even as that will is obedient to the rules and rulers of war. This military body is the perfect instantiation of philosophical fantasy. Abstract, ready to be counted, yet not counting' (199). This leads to the second instance in which reason's body contributes to the military body, namely the erasure of the body in actuality. Here Ruddick refers to the techno-rationality or military strategists whose discourses of logistics, weapons systems and abstract enemies 'divert attention from what actually happens to real bodies' (198). In this regard Ruddick takes her lead from the work of Carol Cohn whose research into the language and community of military strategists reveals how it is possible for those prosecuting a war to avoid acknowledging the fact that their decisions lead to the smashing, tearing, cutting, dismembering and burning of actual people.

One such piece of Cohn's research was based on participant observation in a community of US nuclear defence intellectuals. What she found there was a gendered discourse that was not about how men or women respectively talked to one another, but the way in which certain attitudes or responses were regarded as masculine and legitimate, or feminine and illegitimate. For example, talking about the actual effects of weapons systems on actual people, or as she puts it, voicing concern about the number of casualties on the enemy's side 'is out of bounds' (1993: 232). Speaking of psychological effects on all sides is also unacceptable. 'What gets left out, then, is the emotional, the concrete, the particular, the human bodies and their vulnerability, human lives and their subjectivity – all of which are marked as feminine in the binary dichotomies of gender discourse' (232). Gender discourse thus creates omissions and silences and 'becomes a "preemptive deterrent" to certain kinds of thought' (232). The specific example Cohn offers is participating in a war game in which Cohn's team pulled troops out of Afghanistan and removed troops from Eastern Europe, and despite this de-escalation could not prevent the game ending in nuclear war. During the debriefing session the leader of the opposing team explained how the withdrawal was interpreted as weakness; they had ' "wimped out" ' (234) and could be taken for everything they had. Cohn explains how every action requires interpretation and that being a wimp, that is, being insuffi-ciently masculine, is a readily available interpretive code. Rather than seeking to understand why the opposing team were acting as they were and seeking other options than annihilation, the gendered perception of non-aggression as weakness encouraged the war gamers to seek to wipe them out. The appearance, then, of actions deemed to be feminine were the trigger to actually stop thinking and just go for the kill. And as Cohn points out, such machismo cannot simply be addressed by employing more women because they will simply be co-opted by the discursive regimes, and it is these that need opening up.

This discursive management is exemplified in a second study by Cohn in which she seeks to address how the awesome lethality of nuclear weaponry is hidden by the language of strategists. What concerned her was the fact that the language of the centre soon became something she learned and enjoyed using. The lexicon of acronyms that disguised any lingering sense of what these weapons might actually do was fun to use. 'The words are quick, clean, light; they trip off the tongue [...]. Part of the appeal was the thrill of being able to manipulate an arcane language, the power of entering a secret kingdom. [...] The longer I stayed, the more conversations I participated in, the less I was frightened of nuclear war' (1996: 178). Rather than thinking about what these weapons might actually do to people on the receiving end, Cohn found herself caught up in developing language competence. And once this competence was gained the content of what could be spoken about was radically changed. For example, in techno-strategic speak there is no word for 'peace'. The nearest one gets is 'strategic stability'. But most importantly the subject of the discourse is always the weaponry. In other words, when considering a post-nuclear environment, the subject is not the people whose skin has been melted away, but the weapons systems, that is, the problems for the control, command and communication network. Where materiality did appear it was in the guise of the sexual allusion deployed to suggest the fecundity of the techno-strategists. 'More bang for your buck', 'vertical erectors', 'deep penetration' and putting missiles 'down holes' were all part of the regular language. This was very much in keeping with weaponry being treated as the militarists' offspring, the most obvious being the reference to the atomic bomb as 'Oppenheimer's baby', and later the 'Little Boy' that devastated Hiroshima, a nomenclature perhaps expressing the desire to appropriate women's life-giving power.[3]

For Ruddick, maternal thinking is diametrically opposed to the abstract and alienated mindset of military strategists. Whereas militarists exploit the body's capacity for pain, maternal thinking begins with the fact of corporeal vulnerability. It is premised on the responsibility of care brought about by the notion that 'children "demand" that their lives be preserved and their growth fostered' (1989: 17). While I do not wish to explore the degree to which Ruddick's work suffers from essentialism, it is important to offer some qualifying remarks concerning her use of the term 'maternal'. First, while 'preservative love' is 'the central constitutive, invariant aim of maternal practice' (19), it is not an automatic response. Preserving and nurturing are both dependent upon a social milieu. They are aspects of our socialized, learned behaviour and are not inherent in every woman simply because she is a woman. Secondly, to be a 'mother' does not require one to be a woman. In fact quite the opposite is the case. Given that mothering is not inherent, all mothering is 'adoptive', that is, mothering is a commitment and not an unthinking instinct. This means that men and women can be mothers, as well as all other members of a kinship group. A mother, Ruddick argues 'is a person who takes on responsibility for children's lives and for whom providing childcare is a part of her or his working life' (40). Ruddick chooses to retain the word 'maternal' because it connotes a specific set of activities that are different from the common-sense assumptions regarding the role of the father. To collapse mothering into parenting would be to once again dismiss mothers and play into the hands of patriarchal categories, including a fear of femininity. Whether or not these caveats are successful in rescuing Ruddick's work from the charge of essentialism I am unsure. However, this is not the issue. What I wish to do is draw out those aspects of maternal thinking that I believe are helpful given our current context.

Let us start with a mother's power. Although Ruddick acknowledges the socio-economic distribution of this power, she defines it as the ability to name, to name what is 'unavoidably given and what can be changed; who is to be feared and whose authority is only a sham' (35). Further to this she asks us to think about the creativity, rather than productivity, or even the reproductivity of birth; to think about the emotional, symbolic and political significance of this innovative act. Deploying an Arendtian vocabulary she critiques the technologists framing of birth as controlled production, as well as the common-sense discourses of reproductive rights in which the vocabulary of reproduction asserts 'its heavy emphasis on repetition and its indebtedness to the material production of inanimate goods, [which] misses altogether the originality of birth' (49). Somewhat later in the book Ruddick deploys the Arendtian concept of natality, and while Arendt uses the term to speak of human freedom rather than the necessity implicit in the natural act of birth, Arendt nevertheless uses the metaphor of birth as an analogy for the initiating capacities of humans. Natality represents the capacity for humans to insert themselves in a world through speech and action, an insertion through which, 'like a second birth [...] we confirm and take upon ourselves the naked fact of our original physical appearance' (Arendt, 1987: 39). Most important for Arendt is the fact that this speech and action that is the innovation of human freedom is unpredictable. Unlike the laws of nature that govern necessity, human freedom is without rule, it opens into a network or web of other initiating agents and the course of any one act can never be known in advance. While Arendt only uses birth as an analogy for (political) action Ruddick discovers in the practice of maternal care a logic similar to the unpredictability of Arendtian action. Only in relation to a child is it possible to experience unconditional love. With partners, parents, brothers, sisters, and friends, love is always tied to some sort of reciprocal action in which ties may be broken should that reciprocity ebb away. With a child, however, the mother, in Ruddick's sense of adoptive mother, must commit without knowing what the return will be, or if there will be any return at all. As Ruddick explains: 'Birth is a beginning whose end and shape can be neither predicted nor controlled. Since the safety of human bodies, mortal and susceptible to damage, can never be secured and since humans grow variously, but always in need of help, to give birth is to commit oneself to protecting the unprotectable and nurturing the unpredictable' (1989: 209).

In response to the unpredictability of action Arendt spoke of a grammar and syntax of action (1958) in which the central operations are forgiveness and promising. In response to the fact that action cannot be withdrawn, forgiveness is important as it permits an error that otherwise might disable future action. Also, because every deed is a beginning, forgiveness can interrupt a cycle of action and reaction. Forgiveness, then, is the possibility of a radical intervention in an ongoing situation and the creation of an alternative. Likewise, due to the unpredictable nature of action, promising functions so as to constitute 'a stable worldly structure' (Arendt, 1990: 175). This promise is inherent in the practice of mothering when, by adopting an infant the adoptive mother commits herself to protecting the vulnerability and unpredictability she has created. In the actual practice, or world-creation of mothering the unpredictability of birth and the promise it demands includes other qualities that Ruddick believes are integral to countering militarism. 'What we are pleased to call "mother-love"', she remarks, 'is intermixed with hate, sorrow, impatience, resentment, and despair; thought-provoking ambivalence is a hallmark of mothering' (1989: 68).

What, a little earlier in the book, she referred to as 'disciplined reflection' (24) indicates how, for Ruddick, the work of mothering is a decentring process, not only ontologically in that the mother is committed to preserving and nurturing the life of another, but also epistemologically as the mother is required to work through a complex range of emotions, and make decisions and set criteria for the course of a future life that by its very nature is interruptive of regular, predetermined patterns. Most importantly, to return to this issue of unpredictability, Ruddick argues that to give birth is 'to create a life that cannot be kept safe [and] whose unfolding cannot be controlled' (72). In response, the scrutiny of a mother must be tempered by humility: 'In a world beyond one's control, to be humble is to have a profound sense of the limits of one's actions' (72). Through humility the mother must accept limitations to her will and respect the independence of a life she is committed to preserve but cannot control.

This respect for the independent and uncontrollable will of another person is a virtue developed from within the world of maternal work. Because of this Ruddick is quick to articulate the difference between nurturing and development. Development, she argues, is something that has taken on negative consequences, associated as it is with technocratic and imperialist experts who 'impose on others inappropriate plans' (82). In this sense, maternal work and maternal thinking is a guard against imperialism, expansion and domination. It rejects the imposition of what would be alien trajectories on a subject required to find its own path. As a consequence a mother must accept change, difference and singularity, which is only possible through a 'radical self-renunciation' (122) and an openness to the future. In this way, maternal work invokes the ethics of hospitality so central to Jacques Derrida's later work. Ruddick's humility regarding a commitment to something she cannot entirely control surpasses what Derrida calls 'conditional hospitality', in which the host remains master of the house, and approaches 'unconditional hospitality', which is being prepared to give up such mastery and welcome 'not the invited guest, but the visitor' (1999: 70); it is 'an opening to the newcomer whoever that may be' (70).

After Simone Weil, Ruddick speaks of maternal work as attentive love; intense, disinterested and generous. It is the antithesis of fantasy, which is the capacity to put imaginative activity blindly into the service of 'consolation, domination, and aggrandizement' (1989: 120). Fantasy is the creation of an abstract scheme through which the child will live out the wilful projections of mother, family, community or nation. Fantasy is self-satisfying. The virtue of humility that is a prerequisite for the maternal work committing itself to something it cannot completely control is the antidote to the militarist desire for world mastery. 'In learning to welcome their own and their children's changes, mothers become accustomed to open-ended, concrete reflection on intricate and unpredictable spirits. Maternal attentive love, restrained and clear-sighted, is ill adapted to intrusive, let alone murderous, judgements of others' lives' (150). Such virtue was clearly absent in the invasion of Iraq. Instead, the invasion epitomizes the politics of fantasy in which Bush and Blair clearly set out a scheme through which Iraq will be the mirror image of its Father. The Father, as Ruddick defines him is not simply the male counterpart to the mother (such a counterpart would in turn be a mother). The Father represents the world as it is; its work, its language and its rule. The Father is not humble, but an enforcer, assuming an abstract authority he does not have. The child of the Father *will* comply with the world as it is given. In the case of Iraq, it will be fully marketized and *formally* democratic in a manner that reflects the perpetuation of the desires and interests of the Father. Rather than being the female counterpart of the Father, that is, a person who demands of their children an unquestioning obedience and replaces conscience with submission, the mother should promote her child's critical capacities in line with a life that is unpredictable and open-ended. From this perspective, maternal work also fosters a practice of non-violence.[4] Such a practice extends directly from the maternal commitment to self-renunciation, humility, criticism of unthinking authority, a celebration of difference and change, negotiation and the distribution of goods and privileges that is the mother's responsibility. These practices stem from modes of reasoning developed within 'ongoing changing relationships [...] in the context of collective and often passionate and conflictual enterprises' (Ruddick, 1993: 116). Maternal work is thus concrete, dialogic, open, fluid, de-centred, exposed, disinterested and dissident, and seeks peace that is neither appeasement nor totalitarian compliance. For Ruddick, it constitutes a world opposed to militarism.

Mourning

For Jean Bethke Elshtain (1987), Ruddick's work with its commitment to a critique of war from a maternal perspective repeats the Manichean view of 'us', the good, versus 'them', the bad. Despite Ruddick's attempt to make mothering non-gender specific, Elshtain believes she still slips into an oppositional view that is as comfortable as it is 'false and dangerous' (3). Furthermore Ruddick's reproduction of the dichotomy between war and peace means that she continues 'to locate [us] *inside* [war's] prototypical emblems and identities' (3). While it is true that the purpose of Ruddick's book is to contribute to a peace politics, this does not mean that Ruddick eschews conflict. In fact quite the opposite is the case. Ruddick often returns to the claim that mothering is about fighting and teaching children how to fight for what they believe in. The key, of course, is that such fighting ought to be non-violent. Peacefulness for Ruddick is not an indifferent turning away, but a form of confrontation itself. Nevertheless Elshtain still believes that any politics aimed at peace is problematic. 'Peace', she comments, 'is an ontologically suspicious concept, as troubling in its own way as war. War's historic opponents – those who want peace – are inside a frame with war. These two, peace and war, help structure Western civil society's view of itself, with protests against war couched in terms that mirror that which they oppose: peace to war; anti-bellicist femininity to bellicose masculinity; harmony to disorder; homogeneity to heteronymy; and so on' (253). In other words, peace cannot exist without war.

Central to the Manichean view is the conception of men and women as 'Just Warriors' and 'Beautiful Souls' respectively. These are culturally constructed myths and narratives that help recreate and secure the functions of female non-combatants and male combatants in a time of war. In the first instance, Elshtain is keen to dispel the myths by telling the stories of combative women and pacific men, but the purpose of deconstructing these two myths is to dismantle, or as she says, disarm the grand narrative of armed civic virtue in favour of a politics beyond war and peace that refuses to think in binaries, that refuses the arrogance of certitude and 'that refuses to see *all* right and good on one side only' (257). Like Ruddick, indeed, the one aspect of maternal thinking that she would support is the argument for a moral humility 'that repudiates the fiction that any means are possible if one declares one's ends to be good and just' (257). Unlike Ruddick, however, for whom mourning is central to the act of mothering that promises to nurture life and to attend to every death, Elshtain attributes the role of mourner to the myth of the female 'Beautiful Soul' and thus renders it complicit in the grand narrative of armed civic virtue. In this section I would like to suggest, by turning to the recent work of Judith Butler (2004) on the subject of the war against terror, that mourning may actually do much more for the politics that Elshtain espouses, and that, in fact, it might take us further down the line of a politics of humility. Before this can be done, however, it is important to give an account of Elshtain's reading of the grand narrative of armed civic virtue.

This narrative first appeared in the dialogues of Socrates where, in contrast to the Homeric discourse that tied the warrior into a specific pattern of heroic activity that gave each person (predominantly men) social standing and a place in a community, war becomes a collective undertaking for the sake of the *polis*, epitomized by the status afforded to the guardians in *The Republic*. Elshtain notes how this turn away from heroic society was continued by Aristotle who criticized Sparta for only being able to function while at war and collapsed during the time of its imperial peace. In this conception the idea of heroism as an end in itself is translated into the guardian that fights to secure an end external to the war. The guardian-warrior is a servant of the city, which politicizes, civilizes and tempers the passion for war itself, reserving and directing the guardian's ferocity for those who threaten it. For Elshtain the next key figure is Machiavelli, whose *Discourses* claim that the defence of the state requires no consideration other than everything being done, ' "lawful or unlawful, gentle or cruel" ' (in Elshtain, 1987: 57) to preserve its freedom. Likewise, Rousseau in *The Social Contract* talks of an undivided national will committed to defending the unified political body against division within as well as threats from without. His famous critique of Christian mildness and resignation, whose society would not be a society of men but a society devoted to an extra-worldly paradise, demonstrates what is central to armed civic virtue. Christians will do their duty by fighting a war, but it will be done without passion for victory because, he argued, Christians are more attuned to dying than conquering. 'Set them at war against a generous people whose hearts are devoured by an ardent love of glory and their country [. . .] and your pious Christians will be beaten, crushed, destroyed before they have time to collect their wits, or they will owe their salvation only to the contempt which their enemy feels for them' (Rousseau, 2004: 163–4). While Plato took legitimacy from a knowledge that bestowed order on the well-designed republic, legitimacy for Machiavelli, and for Rousseau after him, stems from the *wilful*, collective struggle for civic autonomy, and these Machiavellian themes 'echo', as Elshtain notes, 'throughout the subsequent history of political discourse in the West' (1987: 59), becoming one of the cornerstones of 'realism', 'the professionalized war discourse' (90) of international relations that views the world as a perpetual conflict, or perpetual conflict in abeyance, between individually wilful states.

While history has shown that men and women do not readily fit into the combative and pacific roles that underpin the discourse of armed civic virtue, Elshtain maintains that the myths of the 'Just Warrior' and the 'Beautiful Soul' are integral to the uncritical acceptance of war, and even its periodic welcoming. While, as Elshtain puts it, we readily accept the division between male life takers and female life givers, these divisions are never clear-cut. The myth of the male 'Just Warrior' is not only discredited by the numerous men who have resisted the draft and suffered prison sentences for their pacifism, it has itself been profoundly challenged by conflicts such as the Vietnam War in which the 'Just Warrior' attributes of righteousness, moral rectitude and civic commitment were all severely tested by a war that was cruel, barbaric, and perceived by the mass of the populace as being pointless in relation to the immediate concerns of the American *civitas*. Interestingly enough, so tied up with the conceptions of masculinity and authority is the idea of the 'Just Warrior' that, as Lynda E. Boose has argued, the perceived moral as well as military failure that was the Vietnam War saw the 'assassination of the national father [and the] literal and symbolic evacuation of authority' (1993: 88). The narrative of the 'Just Warrior' and armed civic virtue is absolutely commensurate with the biography of the US itself, as it is with the formation of the majority of modern states, born as they are of that Machiavellian spirit of civic autonomy. From the War of Independence to the Second World War, almost every generation of Americans had a bloody, but a good war to fight. What the soldier of the Vietnam War suffered was being born to the generation without any good wars and who was subsequently refused the parade and 'the hero's glory they had from boyhood grown to expect' (86). Only with the success of Gulf War I has 'the patriarchal military state [...] been returned to its pre-Vietnam status of wise father' (88) and the figure of the 'Just Warrior' been reinstated.[5]

Irrespective of the historical and contemporary evidence of warrior women that renders the 'Beautiful Soul' a cultural fiction, it remains the case that female violence is regarded as aberrant. Male violence is usually structured into an ordered and legitimate activity, that of war, while female violence always seems to suggest the breakdown of that order itself. Primarily this is because the woman, as a 'Beautiful Soul', not only lends support to male violence, cheering their heroism and supporting their ideals, but in many respects women actually come to represent those ideals themselves. The 'Beautiful Soul' 'serves as a repository of innocent convictions' (Elshtain, 1987: 140), they represent the purity, vulnerability and pacific creativity that the men are fighting for.

They thus become the emblem of the ethical dimension of war. In many respects the sacrifice of fighting men is tainted with the death they have wrought on others. For the women who do not fight, their sacrifice, their loss of husbands, sons and brothers, is untainted by any violent act. It is this image of them as mourners, as 'keeper[s] of the flame of nonwarlike values' (144), that gives extra moral weight to the image of the 'Just Warrior' and reproduces, or performs, the legitimacy of the *polis*, republic or state.

For Elshtain the exemplary narrative of women's sacrifice is the story of Mrs Bixby who lost five sons in the American Civil War. Her exemplary status is afforded not only by her exceptional and unimaginable loss, but by the fact that President Lincoln's words to her have been recorded for posterity. These words reappeared on the memorial to the dead of the Pacific Theatre in the Second World War. The memorial is dominated by a helmeted female figure carrying a laurel branch in her left hand. Beneath her is the inscription of Lincoln's words to Mrs Bixby: 'The solemn pride that must be yours to have laid so costly a sacrifice upon the altar of freedom.' As Elshtain notes, the helmeted female figure is not a passive figure, but a figure symbolizing resolve. Sacrifice is thus stripped of the material, physical, corporeal loss and sublimated as an ethical ideal without which the body politic would be threatened with collapse.[6] This discourse of sacrifice and armed civic virtue, however, can no longer sustain us, Elshtain argues. Neither notions of a robust community nor robust individualism are suitable political frameworks for they fail to attest to the 'inherent tragedy of political action' (1987: 250). Such awareness is, according to Elshtain, what made Lincoln the greatest American leader. While he has provided America with the exemplary eulogy for sacrifice, he nevertheless resisted the discourse of armed civic virtue; 'grand visions of wholesale *civic unity* fall through the cracks of Lincoln's recognitions. [...] The civil war was not fought between one side that was righteous and another that was not; rather, "Both read the same bible, and pray to the same God" [...]. It means that *power* and *interests* alone cannot and need not define politics' (251). With Lincoln we must 'chasten the nihilistic disillusionment of blind triumphalism' that victory in war invites, which means we must 'put away the grand narrative of armed civic virtue' (251).

At the time of writing *Women and War*, Elshtain noted a wave of 'new patriotism', but remarked that it looks suspiciously like the old nationalism to me, an aggressive self-identity that courts arrogance through [...] identification with the state's awesome preserve of force'

(252). Patriotism, she suggests, can and should be critical of the nation/
country when required. Her example is Martin Luther King Jr and his
1967 'Beyond Vietnam' speech in which he criticized his country out of
a passionate love for it. Where nationalism constructs foreign enemies
as 'implacable, demonized foes' (252), King's patriotism does not condemn
Hanoi, but tells America it has ' "the greatest responsibility in ending a
conflict that has exacted a heavy price on both continents" ' (252). Such
words exemplify Elshtain's model for moving beyond the dyad of war
and peace, a model she names the 'chastened patriot', a person who
modulates 'the rhetoric of high patriotic purpose by keeping alive the
distancing voice of ironic remembrance and recognition of the
way patriotism can shade into the excesses of nationalism [...]. The
chastened patriot is committed *and* detached: enough apart so that she
and he can be reflective about patriotic ties and loyalties, cherishing
many loyalties rather than valorizing one alone' (252–3). This, then, is
Elshtain's model of moral humility.

In Ruddick's discussion of maternal thinking, '[e]very body, and
therefore every death, counts; the promise of birth includes a dying well
tended and a death well mourned' (206). But as has been shown,
Elshtain is wary that such mourning, and its positioning within a
maternal discourse that reproduces the discourse of the 'Beautiful Soul',
ought to be challenged. But if we turn to the recent work of Judith
Butler on the question of mourning after the events of 11 September
2001, it is possible to see how the experience and practice of mourning
can move us much further in the direction of moral humility than
Elshtain's chastened patriot, a concept which has not prevented her
from currently being an apologist for one of the most belligerent and
militarist US administrations.[7] For Ruddick the fact that a maternal
history is one that mourns every death situates the mother in the
position of the dissident. Amid the righteous rhetoric of the war against
terror, for example, the dissenting voice is precisely the one demanding
that all the dead be counted. The figure of Antigone appears here, the
woman who in defiance of Creon's decree buried her brother and
transgressed the law of the city. Sophocles's play brilliantly demonstrates
the powerful and often resistant work of mourning in a manner that
remains compelling today. In December 2004 the Count the Casualties
Campaign sent a letter signed by high-ranking diplomats, civil servants,
academics and jurists, to the British government asking Tony Blair to
set up an independent enquiry into the number of Iraqi dead. This
request was dismissed by Blair who claimed the British government
were under no obligation (a reference to the obligation under international

law to protect civilians under occupation) to set up such an enquiry and that it was a matter for the Iraqi authorities.[8] Such a dismissal, of course, is in stark contrast to his words of gratitude for the members of the Black Watch who lost their lives during their move into central Iraq to support the US-led attack on Fallujah in November 2004. In this instance he presented himself as a man struggling to hold back his tears. But the fact that Blair should dismiss the need to count the dead Iraqis is perhaps not surprising given that these counter the techno-strategic myth of clean wars and his deployment of the humanitarian grounds for the invasion. Nevertheless these two examples do indicate the importance of mourning as it is deployed to bolster the resolve for war and its sacrifice, or to critique war and its moral duplicity.

Butler's work of mourning begins by considering the way in which the narrative of the war against terror works as a framing device that decides 'in a forceful way, *what we can hear*' (2004: 5). To begin at the beginning, she notes, is to go no further back than 11 September 2001: 'It is this date and the unexpected and fully terrible experience of violence that propels the narrative' (5). What is more the narrative is a first person account complementing the temporal fixity of the narrative with its telling as a monologue. There is no pre-history that is relevant to the attacks. There can be no other telling of the story, Butler remarks, because this would introduce the kind of moral equivocation at odds with the moral righteousness that underpins the reprisals. However, to act effectively demands that some reflection take place and this requires either the recognition of some pre-history, or the story being told from another perspective. 'The ability to narrate ourselves not from the first person alone, but from, say the position of the third, or to receive an account delivered in the second, can actually work to expand our understanding of the forms that global power has taken' (8). Such a second person narrative was offered by Ariel Dorfman (2002) on the first anniversary of the attacks in New York and Washington. He sought to remind Americans of another 11 September, one that occurred in 1973, the day that Pinochet seized power in Chile with the active support of the US government and then proceeded to murder or 'disappear' thousands of people. The message of Dorfman's 'Open Letter to America' was the simple one that there are other victims to mourn and other executioners to condemn. This telling of another story intent to disrupt the closed narrative of America as absolute victim is precisely the kind of narrative that contributes to a greater under-standing of global power, but as Butler is determined to point out, these other narratives that might include voices from Palestine, Saudi Arabia,

Vietnam, Panama, Iran, India and numerous other places ought not combine to form their own closed counter narrative that says everything is the fault of the US. Such explanations are simply one other way 'of asserting US priority and encoding US omnipotence' (9). A multiplicity of narratives from the perspective of first, second and third persons is required to develop the necessary apparatus for understanding the history that has brought about this situation.

Central to these historical considerations is the question of the human, that is, who counts as human? Whose lives count as lives? And what makes for a grievable life? These are the three questions that compose Butler's considerations of the work of mourning. Immediately she argues that mourning can appeal to a 'we' that transcends all geo-political and ideological boundaries because all of 'us' have some experience of loss, which means also that each of us is constituted in part by virtue of our vulnerability, either as bodily injury or social/familial dependency. Butler notes that for Freud the completion of the mourning process was the successful substitution of one object for another. In contrast she would like to think of mourning as the accept-ance of a change that radically alters the subject, perhaps permanently. 'Perhaps mourning has to do with agreeing to undergo a transformation (perhaps one should say *submitting* to a transformation) the result of which one cannot know in advance. There is losing, as we know, but there is also the transformative effect of loss, and this latter cannot be charted or planned. One can try to choose it, but it may be that this experience of transformation deconstitutes choice at some level' (21). In this manner mourning is also akin to Ruddick's formulation of the maternal promise that commits to protecting the unprotectable. In grief and mourning, one may start off the day with a project, but as Butler notes, one always 'finds oneself foiled. One finds oneself fallen' (21). Mourning is thus 'a mode of dispossession' (28). This defeat experienced by those who mourn, overcome by something more powerful than the mourner's own resources, is compounded by the ambivalence of the loss. Butler comments on Freud's claim that we do not know what it is in the person that we have lost: 'something is lost within the recesses of loss' (22). Perhaps the something lost is precisely the relationality between the self and an other, '*the tie* by which those terms are differen-tiated and related' (22).

This relationality revealed in the work of mourning moves it from the private and creates instead 'a sense of political community of a complex order' (22). Mourning reveals our relations with others that question our autonomy, self-sufficiency and control. Mourning seems to be a condition in which one can no longer tell one's own story, so tied-in is that story with the now absent life of another. This absent other does not reduce me to speechlessness, 'but does clutter my speech with the signs of its undoing' (23). Mourning is thus an ecstatic relation, literally a *being outside* oneself. To mourn others whom we are not supposed to mourn is not the question of respecting their rights, for such a discourse cannot represent the passion, rage and grief that has us *beside ourselves*, interrupted, disrupted, splintered, constituted heteronomously rather than autonomously. Is there, Butler asks, in this vulnerability, this being-outside-oneself, 'another kind of normative aspiration within the field of politics?' (26). In line with Emmanuel Levinas's ethics of alterity, Butler argues that claims to autonomy, to the self-enclosed space of a bounded individual, community or nation can only come if the subject refuses the prior relations it has with others, the physical proximity and anteriority of others and the relations with them that constitute us. At this point Butler also deploys the analogy of the newborn, 'laid bare from the start' (31). She reiterates Ruddick's argument that mothering is adoptive and due to social conditioning is not always given, yet this does not escape the fact that every newborn is 'given over', whether this be to the care of an adoptive promise, or to aban-donment, the newborn remains given over to an other and 'signifies a primary helplessness' (32).

Can this revelation of a fundamental dispossession and vulnerability be used to contemplate the current global situation and an alternative sense of worldhood? Can it be part of a framework rethinking international ties in terms of collective vulnerability? 'To foreclose that vulnerability, to banish it, to make ourselves secure at the expense of every other human consideration is to eradicate one of the most important resources from which we must take our bearings and find our way' (30). This failure to recognize vulnerability, the fact that there are no obituaries for those killed in Iraq by US or British soldiers, forces Butler to ask how these people have fallen outside the 'human'? These bodies have been made unreal, not worth recognizing, and they have received the violence that accompanies such de-realization. Women too have known this vulnerability of de-reali-zation often 'wishing for death or becoming dead, as a vain effort to pre-empt or deflect the next blow' (42).[9] There is a disturbing logic at work here that only the recognition of universal vulnerability can break, for the belief that certain lives are not lives at all, and therefore do not even need counting, let alone mourning, 'gives rise to a physical violence that in some sense delivers the message of dehumanization that is already at work in the culture' (34). What is more, this violence is without end.

If violence is done against those who are unreal, then, from the perspective of violence, it fails to injure or negate those lives since those lives are already negated. But they have a strange way of remaining animated and so must be negated again (and again). They cannot be mourned because they are always already lost or, rather, never 'were', and they must be killed, since they seem to live on, stubbornly, in this state of deadness. Violence renews itself in the face of the apparent inexhaustibility of its object. The derealization of the 'Other' means that it is neither alive nor dead, but interminably spectral. The infinite paranoia that imagines the war against terrorism as a war without end will be one that justifies itself endlessly in relation to the spectral infinity of its enemy, regardless of whether or not there are established grounds to suspect the continuing operation of terror cells with violent aims. (33–4)

The work of mourning thus operates against this logic. In the first instance it seeks to guard against the dehumanizing tendencies of global power. Secondly, with regard to the loss and mourning of US security, it is seen to be an opportunity to form new relations with the world. Mourning should be allowed to do its work and expose 'my own foreignness to myself [that is] my ethical connection with others' (46). Returning briefly to the image of the grieving Antigone outside the city walls, Gillian Rose has spoken of mourning as 'that intense work of the soul' (1996: 35) that is the gradual rearrangement of its own boundaries. Likewise, when mourning is completed the mourner returns to the city 'to negotiate and challenge' (36) *its* boundaries and question the law that excluded it. For Butler, however, instead of the work of mourning negotiating new boundaries and new ties based on the experience of its vulnerability, the boundaries prior to 11 September 2001 have been remade, only this time stronger and *less* permeable. The new subject that has installed itself 'at the national level' is not open to its dependencies, not exposed to its relationality, and has done with mourning to rebuild even more powerfully than before, a self-centred, violent, and this time 'extra-legal subject' (41), determined to restore the fantasy of mastery.

Injuring

The 'paths' by which the de-realization of bodies takes place is examined by Elaine Scarry in her remarkable book *The Body in Pain* (1985). Her analysis of how injury is hidden in the discourses of war complements the discussions of natality and mourning offered above. With regard to the practice of mourning, it was noted how mourning the loss of a brother, husband, wife or daughter is often curtailed and prevented from exposing the subject's dependency on others through the sublimation of sacrifice that is a central component of armed civic virtue. It was also noted in the analysis of Ruddick's work that militarism functions in part by abstracting from the singularity and particularity of actual bodies. This, she argued, is part of a long tradition of forgetting human flesh, a tradition that might be interrupted by thinking through the work done by mothers; their labour and their adoptive promise. For Ruddick, the representative image of the maternal promise is Käthe Kollwitz's *mater dolorosa*, which 'stands for the refusal to subordinate pain to tales of victory or defeat' (1989: 149). Such a refusal is at the heart of Scarry's work.

In studying the structure of war, Scarry takes as her first premise the claim that war is 'the activity of reciprocal injuring where the goal is to out-injure the opponent' (1985: 63). This structure of reciprocal injuring is complemented by the rhetorical necessity of finding ways of disowning injury, or making injury disappear. Scarry documents six paths by which bodies are disowned. In the first two the body is completely erased. The first path of 'omission' requires no analysis.[10] The second path Scarry calls 'redescription'. This is the way in which the language of war is 'formalized into a conventional mode of perceiving' (67). Two strategies that Scarry notes, and two strategies that were central to Bush and Blair, include deploying the terms 'disarm' (or even 'degrade') and 'free' rather than injure. In the discourse of freeing, injuring is misrepresented as a subordinate term rather than the primary function of warfare, while the discourse of disarming hides the fact that the side doing the disarming is actually seeking to gain immunity from being injured while inflicting injury on the other. This rhetoric of disarmament, then, is more akin to the 'dream of an absolute, one-directional capacity to injure [and] may begin to approach the torturer's dream of absolute nonreciprocity' (80). The third path is the one in which injured bodies are understood as 'by-products' of war; the analogy being the desire to make paper not destroy trees. The fourth path is the one in which injury is likened to an interruption on the road to something else, when in fact injured bodies 'are the material out of which the road is built' (74). The fifth path is to recognize that injury is a product of war, but to hide it by referring to it as a 'cost'.[11] The six path Scarry refers to as 'extension'. Similar to the earlier strategy of redescription, extension is calling war the continuation of something

else; in Bush's rhetoric the continuation of peace. In this way Scarry
offers us a detailed analysis of the ways in which bodies are de-realized,
but the significance of this process only really appears when considering
Scarry's second premise of war, namely that war is a contest.

War is a contest because combat is an activity in which two sides seek
to '*out-perform* the other in the appointed labor' (84) of injuring the
opponent with a view to deconstructing or unmaking their world. This
leads to the second aspect of the contest whereby war is the arrangement
of two sides against one another for the purposes of designating a
winner and a loser. In a time of war, two sides enter into an 'intolerable
duality' (87), a conflictual binary that must be transformed into a
unitary state. 'This insistent duality will reign until the end of the war
when it will become clear that the concussive state of doubleness was
all the while in the process of eliminating itself [and] the belligerent
equality transforming itself into the peaceful inequality that entails the
designation of one as "winner"' (88). The winner is the agent able to
best perform the work of out-injuring the opponent to the point of
acceptable damage. In other words, war is a contest seeking to injure
the opponent up to and possibly beyond the level of injury deemed
acceptable. Importantly, however, this level of injury is also required to
be the point at which the opponent's self-description is affected. This
idea of the work of injuring as world-unmaking labour is important
because for Scarry a declaration of war is a declaration that 'reality' is
'up for grabs' (137). The deconstruction of 'reality' that ensues is
designed to be carried far enough so that the loser will be better able to
accommodate the loss of its self-definition that it would have had prior
to the war, which is, of course, a key component in the outcome
enduring over time. The next question then becomes the need to determine why the contest of out-injuring and world-unmaking is the only
possible contest that can secure the endurance of unequal peace, that is
the distinction between winner and loser as an 'abiding designation' (95).

To address this, let us first of all set out Scarry's version of the
interpretive confrontation that is war:

> In the dispute that leads to war, a belief on each side that has
> 'cultural reality' for that side's population is exposed as a 'cultural
> fiction': that is, by being continually called into question, it begins
> to become recognizable to its own population as an 'invented structure'
> rather than existing as it did in peacetime as one that (though on
> reflection invented) could be unselfconsciously entered into as
> though it were a naturally occurring 'given' of the world. As the

dispute intensifies and endures, the exposed 'cultural fiction' may seem in danger of eroding further into a 'cultural fraud', in danger of eroding from something that is uncomfortably recognizable as 'made' into something potentially identifiable as 'unreal', 'untrue', 'illegitimate', 'arbitrary'. The more the process of derealization continues, the more desperately will each side work to recertify and verbally reaffirm the legitimacy and reality of its own cultural constructs. Although at a distance human beings take pride in being the single species that relentlessly recreates the world, generates fictions, and builds culture, to arrive at the recognition that one has been unselfconsciously dwelling in the midst of one's own creation by witnessing the derealization of the made thing is a terrifying and self-repudiating process. (128)

Injury, therefore, is not only the means of producing an enduring marker of defeat or victory, it also becomes the means by which a 'cultural fiction' is substantiated and the process of worldly de-realization or unmaking brought to an end. Scarry notes that the point of out-injuring is not to place the opponent in a position where they cannot pursue the conflict further, that is, to the point where they are unable to regroup or reproduce and thus recommence the fighting, it is rather to injure beyond the point that is acceptable. Physical injury to bodies, destruction of the environment and the deconstruction of a culture all testify, permanently if required, to the distinction between winner and loser. In this regard, war differs from any other form of contest. Here the decision regarding winner and loser has 'the power of its own enforcement' (108) because the outcome of war is made substantial through 'a process of perception that allows extreme attributes of the body to be translated into another language' (124), that of victory or defeat. Through what Scarry calls 'the "*as if*" reflex' (108) the opponent perceives the enduring reality of injury and takes it for the enduring reality of defeat because 'the open body has lent [defeat] its truth' (125). What is more, the 'open body' will not only lend itself to the reality of the designation loser/victor it will also lend itself to the realization or *substantiation* of the victorious 'cultural fiction', whether that be freedom, democracy, equality, justice, or any of the other numerous ideas for which we fight.

Scarry notes that this attempt 'to bestow the force of the material world on the immaterial' (127) by the sacrificial use of a body is a central component in all rituals that are enacted due to 'a crisis of substantiation' (127). Anthropological studies are replete with examples of rituals and oaths where the body, its flesh and blood are used to give force to an identity, a commitment, even a description of the world. In Scarry's words, injuring 'provides, by its massive opening of human bodies, a way of reconnecting the derealized and disembodied beliefs with the force and power of the material world' (128). And the greater the threat to the object, that is the more the idea being fought for is seen to be a 'cultural fiction', the more bodily injury is required to substantiate it. The fact that the cut, burned, decapitated and open body then disappears from the language of war is because of a second *as if* reflex, or rather the way in which the *as* if' reflex is completed. The injured and dead bodies are de-realized along the six paths identified earlier because the victorious 'fiction' must stand *as if* that victory was secured through the force of its own 'truth'.

As a possible alternative to the ritual of war, Scarry offers the relatively benign example of coin tossing. The situation could not be resolved by one toss of a coin, only by an extensively prolonged and extraordinarily elaborate means of tossing coins that might 'engage over time a depth of attention consonant with the depth of imaginative reorientation' required in war. Secondly, as the decisive week approached, people would be required to wear signs objectifying the fact that a contest took place, some form of armband, for example, that cut into the skin and modified it in some way, thus producing the memorial function of enduring injury. They would also then be required to gather in large groups in their homeland and each person would hold up 'an animal organ or entrails in confirmation of the idea of winning and of the issue that was the winner and henceforth "real"' (138). Such a ritual would entail the massive slaughter of animals, but it would be more civilized than war, Scarry contends, having at least substituted animal for human sacrifice.

While this is not intended to be a genuine proposal for an alternative to war, it does serve to illustrate why war as a contest premised on out-injuring your opponent remains integral to world-creation, and also serves to intimate just how many bodies would need to be waged in a clash of civilizations. But as was suggested in the opening chapter, rather than seeking alternative forms of contest, a contribution towards lessening our disposition for war might come from resigning ourselves to the 'fiction' that is our world. While Ruddick's analysis of maternal thinking remains open to charges of essentialism, as well as Elshtain's charge that her focus on peace is the mirror image, and thus the consti- tutive outside, of war, her phenomenology of the promise, in which the adoptive mother is decentred through the commitment to protect the unprotectable, sets out the moral humility that is required if the de-realization of our world is not to be met with violence. Likewise, Butler's consideration of mourning exposes the relationality that produces each and every identity. Again it offers us a means of understanding ourselves as always already decentred such that threats to our perceived identity are not so undermining that self-preservation in a cultural sense demands the annihilation of the other. In this respect the reflections of these writers on what might generally be called the de-realizing discourses of militarism expose some of the spaces within which an alternative practice might be founded, and such a foundation is very far from the abstract, binary fundamentalism that currently governs our world-making.

6
Friend and Enemy

The humility that Sara Ruddick describes as essential for a critique of militarism is missing from the rhetoric in the war against terror. Such humility, she argues, would produce a politics that is decentred, open and non-doctrinal, instead we have what is best described as a clash of fundamentalisms (Ali, 2002) between two opponents eager to represent the other as the epitome of evil. Where the gesture of humility does appear in this rhetoric it is simply a veil for a politics of certainty and righteousness. George W. Bush is no doubt humbled by the fact that he is the chosen instrument of God, delivering His gift of freedom to the world, but this humility is anything but pacific, used as it is to support a massive military budget, pre-emptive strikes and the moulding of the world in accordance with US economic interests. While the identification of a new enemy is undoubtedly the cover for the expansion of these interests, something I will address in the final chapter, the naming of this new enemy has a number of other functions, not least the continuation of the existential struggle against the forces of darkness. These forces may be couched, as we shall see, in theological garb in which the enemy is quite literally Satan, or in more secular terms as the atrophe of the human spirit in the absence of a struggle.[1]

In the light of this, it is important to consider the influence of Carl Schmitt's work on the thinking of the architects of the war against terror. Schmitt's famous definition of the political as the distinction between friend and enemy is the overriding model of international relations that informs the Bush administration. The vehicle for the transmission of this fundamental distinction to heart of the US government was the exiled German philosopher Leo Strauss, who while radically different to Schmitt in many respects, especially regarding the importance of reason over revelation, nevertheless believed that the friend and enemy distinction was precisely what was at stake in the world. In a fascinating study of the influence of the 'Straussians' in the US, Anne Norton (2004) shows how Leo Strauss (and that other famous German exile, Hannah Arendt, both of whom were students of Martin Heidegger) reinvigorated the discipline of political theory against the sterile positivism of political science that had taken over the US academy.[2] Aside from Straussians such as Robert Kagan, William Kristol and Gary Schmitt, all of whom are members of the *Project for the New American Century*, the most notable is Paul Wolfowitz, now head of the World Bank.

To give a sense of Carl Schmitt's influence on the forces currently shaping the world, it is useful to see how Joseph Cropsey, who studied and worked with Strauss and taught Paul Wolfowitz, conceptualized the importance of the distinction between friend and enemy. In his foreword to Heinrich Meier's book on the dialogue between Schmitt and Strauss, Cropsey writes:

> It belongs only to human beings to make war, not only to kill but to die, for a high cause and ultimately for the highest cause, which is their faith. Schmitt can agree with those who have perceived the human record as a history of bloodshed, but far from interpreting the fact as a sign of God's neglect or punishment, he sees it as evidence of God's providence. By a dialectic of conflict, of 'ideals' that men take seriously enough to contend over, and not by any mere dialectic of reason, mankind is preserved from the lassitude of indifference that is the soul's death. (in Meier, 1995: x)

In the course of this chapter, then, we will explore the war against terror in terms of this existential and theological struggle for the highest cause.

Before this is commenced, however, one further important factor needs to be introduced. Something that is integral to the naming of an enemy is the corresponding announcement of a state of emergency, or what Schmitt referred to as the state of exception, the quasi-legal condition in which the validity of the juridical order is itself suspended. In Britain, this is best known as the implementation of emergency powers or martial law; a period of time in which normal legal entitlements and civil liberties are suspended, or it can be understood as the expansion of the powers of the executive into the legislative sphere, something that happened during the military emergencies of the two world wars and continued in line with the economic emergencies that emerged in their aftermath. With regard to the West, and the US in particular, it is possible to show how a catalogue of very different enemies have ensured a permanent state of emergency from 1914 to the present day. For seventy of the last ninety years the chief enemy has been the Soviet Union. Even when they were part of the Axis powers during the Second World War, and arguably did more to defeat Hitler than any other nation, they remained the enemy given that the goal of communism was the defeat of capitalism and the world it created. Despite the brief tactical alliance in the early 1940s, Soviet Russia represented an anonymous Bolshevik mass determined to assimilate and eradicate the freedom and dignity of the individual. The year 1989 thus represented a peculiar crisis in that it threatened to undermine the crisis itself and the legitimacy of the state of emergency. For a very brief time between the fall of the Berlin Wall and the invasion of Kuwait, the West had no enemy: enter the 'Rogue Doctrine', which, amid fears of nuclear and chemical weapons proliferation, was to present failed or despotic states as the new threat to world security and find its symbolic figure in Saddam Hussein. Since then the threat of the Soviet mass has been replaced by the Islamist hordes; a cult of death out to destroy our way of life in an infinite war of terror. We now have the perfect enemy, anonymous, ubiquitous, absolutely evil, permanently present and definable simply as that which is not (with) us.

Enemy

Carl Schmitt's *The Concept of the Political* first appeared in 1927 with revised versions appearing in 1932 and 1933, the year he joined the National Socialist Party. The 1933 edition is also important because it is the revised version he published in response to Leo Strauss's review in 1932. The dialogue between Schmitt and Strauss, brilliantly set out by Heinrich Meier, will be important to the argument here as we move from the political to the theological, but let us first consider the nature of the political according to Schmitt. Any consideration of the nature of the state, he argues, 'presupposes the concept of the political' (1996: 19). Schmitt notes that modern linguistic usage understands the state as 'the political status of an organized people in an enclosed territorial unit' (19), but this fails as a definition if it does not properly consider the nature of the political. The political is independent of the moral, aesthetic and economic realms and has its own criteria, resting, he argues, on its own ultimate distinctions. If the moral is understood as the antithesis between good and evil, the aesthetic as the antithesis between beautiful and ugly, and the economic as the antithesis between profitable and unprofitable, then the political is the antithesis between friend and enemy. If each of these realms is independent because its criteria cannot be reduced to or conflated with the criteria of the other realms 'then the antithesis of friend and enemy must even less be confused with or mistaken for the others'. The specificity of the political antithesis is, Schmitt continues, based on the fact that the 'distinction of friend and enemy denotes the utmost degree of intensity of a union or separation, of an association or dissociation' (26). While the political cannot be reduced to the other antitheses, the primacy of the political is indicated by the fact that the economic and the moral, for example, can intensify to the point where they become political and 'bring about the decisive friend–enemy constellation' (36). It is thus the polemical that defines the political, and the state is the ultimate authority that decides the case of friend or enemy. Non-polemical definitions are 'legal or administrative' (21), but are not political and do not give us a definition of the state.

The peculiarly intense antithesis of the political stems from the fact that an enemy 'exists only when, at least potentially, one fighting collectivity of people confronts a similar collectivity' (28). Schmitt is very clear that the political is the confrontation between worlds. It is the threat of another way of being and a different mode of valuing. It is a clash of differing belief systems, of differing ideals that demand the intensity of a fight to the death. That the friend and enemy distinction is based upon the simple binary of identity and difference is evident in the following clarification of the nature of the enemy: 'The political enemy need not be morally evil or aesthetically ugly; he need not appear as an economic competitor, and it may even be advantageous to engage with him in business transactions. But he is, nevertheless, the other, the stranger; and it is sufficient for his nature that he is, in a specially intense way, existentially something different and alien, so that in the extreme case conflicts with him are possible' (27). Specifically, the possibility for combat is determined by whether or not 'the adversary intends to negate his opponent's way of life and therefore must be repulsed or fought in order to preserve one's own form of existence' (27). And just so that no one be under any illusions about what Schmitt means by combat, he explains that by combat he 'does not mean competition, nor does it mean pure intellectual controversy nor symbolic wrestlings, in which, after all, every human being is somehow always involved, for it is a fact that the entire life of a human being is a struggle and every human being symbolically a combatant. The friend, enemy and combat concepts receive their real meaning precisely because they refer to the real possibility of physical killing' (33). For Schmitt, in its pursuit of pacific fraternity, liberalism has completely lost sight of this necessity to kill or be killed that is at the heart of the political. For liberalism the enemy is precisely nothing more than an economic competitor or intellectual adversary. In this sense, liberalism has lost sight of this most intense and extreme antagonism. Liberalism is thus apolitical and ultimately weak.

One further definition that clarifies the nature of the enemy and transcends the individual centred thinking of liberalism is the notion that the enemy is always the enemy of a collectivity or a people and is thus a public rather than a private enemy. Here Schmitt notes that both Latin and Greek are sensitive to this distinction in a way that German (or indeed English) is not. In Latin the enemy is *hostis*, not *inimicus*; while in Greek it is *polemios* and not *echthros* (ἐχθρός); and claiming support from the Scriptures he argues that the famous passages from Matthew, 5: 44 and Luke, 6: 27 that petition Christians to 'Love your enemies' reads *diligite inimicos vestros* and not *diligite hostes vestros*, with the distinction maintained in the original Greek. The petition is thus to love one's private or personal enemies and not the public enemy: 'Never in a thousand-year struggle between Christians and Moslems did it occur to a Christian to surrender rather than defend Europe out of love toward the Saracens or Turks' (29). Support for Schmitt's interpretation is also to be found in Plato, he claims, who considers real war as only possible between natural enemies such as the Hellenes and the Barbarians. In a footnote to the above he writes: 'a people cannot wage war against itself', such a 'self-laceration' is better understood as rebellion, insurrection or civil war, that is *stasis* and not *polemos*. In the light of this, the state is thus defined as the decisive entity, to which as a 'political entity belongs the *jus belli*', this is the capacity to decide 'in a concrete situation' (45) who is the enemy as well as the right to demand from the people comprising the state 'the readiness to die and unhesitatingly to kill' (46). For Schmitt, the elimination of war and the pacification of the globe, a project fundamental to both economic and political liberalism, would thus remove the 'meaningful antithesis whereby men could be required to sacrifice life, authorized to shed blood, and kill other human beings' (35).

The word 'meaningful' is very important here for it links the potential for physical combat to the 'symbolic wrestlings' that is our interpretive confrontation to win a world. While Schmitt places the definitive moment of the political on the identification of a real enemy that may demand from every member of the political entity the need to kill or be sacrificed, this killing is necessitated by the need to preserve the hermeneutic project that is a world. Indeed the ontological nature of the political comes to the fore here, and one can understand why Heidegger would find Schmitt's treatise so compelling in 1933 given that it takes polemos to be a sovereign principle.[3] The fact that Schmitt's treatise is not, in Heidegger's terms, purely ontical, but is also ontological is revealed towards the end of Chapter 5 of *The Concept of the Political* when he explains that to disarm would not mean depoliticization, or that the search for peace could not be seen to solve the antithesis between friend and enemy, which for liberals might be understood as a 'problem': 'it would be a mistake to believe that a nation could eliminate the distinction of friend and enemy by declaring its friendship for the entire world or by voluntarily disarming itself. The world will not thereby become depoliticized, and it will not be transplanted into a condition of pure morality, pure justice, or pure economics' (51–2). The contestation between friend and enemy will arise even if it appears in the counterforces of economics, culture or religion. As an ontological principle it cannot be dodged. If any entity relinquishes its sovereign capacity to decide, it is no longer free and will be 'absorbed into another political system' (49). In many respects, this is a key component in the neo-conservative antipathy to all things universal, fraternal and pacific and is central to understanding the rationale for exponential military growth. The US administration not only wants the physical capacity to defend itself against any enemy, it also wants to be able to fight two or three simultaneously in multi-theatre warfare because the enemy does not come along one at a time, nor challenge in one place alone, the enemy is a permanent and omnipresent threat. Should the US, indeed should any political entity lose sight of itself as political, then another will appear to take over political rule and provide protection while demanding obedience.[4] Interestingly enough, however, Schmitt argues that to engage with the political is not to support the belligerence of militarism, it is rather a moment of integrity, for where the political is seen to disappear it only becomes hidden.[5] When, for example, economics rather than politics becomes destiny a new vocabulary is invented: 'War is condemned but executions, sanctions, punitive expeditions, pacifications, protection of treaties, international police and measures to assure peace remain. The adversary is thus no longer called an enemy but a disturber of the peace and is thereby designated to be an outlaw of humanity' (79).

Schmitt qualifies this further by arguing that a war in the name of humanity is illogical because humanity being universal cannot have an enemy.[6] That the war against terror is often portrayed as a war in defence of humanity thus indicates a point of contradiction in the rhetoric viewed from a Schmittian perspective, but it also opens on to a problem with Schmitt's concept of the political itself. Specifically Schmitt's concept of the political runs into problems the moment it speaks of the concept of the political defined as the capacity to decide 'in a concrete situation'. For Jacques Derrida the difficulty lies in the impossibility of maintaining the purity of a concept or the purity of a discourse when it is put into practice, one cannot implement 'the rigour of such a conceptual limit' (1997: 114), he argues. It is, Derrida notes, the point of an incommensurability between *praxis* and *lexis*:

> As a result, the purity of *polemos* or the enemy, whereby Schmitt would define the political, remains unattainable. The concept of the political undoubtedly corresponds, as concept, to what the ideal discourse can *want* to state most rigorously on the ideality of the political. But no politics has ever been adequate to its concept. No political event can be correctly described or defined with recourse to these concepts. And this inadequation is not accidental, since politics is essentially a *praxis*, as Schmitt himself always implies in his ever-so-insistent reliance on the concept of *real, present possibility* or *eventuality* in his analyses of the formal structures of the political. (114)

If we take the concrete situation of the war against terror, a decision has been made regarding the enemy: it is terrorism. Already there is a drift from the concrete to the abstract, a slippage the rhetoric is both unable to avoid because it cannot actually identify the specific entity or collective that it is at war with, but it is also purposive in that it permits an open-ended war that can be directed at any location the sovereign, in this case the US president, decides. One further problem, and this is the problem that Derrida outlines above, when the US actually names the enemy in the concrete, the distinction between friend and enemy can no longer be made with the purity Schmitt demands given that Al'Qaeda, for example, the nearest the rhetoric comes to naming the hostile entity, were until very recently friends of the US administration.

The US is also friends with Saudi Arabia, a profoundly anti-democratic state that encourages the extreme form of Islam known as Wahabism that guides the actions of Osama bin Laden. These are only two ways in which the identification of an enemy in the concrete makes impossible the ideal purity of the distinction. In a more recent interview, Derrida considers the impossibility of a pure distinction in terms of 'autoimmunity' (Borradori, 2003). In relation to the attacks of 11 September 2001, the problem of autoimmunity is revealed in the US having funded and trained Al'Queda. It can also be seen in the use of US resources by the terrorist to train for the attacks, but most significantly the autoimmunitary logic is most pronounced in the declaration of a war in which 'the "bombs" will never be "smart" enough to prevent the victims [...] from responding, either in person or by proxy, with what it will then be easy for them to present as legitimate reprisals or as counterterroism' (Derrida in Borradori, 2003: 100). As Borradori comments, in Derrida's understanding, autoimmunity thus becomes a third term between friend and enemy, and like concrete politics destabilizes the distinction. The inability, then, to work at the level of the concrete thus demands the move to abstractions. As Suman Gupta has argued in his excellent analysis of the rhetoric, 'The confrontation of *principles in abstract* translates the complex network of the material and the theoretical, the practical and the ideological' into two absolutely opposed normative positions that then translate into two absolutely opposed ethical positions (2002: 76). To escape the complexity of the concrete the rhetoric speaks of democracy versus terror (fanaticism) and good versus evil. It also requires Bush and Blair to speak and wage war in the name of humanity, for only at this level can they avoid the slippage and the contamination of the concrete.

What does remain clear in all of this, however, is that a distinction *is* made, war is declared and emergency powers assumed. As Schmitt argues, what matters 'is the possibility of the extreme case taking place, the real war, and the decision whether this situation has or has not arrived' (35). In other words, sovereignty is the capacity to decide on the extreme case, that is to designate an enemy and declare the opening of hostilities. Furthermore, that the extreme case 'appears to be an exception does not negate its decisive character but confirms it all the more [and] exposes the core of the matter' (35). Before turning to the unveiling of the religious dimension in Schmitt's analysis of the political it is important to consider the nature of this exception, what it means for the juridical order of the state, for the status of the enemy and how it relates to the war against terror.

Emergency

One of the major results of the events of 11 September 2001, as David Lyon notes, was that civil liberties fell on hard times as new laws and technologies increasingly disregarded them (2003: 42). The desire for 'maximum security', that is the attempt to shore up US territorial sovereignty, was to override any question of personal sovereignty.[7] Securing borders, airwaves, digital networks and people meant that liberty was to give way to control. The USA PATRIOT Act and the EU's Framework Decision on terrorism are significant examples of this. The USA PATRIOT Act, according to the Center for Constitutional Rights (CCR), is part of a raft of legislation that contravene Amendments one (free speech, assembly and press), four (protection against unreasonable searches and seizures), five (protection regarding criminal punishment, including Due Process) and six (unbiased and timely completion of criminal proceedings) of the US constitution, and greatly expands the powers of the executive branch of US government. According to a report published by CCR the fact that the war against terror is fought by executive fiat is 'a serious abrogation of the rights of the people and the obligations of the federal government'.[8] Contraventions of the fourth amendment, for example, are related to the growing use of profiling in which religious and racial categories such as 'Muslim-Arab' are used to define potential threats. Such profiling also involves consumer screening whereby 'CEOs and other company officials declare themselves as combatants in the war against terrorism, joining the data gathering effort as allied collaborators' (Lyon, 2003: 57). Our movements are now not only tracked by CCTV and digital passports, but by a host of databases used for consumer screening including the use of information from credit cards, library cards, phone bills, e-mail and Internet usage. And, as Lyon argues, as this surveillance becomes increasingly integrated with other monitoring systems it also becomes more opaque. 'This is because system designers and computer programmers play a greater role in creating the categories which are the criteria for discrimination. In other words, the processes by which unusual or abnormal behaviour is defined are tasks for "technical experts" rather than ones in which there is ethical scrutiny or democratic involvement' (135).

But perhaps the greatest concern for those committed to democratic freedoms is the creation of a new crime by the USA PATRIOT Act called domestic terrorism, a category that blurs the line between the civil rights provided under the First Amendment and criminal activity.[9] Given the illiberal pedigree of the Bush administration this is hardly surprising, but similar concerns are also raised by Statewatch in relation to the new EU definition of terror. While intent is a key component of the definition of terrorism in the EU Framework Decision, it defines terrorism as acts aimed at (i) seriously intimidating a population, or (ii) unduly compelling a government or international organization to perform or abstain from performing an act or (iii) destabilizing or destroying the fundamental political, constitutional, economic or social structures of a country or international organization. What is of central importance here is that this legislation seems to conveniently threaten a broad range of political activism prompting the legitimate charge that the state of emergency is as much an opportunity to stifle dissent as it is about preventing terrorism. The irony of all this is that both the US and the EU have continually deployed the rhetoric of democracy and yet this legislation would ban the kind of political activity that actually gave birth to democracy. While progressive academics such as Seyla Benhabib (2002) still argue that it is terrorism that threatens democracy, a more nuanced and responsible position would be that argued by Andrew Arato: 'We must consider the precise nature of the identity we wish to defend, and prove that there are forms of protection that represent dangers equal to the explosives of our enemies' (2002: 50).[10]

What defines a state of emergency, then, is not the emergency it is supposed to be a response to, but the suspension of the law and the nature of the sovereign charged with the powers to enact such a suspension. For Schmitt, both sovereignty and emergency are mutually implicated in each other, for as he famously declared in 1922 with the publication of *Political Theology*: 'Sovereign is he who decides on the exception' (1985: 5). The sovereign decides whether 'a normal situation exists' (13) and therefore the normal legal order can function, or whether a threat to the state exists and the normal legal order is to be suspended. In legal terms this is something of a paradox given that the sovereign decision is immanent to the legal order and yet can neither be 'codified' in it nor be 'made to conform to a preformed law' (Schmitt, 1985: 5). Furthermore, the decision is not a legal one but a political one based on the judgement of a threat and the determination of an enemy. For Giorgio Agamben, the exception made manifest in the declaration of a state of emergency is therefore a juridical measure that cannot be understood in legal terms; 'it defines law's threshold or limit concept' (2005: 4). He notes how, given the extensive use of emergency powers during and after the two world wars, the 1940s saw an increased academic engagement with the problem through the work of Frederick M. Watkins, Carl J. Friedrich and Clinton L. Rossiter. In these works

Schmitt's distinction between commissarial dictatorship and sovereign dictatorship is represented as a distinction between constitutional and unconstitutional dictatorship in which the sovereign as a constitutional dictator seeks to protect democracy by temporarily suspending it, a logic that is manifestly at play in the war against terror as both Bush and Blair sacrifice certain democratic principles in order to supposedly preserve them, but as we saw above in the quote from Andrew Arato, the expediency of this logic is by no means uncontested. However, the concept of commissary or constitutional dictatorship does help us define the state of exception as a situation in which the norm is in force but is not applied and actions that do not have the value of law acquire its force. 'The state of exception is an anomic space in which what is at stake is a force of law without law' (Agamben, 2005: 38), and in the war against terror nothing encapsulates this force of law without law more than the camps at Guantánamo Bay.

For Agamben, the complexity of sovereignty lies in the fact that it is both inside and outside the juridical order as both its founding event and its suspension. It is, therefore, both a structure of inclusion and exclusion. The sovereign decides who is the enemy and incorporates them within the juridical order through the logic of exception, or under what Agamben calls the sovereign ban, a situation where the law applies by no longer applying. The enemy, for example, is the person who can be legitimately killed at a time (during the state of emergency, or after a declaration of war) announced by the sovereign. Sovereignty is thus the command over life, suggesting for Agamben that the distinction between friend and enemy is actually based on something more primary. In the introduction to *Homo Sacer*, Agamben highlights the distinction in Aristotle's *Politics* between *zoē* and *bios*, where *zoē* is 'the simple fact of living common to all beings (animals, men, or gods), and *bios* [is] the form or way of living proper to an individual or a group' (1998: 1). In this situation, *zoē* is excluded from the *polis* and is confined to the *oikos*, or the sphere of the home, a distinction that has remained integral to Western conceptions of the political through the division of private and public. Thus Agamben can argue that it is the exclusion of bare life (*zoē*) that founds the city of men: 'There is politics because man is the living being who, in language, separates and opposes himself to his own bare life and, at the same time, maintains himself in relation to that bare life in an inclusive exclusion' (8). And it is this categorical pairing, rather than the distinction between friend and enemy, that is for Agamben the foundation of the political in Western philosophy. To put it another way the distinction between friend and enemy is derived from the distinction between *zoē* and *bios*. In a later work, Agamben goes so far as to say that 'the decisive political conflict, which governs every other conflict, is that between the animality and the humanity of man' (2004: 80). Sovereign power, therefore, decides who qualifies for, or belongs to the political community with its protection under law, and those who can be reduced to the bare life of their animal existence and from whom the law withdraws. What is so important about this interpretation of sovereign power is that it contravenes the dominant humanist position whereby the violation of persons and/or peoples are an *aberration* of the liberal ideal, which has tolerance, compassion and reasonableness as its default position. Instead Agamben's reading argues that this exclusionary practice which at best seeks to discipline and manage 'lesser beings' (the proletariat, the African) and at worst annihilate the bestial or non-human (the Jew) is not an anomaly but is the normal proceedings of sovereign power; and in this regard 'the camp' becomes the paradigm case for the structure of our political space.

From this perspective the horrors of the Nazi concentration camps are the exemplary expression of sovereign power. '*The camp is the space that is opened when the state of exception begins to become the rule.* In the camp, the state of exception, which was essentially a temporary suspension of the rule of law on the basis of a factual state of danger, is now given a permanent spatial arrangement, which as such nevertheless remains outside the normal order' (1998: 169). Inside the camp the prisoners are stripped of their political status and reduced to bare life where power confronts them 'without any mediation' (171) and where acts can be committed against them without being considered a crime. While obviously incomparable in scale and brutality to Nazi concentration camps, the paradigm spaces for the current state of emergency are the camps (X-ray and Delta) at Guantánamo Bay in Cuba, Belmarsh Prison in London and the prison at Abu Ghraib, which was just one of a network of prisons holding inmates without charge in Iraq. While prisoners at Guantánamo Bay are clearly not reduced to bare life, for their religion is at least recognized, they are nevertheless literally and figuratively suspended outside the law, excluded from a juridical order that they are deemed to be not worthy of, and yet which at the same time their exclusion makes sacred. Held in Cuba to ensure they are not entitled to protection under US law, and given the nomenclature 'illegal combatants' to ensure that the Geneva Convention does not apply to them, the inmates of the camps are beholden to the whim of what Amnesty International has called 'unfettered executive power'; denied access to court and counsel, and thereby condemned to a legal black hole for the duration of an endless war against terror.[11]

The prisoner abuse at Abu Ghraib, as well as reports concerning the CIA's preferred practice of 'rendering' prisoners, which is the transfer of uncooperative prisoners to the custody of foreign intelligence services in Egypt, Jordan, Saudi Arabia and Morocco where torture is widely practised, demonstrates that sovereign power is not only the withdrawal of the law from those people deemed somehow less human, it is also exemplified in the use of, and monopoly over the use of violence. As we shall see in relation to the declaration of war, sovereignty is also 'the point of indistinction between violence and law, the threshold on which violence passes over into law and law passes over into violence' (Agamben, 1998: 32). This is Agamben's reading of the Hobbesian justification of sovereignty. Hobbes writes that 'during the time men live together without a common power to keep them all in awe, they are in that condition which is called war, and such a war as is of every man against every man'. And it should be noted here that this most famous of passages from Hobbes's *Leviathan* continues in a manner that is highly pertinent to our current discussion of emergency: 'For War consisteth not in battle only, or the act of fighting, but in a tract of time wherein the will to contend by battle is sufficiently known. And therefore, the notion of *time* is to be considered in the nature of war, as it is in the nature of weather. For as the nature of foul weather lieth not in a shower or two of rain, but in an inclination thereto of many days together, so the nature of war consisteth not in actual fighting, but in the known disposition thereto during all the time there is no assurance to the contrary' (1994: 76). In this manner the violence of the state of nature justifies the absolute power of the sovereign, and the violence that is forbidden by the institution of the law is preserved in the sovereign's rule who may legitimately use 'terror' in the pursuit of conformity, and 'use the strength and means of [the multitude] as he shall think expedient, for their peace and common defence' (190). In the Hobbesain worldview, then, an endless war (against terror) equates to an endless rule of sovereign power/violence in the name of peace. As Judith Butler has argued, the images of detainees at Guantánamo function as an illustration of the permanence of the threat. The prisoners are presented as animals 'out of control [and] in need of total restraint' (2004: 78). The detention is portrayed as actually stopping the killing. 'If they were not detained, and forcibly so when any movement is required, they would apparently start killing on the spot' (78).

In many respects the images of the prisoners at Guantánamo and the rhetoric of the war against terror more broadly work off and promote both profound fears and anxieties born of our openness to a world that is uncertain and yet to be decided. In *Being and Time*, Heidegger describes both fear and anxiety as modes of disclosure. Where fear is 'fearing *in the face of* something [...] which is detrimental to Dasein's factical potentiality-for-Being' (1962: 391), anxiety is an exposure to the 'insignificance of the world' or being 'anxious in the face of the "nothing" of the world' (393). In this regard the face of Osama bin Laden becomes the 'known' object of fear, the *hostis*, the enemy of the community, while the challenge to American hegemony and the American way of life generally opens up as an incomprehensible yet now ever-present anxiety. As Paulo Virno has eloquently put it, 'Fear is always circumscribed and nameable; anguish is ubiquitous, not connected to distinctive causes; it can survive in any given moment or situation' (2004: 32). He continues: 'The distinction between circumscribed fear and unspecified fear is operative where there are substantial communities constituting a channel which is capable of directing our praxis and collective experience. [...] The counterpart of fear is that security which the community can in principle, guarantee; the counterpart of anguish (or of its showing itself to the world as such) is the shelter procured from religious experience' (32).

Evil

Towards the end of Leo Strauss's 'Notes' on *The Concept of the Political*, he points out that Schmitt is really battling not with liberalism but with the order of human things, a position that is only briefly admitted in the afterword to Schmitt's 1932 edition. For Strauss the 1932 edition can only be Schmitt's first word against liberalism because he only identifies the problem without getting beyond it. In other words the affirmation of the political as such equates to a respect for all who want to fight and proves to be a form of liberalism only with 'the opposite polarity' (Strauss in Schmitt, 1996: 105). That Schmitt himself admits to being concerned with the order of human things intimates the path beyond liberalism that Schmitt is still to articulate. Strauss writes: 'The polemic against liberalism can therefore only signify a concomitant or preparatory action: it is meant to clear the field for the battle of decision between the "spirit of technicity", the "mass faith that inspires an antireligious, this-worldly activism", and the opposite spirit and faith, which, as it seems, still has no name' (106). This critique heightens the peculiarity of Chapter 7 of Schmitt's treatise, which reads as something of a radical departure from what has gone before. It is still concerned with the friend and enemy distinction, but in this chapter Schmitt makes it very clear that the political is based on something more fundamental, the moral which in itself is also founded on the theological. Chapter 7 is peculiar because it suddenly turns to the question of evil and, one might extrapolate, to the ultimate friend and enemy distinction between God and Satan.

In the opening of this chapter, Schmitt makes the stark claim that all political theories can be tested by their anthropological faith, that is, by their assessment as to whether or not man is 'by nature evil or good, a dangerous or harmless creature' (58); going on to announce that political theories are only 'genuine' if they 'presuppose man to be evil' (61). In the state of nature, humans like animals are stirred by their drives (59) and man's power, his being open and undetermined (something that countless philosophers have referred to as man's freedom) is the locus of evil (60). The political equivalent of the open and undetermined condition is the philosophical and political anarchy that starts from the belief in natural human goodness and ends up by denying the importance of the state. While Schmitt reasserts the primacy of the political by working backwards from the fundamental enmity that means political theory cannot, if it is to remain political, start with anthropological optimism, it becomes clear that the primary concern is the moral-theological in that the real enemy is the evil of disorder. In the 1932 edition he remarks that what denial of original sin means can be seen in examples of sects, heretics, romantics and anarchists (65). In the 1933 edition this is strengthened by the additional phrase that the example of sects, heretics, romantics and anarchists have shown that ' "the denial of original sin destroys all social order" ' (in Meier, 1995: 53). At this point Schmitt also likens the methodological kinship of theology and politics. As a political theorist ceases to be a political theorist as soon as he fails to distinguish between friend and enemy, so a 'theologian ceases to be a theologian when he no longer considers man to be sinful or in need of redemption and no longer distinguishes between the chosen and the unchosen'. As Meier notes, Schmitt 'embarks upon his confrontation with liberalism in the name of the political, and pursues it for the sake of religion' (30). His statement concerning original sin 'tolerates no contradiction' (53), the couplet friend and enemy equates to credo or non-credo, order or disorder. Without faith in original sin and the primacy of enmity the result is chaos. The distinction between friend and enemy in the political sphere ultimately corresponds to a decision between God and Satan in theological sphere. In a later work Meier contends that the intensity of the bond or separation can thus be equated with the Fall of Man and the need for salvation (1998: 68). This kinship between the theological and the political is made explicit in the close to Chapter 7 where Schmitt briefly discusses the 'high points of politics [...] in which the enemy is, in concrete clarity, recognized as the enemy' (1996: 67). All such outbreaks of enmity, he claims, are surpassed by Cromwell's enmity towards papist Spain documented in his speech of 17 September 1656. In this speech Cromwell stresses the first lesson of nature is the preservation of existence and the conservation of National Being. Schmitt's rendition of Cromwell's speech is as follows:

'Why, truly, your great Enemy is the Spaniard. He is a natural enemy. He is naturally so; he is naturally so throughout, – by reason of that enmity that is in him against whatsoever is of God. "Whatsoever is of God" which is in *you*, or which may be in you'. Then he repeats: 'The Spaniard is your enemy', his 'enmity is put into him by God'. He is 'the natural enemy, the providential enemy', and he who considers him to be an 'accidental enemy' is 'not well acquainted with Scripture and the things of God', who says: ' "I will put enmity between your seed and her seed" (Gen. 3, 15)'. (68)[12]

While Strauss challenged Schmitt by arguing that the grouping of friend and enemy 'owes its legitimation to the seriousness of the question of what is right' (Schmitt 1996: 103), Schmitt responded that is was 'the battle of *faith* against *faith*' (Meier, 1995: 72). In the 1933 edition Schmitt revisits his discussion of Hobbes and the state of nature as the antagonism of animal drives and in response to Strauss writes: 'The political distinction between friend and enemy is to the same degree deeper than all oppositions that exist in the animal world, as the extent to which man, as a being who exists spiritually, stands above the animal' (58–9). Thus the challenge of political philosophy is met at the level of political theology. For Schmitt, there is still too much autonomy and freedom pertaining to the question of what is right, faith on the other hand 'is not a question *asked by man* but the question *put to man*, whether he will obey God or Satan' (Meier, 1995: 42). In this respect the distinction between friend and enemy could come to an end only if there were no Providential enemy. Political theology thus sets in place a metaphysical antagonism between authority and anarchy, spirituality and animality, between faith and atheism, and obedience to and rebellion against the sovereign.

Meier concludes that Schmitt's critique of liberalism, which begins with the political distinction between friend and enemy is ultimately played out on the theological stage as a confrontation between good and evil. Schmitt struggles against the liberal universal fraternity and world-state because it is ungodly. The religion of technology diverts man's attention from the true religion and generates the false belief that man can create a paradise on earth. In turning himself into a God, man loses sight of his obligation to make a fateful decision between God and Satan and it is the Antichrist who ultimately establishes dominion. Meier quotes from Schmitt's 1916 work *Theodore Däublers 'Nordlicht'* in which he writes: ' "[The Antichrist's] mysterious power lies in the imitation of God. God created the world, the Antichrist counterfeits it [...] Men who allow themselves to be deceived by him see only the fabulous effect; nature seems to be overcome, the age of security dawns; everything has been taken care of, a clever foresight and planning replace Providence; the Antichrist 'makes' Providence as he makes any institution" ' (48). And Meier continues: 'The Antichrist would triumph – and in the long run could *only* triumph – if he succeeded in convincing men that the opposition between friend and enemy has been overcome once and for all, that they no longer need to decide between Christ and the Antichrist' (48–9). Finally, then, the political is destiny 'because it keeps men [...] in the condition of historicity and Judgement' (70).

To return to the war against terror, the fact that the rhetoric is couched in terms of a confrontation between Good and Evil has been shown to result from the impossibility of defining the enemy in the concrete. It might also be said that the rhetoric is merely a cover to hide the true motivations and interests which are economic. However, there is a body of evidence to support the argument that many people in the US, and indeed some members of the Bush administration, do believe the war against terror to be part of a literal battle with Satan, a battle to be decided in the final conflagration. In a study that traces the rise of millenialism in the US, Michael Northcott (2004) has shown how a significant percentage of the US population believe they are living in the end times and that the increase in war, violence, natural disaster and social decay are all signs that Armageddon is nigh. Significantly, however, within this narrative the US is the divine instrument charged with securing this Providential path.

Northcott opens his study with a quotation from Bush's inaugural speech of 20 January 2001 in which he declares that America's destiny to shape the world according to its interests will take courage and perseverance, but it will be successful 'because it is "the angel of God that directs the storm"' (6). This phrase is adapted from a letter written by John Page to Thomas Jefferson shortly after the Declaration of Independence in which Page declares: '"We know the race is not to the swift nor the battle to the strong. Do you not think an angel rides in the whirlwind and directs this storm?"' (6). The repetition of Page's revolutionary faith restates the belief that America was from its founding and will be into the future the instrument of God's will on earth. Where all nations had previously failed, America would be the exception in the human quest for the good society, and today Bush continues to appeal to the 'transcendent significance of the experience of being American' (100), assured that the spread of American values is Christ's mandate. Northcott's argument, however, is that in assuming to be the instrument of God's will America has perverted the Christian message, converting the Christian community from 'counter-cultural egalitarianism, economic sharing and practical care for the orphan, the poor, the sick and the widow' (12) into an imperial cult.

According to Northcott, 40 per cent of Americans describe themselves as evangelical Christians and a quarter believe they are living in the end times. This belief in the end times is a specific strain of millennialism known as premillennialism or dispensationalism. It has become the most popular version of millennial belief and, unlike postmillennialists who believe they are building a godly commonwealth and ushering in the thousand-year rule of the saints, premillennialists believe the Judgement will happen before the thousand-year rule and that the Judgement and the Second Coming will be preceded by the final decisive battle against Satan. However, despite their differences, Northcott notes: 'Both varieties of New World millennialism involve the claim that Americans are in some exceptional sense in charge of human history, that their story represents the fulfilment of Biblical passages about the end of history, the last judgement and the final revelation [...]. Americans in this millennial reading of history come to see America as the "redeemer nation", the first nation fully to realise the true salvic intent of human history' (15). For the postmillennialist the kingdom of God would be built in America and beyond. In 1899, for example, Albert Beveridge described the logic of the American Greater Republic: '"God did not make the American people the mightiest human force of all time simply to feed and die [...] He made us the lords of civilization that we may administer civilization"' (in Northcott, 2004: 24), a sentiment echoed in Dick Cheney's Christmas card in 2003, which included the inscription: 'If a sparrow cannot fall to the ground without His notice, is it probable that an empire can rise without His aid?'. In this vision, anything done in American interest even the active support of dictators was, and could only be, for the greater good given the providential role of the US.

Premillennisalism or dispensationalism, however, believes that we are headed for the 'Great Tribulation' that precedes the millennium of peace. The Great Tribulation, Northcott explains, involves an increase in wickedness, war and disaster as well as a falling away of faith. It is known as dispensationalism because of John Darby's interpretation of the seven dispensations of human history in the Book of Revelation. The first is paradise in the Garden of Eden, the seventh and last is the millennial rule of the saints. According to Darby, human history is currently nearing the close of the sixth dispensation. One other important feature of premillennialism is the idea that true believers will be saved from the violence of Armageddon in what is known as the 'Rapture'. According to Northcott, this idea has its sources in 1 Thessalonians, 4: 16–17 where Paul says ' "the dead in Christ shall rise first, and then we which are alive and remain shall be caught up together with them in the clouds, to meet the lord in the air" ' (59). At this moment the fate of righteous individuals is to be 'mysteriously and suddenly plucked from their beds or workplaces by the divine hand and so rescued from the coming conflagration' (88–9). Much like the Calvinist belief in predestination the Rapture is a matter of election and nothing can be done to alter one's fate. No doubt part of the appeal of this idea is the complete abdication of responsibility. Nothing is required of the believer save for his or her unwithering faith, and each new war and every new disaster is just one more sign permitting Reuben Torrey, for example, to declare at the outbreak of the First World War: ' "the darker the night gets, the lighter my heart becomes" ' (Northcott, 2004: 61). That premillennialism should see an increasingly violent world as a good sign is indeed disturbing, but matters are worse when Northcott permits us to see the full extent of this logic. What is most sinister is the idea that because violence and destruction are all providential signs of God's will, premillennialists believe that any programme of wholesale (global) betterment goes against divine purpose and delays the Second Coming. According to James Robison, a religious mentor to Ronald Reagan who prayed with George W. Bush during the presidential campaign in 1999, all peace activists are heretics because the teaching of peace prior to the return of

Christ is against the Word of God (Northcott, 2004: 67). For Northcott, this attitude is exemplified in the words of Lewis Chafer: ' "Satan, like a fond mother, is bending over those in his arms, breathing into their mouths the quieting balm of a 'universal fatherhood of God' and a 'universal brotherhood of man' [...] feeding their tendency to imitate the true faith by great human undertakings and schemes for the reformation of individuals and the betterment of the social order" ' (60).[13] It is also interesting to note how this echoes Schmitt's concerns regarding the complacency of peace.

Given that one of the signs for the immanence of the Judgement and Second Coming is the building of the Third Temple in Jerusalem on the site of the Al-Aqsa mosque, the founding of the Jewish state in 1948 and the occupation of Jerusalem during the six-day war in 1967 were read as epochal events. Writing at this time, Hal Lindsey produced one of the most popular pieces of premillennialist literature entitled *The Late Great Planet Earth* in which he explains both Old and New Testament prophecies and links them with contemporary signs which included amongst others the formation of the UN and the threat of the Soviet Union. Of course the popularity of Lindsey's book was underpinned by the fear of nuclear annihilation, but what is most interesting is the fact revealed by Phillip Melling in his study of American fundamentalism (1999) that it was not until 1989 and the disappearance of the enemy with the collapse of Soviet communism that the popularity of premillennialist literature surged. At this point the threat of secular one-worldism encapsulated the balm of universal brotherhood breathed by Satan.[14] Pat Robertson's book *New World Order* epitomized the premillennialist foreboding regarding the Soviet beast now preaching *perestroika* and *glasnost*. Americans should remain on guard because such one-worldism signals the coming of the Antichrist's dominion. Sales in premillennialist literature were only to increase during Gulf War I, not least because as Fred Henry observed in *The Middle East – Destined*, the war was the confirmation of Revelation 18 that speaks of the destruction of Babylon. As Melling notes, John Walvoord's *Armageddon, Oil and the Middle East Crisis*, first published in 1974, sold 600,000 copies in ten weeks in 1991: 'These book sales were the sign of an expectant people, not one whose victory was already assured by its triumph over Communism or one whose religious beliefs were no longer relevant in a secular age' (Melling, 1999: 82).

Gulf War I can thus be seen as the renewal of the civil religion of America that links nationalist fervour to millennialist belief.

Northcott argues that through embodying the protestant virtues of industry and enterprise as well as privileging private property, autonomy and personal liberty, the American nation, rather than exempting itself from religion, as established in the separation of church and state, was able to become the focus for a civil religion. Religious disestablishment as practised by the Protestant sects that populated the New World was based on the rejection of hierarchy and of the social, political, economic regulation that gave birth to the nation and consecrated its constitution. The result, according to Northcott, was the presence of a distant deity in the values of the Republic. Northcott likens this process to the events that led Constantine in the fourth century to make Christianity the official religion of the Roman Empire. Constantine's vision of the Cross and subsequent use of the *chi-rho* symbol on his soldiers' shields is believed to have contributed to his decisive victory; and it was Eusebius of Caesarea, an early imperial theologian, who Northcott attributes with developing the idea of a subsequent social order sustained by a military power blessed by God.[15] As with Eusebius, it is the current theologians of national destiny who now argue God is determining the outcome of history through its wars with the barbarians (150), but while Rome became the pacifier, Northcott reminds us that the *pax romana* was a violent peace.

In the narrative of permanent hostility, ever-present violence and the decisive fight in which the US keeps evil at bay, the political theology of Carl Schmitt is given a popular form. Schmitt in 1933, like the US administration and indeed a significant percentage of the American population, believed that he must be forever watchful, forever prepared to make that fateful decision regarding the enemy, for if the need for that decision should ever be allowed to lapse then the Antichrist would have dominion. However, in his fight with the bad infinite (Flahaut: 2003) he plunged directly into it. Central to Schmitt's belief in his role and indeed the role of conservative political authority in the shape of the commissarial dictator, the sovereign, the Leviathan and even the Führer is, as Gopal Balakrishnan explains, their function as a restrainer, holding the world in place (2000: 225). But the restrainer also has a theological significance in that it is this figure, the *katechon* in Greek, who according to Paul is also holding back 'the lawless one' (2 Thessalonians, 2: 6–7). However, bearing in mind Schmitt's fateful decision to join the National Socialist Party, and given the Bush administration's willingness to prosecute wars wherever and whenever its interests are threatened, and potentially by any means necessary, including the use of tactical nuclear weapons we ought to give the last word of warning to Heinrich Meier: 'In the event that the battle of decision still lies in the distant future and that what matters here and now is short of the eschatological confrontation, to strengthen the *katechon* [the restrainer] that can subdue the Antichrist for an unknown period, how can the *restrainer* be distinguished from the hastener, and from the *hastener in spite of himself*?' (82).

7
Media and Machine

The relationship between advances in communications and development in warfare are well documented. The link is supposed to be at its strongest during a state of emergency, a time when the state heavily regulates media outlets for the purposes of 'national security' and the necessities of military operations demand innovations in transmission, collection, decoding and interpretation of information, but the link remains tight even during periods of peace. In fact the relationship is so strong that it is becoming increasingly difficult to separate military operations from the everyday practices of the media and entertainment industries locked as they are in a cycle of imitation (Der Derian, 2001). Two events in particular, one anecdotal the other factual, serve to demonstrate the close historical ties between the military and the media. The first event takes place in 1898 and is, as Armand Mattelart (1994) reports it, 'the first great press campaign aimed at inciting a government to intervene militarily on foreign soil' (17). In this instance, William Randolph Hearst was able to force the hand of President William McKinley and bring about the invasion of Cuba based on the surge of public opinion Hearst had created via the use of his media empire. Legend has it that when Frederic Remington, who Hearst had dispatched to photograph the crisis in Cuba, telegraphed him saying: 'Everything is quiet. There is no trouble here. There will be no war. Wish to return', Hearst replied: 'Please remain. You furnish the pictures and I'll provide the war' (in Mattelart, 1994: 18).[1] The second event took place in 1928, the date of the second ever television transmission by engineers at General Electric. This event is not only significant due to the new world of communications that it heralds, it is also significant given that the content of the broadcast was a simulated missile attack on New York City, thus announcing the perpetual fascination that the medium of television would have with war, conflict and violence. As James Der Derian notes, the transmission seems to presage the video footage of smart-weapons and the revolution in military affairs (RMA) first revealed in Gulf War I, and we should add, even more eerily it seems to foretell the media spectacle we now call '9/11'.

Communication

According to Mattelart the first system of telecommunications was set up in 1793, an optical or aerial telegraph between Paris and Lille, which became a key technology for a country at war. Over the course of the next half century the aerial telegraph was used for strategic purposes on a number of occasions, proving decisive, as Mattelart notes, during the colonization and occupation of Algiers in 1842. However, what Mattelart refers to as the first ambitious use of the telegraph was its deployment during the Crimean War in which British and French high commands set up communication routes to relay information about the various operations in the field. In addition to enhancing their command structure the Crimean War was also the vehicle for establishing new laws in relation to wartime censorship due to the fact that the telegraph system was also used to relay stories of the war to the public at home. When William Howard Russell's account of the charge at Balaclava on 25 October 1854 appeared in *The Times* and caused an outcry, it was not long before the British stopped uncensored journalism, and by February 1856 military accreditation of all stories was made mandatory (Mattelart, 1994: 9).[2]

It was not until the outbreak of the First World War, however, that communications were as important, if not more important, off the battlefield as they were on it. The First World War was an ideological war as much as a concern with physically injuring the enemy and the use of propaganda was central to maintaining public opinion and demoralizing the enemy. These exercises in propaganda and the relative success of the British and allied forces, something that Joseph Goebbels later sought to emulate (Taylor: 1995), also precipitated the birth of modern media theory and mass communications research, most notably the post-war work of Harold Laswell. Laswell's contribution to the informational logistics of warfare was the recognition of the necessity for governments to manage public opinion, a process even more important today in an age that has become increasingly mediated by information and where information has so many outlets and carriers. For Laswell, the management of information was needed because the physical mobilization of men and women was not enough. Mobilization of their attitudes and beliefs was just as important for the newly emerging paradigm of total war. Laswell's diagnosis of the problem was as follows:

> Small primitive tribes can weld their heterogeneous members into a fighting whole by the beat of the tom-tom and the tempestuous rhythm of the dance. It is in orgies of physical exuberance that young men are brought to the boiling point of war, and that old and young men and women are caught in the suction of tribal purpose. In the Great Society it is no longer possible to fuse the waywardness of individuals in the furnace of the war dance; a newer and subtler instrument must weld thousands, even millions, of human beings into one amalgamated mass of hate and will and hope. A new flame must burn out the canker of dissent and temper the steel of bellicose enthusiasm. The name of this new hammer and anvil of social solidarity is propaganda. (in Mattelart, 1994: 66)

A decade earlier the US set up its first propaganda agency to ensure public opinion supported America's entry into and continued participation in the First World War. While Mattelart refers to the Committee on Public Information (otherwise known as the Creel Committee) as the first bureau of governmental censorship in the US, Nancy Snow (2003) highlights the fact that it was anything but an agency of censorship. George Creel, who was the key figure behind the Committee, always argued that it was never part of the machinery of concealment or repression. His book, entitled *How we Advertised America: The First Telling of the Amazing Story of the Committee on Public Information that Carried the Gospel of Americanism to Every Corner of the Globe*, argued that the Committee was not about limiting a free press: 'In all things [...] it was a plain publicity proposition, a vast enterprise in salesmanship' (cited in Snow, 2003: 51). But having said this, the object of Creel's attention remained, as it would be for Laswell, the will of the amalgamated masses. ' "What we had to have" ', he wrote, ' "was no mere surface unity, but a passionate belief in the justice of America's cause that moulds the people of the United States into one white-hot mass instinct of fraternity, devotion, courage and deathless determination" ' (in Snow, 2003: 52). What he called 'the *war-will*' required the consecration of body and soul ' "in the supreme effort of service and sacrifice" '. Of course, this approach did not end with the dissolution of Creel's committee in 1919. The rhetoric deployed in the war against terror deploys empty platitudes about freedom and civilization with the regularity of Laswell's tom-tom, and Creel's vision for selling America was inherited by Charlotte Beers, who previously sold disposable razor blades and Uncle Ben's Rice (Snow, 2003: 54), before being asked by George W. Bush to sell America to the Middle East and Asia in October 2001.

Communications technology, in particular radio, but increasingly television, is a key weapon in the psychological operations (PSYOPs) that deterritorialize strategic space (Mattelart, 1994: 100). Most recently the CIA has sponsored the Middle East Radio Network, broadcasting under the name of Radio Sawa, meaning 'together', along with the PSYOPs aircraft *Commando Solo*, which in April 2003 was transmitting nightly newscasts by Tom Brokaw, the NBC anchor, and Peter Jennings, the ABC anchor, into Iraq (Snow, 2003). Of the three paradigms of the information war identified by Robin Brown (2003), information operations, public diplomacy and media management, these exercises in disseminating both America's image and its view of the world are best categorized in the paradigm of public diplomacy, that exercise of 'soft power' (Nye, 2004) in which the US seeks to create 'the kind of international milieu where American values would flourish' (Brown, 2003: 91), but, of course, it is hard to separate this from the hard edged information war in which disinformation and even deception are an important weapon. In this regard the information armoury of the Bush administration received a slight dent when Donald Rumsfled's Office for Strategic Influence (OSI) was shut down after a story was leaked to the press that the OSI was in the business of feeding false stories to foreign news agencies in pursuit of its strategic aims.[3] Obviously, there are moments when the differing paradigms of the information war work against each other. In this instance the information operations had to concede to the soft power of public diplomacy as the news of the US deliberately feeding the world lies did not sit well with its mantra of America as the bastion of truth and democratic transparency.

The difficulty faced by the military today is summed up by the fact that information is becoming an evermore important aspect of the logistics of war, and yet the sources for delivering information have become much more difficult to control as technology blurs the distinctions between official spokespersons, professional journalists and civilian observers publishing on the Web. This has been heightened in the war in Afghanistan and Gulf War II by the presence of Al'Jazeera, the only channel in the Middle East to both challenge the Western monopoly and be independently run (Miladi, 2003; Miles, 2005). As

Frank Webster (2003) has argued, at the symbolic level nation states are becoming increasingly porous, meaning the military are less able to contain information in the manner they might wish, a problem of added significance given the US administration's supposed failings in the information war in Vietnam.

Since then the US administration has practised what were in effect media blackouts in the invasions of Grenada and Panama, but Grenada, in particular lead to such fierce criticism from the press wishing to retain their constitutional rights that the Pentagon introduced a new system for Gulf War I, known as the pool system, where, as Philip Taylor notes an attempt was made to bridge the 'diametrically opposed needs of both the military (secrecy) and the media (publicity)' (1992: 42). Given that the rhetoric of freedom during Gulf War II was even more pronounced than it was in 1991, the Pentagon felt it necessary to make further innovations in which their democratic credentials could not be questioned. The result was journalists 'embedded' with military units, revolutionary in journalistic terms perhaps, but already deployed for propaganda purposes in the Second World War when each German regiment had its own cameraman and propaganda unit to send pictures of battles home to a public eager to see the destiny of the Third Reich being played out. In June 2003 Victoria Clarke, assistant secretary of defense for public affairs at the Pentagon, remarked that embedding journalists alongside the forces was an example of how she, and her boss, Donald Rumsfeld 'tried since the beginning to be very transparent in our business' (in Tumber and Palmer, 2004: 13), but the main purpose was to ensure that reporting continued via official sources.

Information

The nightly broadcast of press meetings lead by Army colonels introducing images of the digital battlefield and smart weapons that lead Jean Baudrillard to liken Gulf War I to 'an assault on the reality principle' (1995: 76) have also been taken as evidence for the latest RMA.[4] While it is important to remain sceptical with regard to this discourse of a revolution, not least because it is a discourse circulated by the military, but also because cyberwar remains tied to the consumption of fossil fuels, especially oil, there is sufficient evidence to suggest that current transformations in weapons systems and military thinking do require sustained analysis if only to expose the vision of the world's single hyperpower. Also, we must not lose sight of the fact that these weapons, no matter how smart, are still about blowing people apart, that is, out-injuring an opponent (Scarry, 1985). In this sense they are as primitive as the bronze-age axe, but the invention of such an axe did not permit those using it to imagine a battle in which their own death would be taken out of the equation. For the changing role and nature of media and military communications, for war as a zero-sum game, for war increasingly at a distance and at increased speed, it is worth thinking through some of the key issues in the current RMA, for as Paul Hirst concedes these innovations suggest a future that will probably see civil and military values increasingly diverge, which 'in some circumstances might lead to a praetorian threat to political order' (2001: 98).

Somewhat ironically, the possibility of this praetorian threat was first announced by President Dwight Eisenhower in 1961. As Brian E. Fogarty notes, the partnership between government and defence contractors, a partnership that Eisenhower himself had encouraged, was by the end of his presidency becoming such a political force that he warned the American public to remain vigilant. In his words: '"In the councils of Government we must guard against the acquisition of unwarranted influence, whether sought or unsought, by the military-industrial complex. The potential for the disastrous rise of misplaced power exists and will persist"' (in Fogarty, 2000: 107).[5] But as Fogarty argues, the failure of the civilian authorities to reign in the power of the military and control weapons acquisition, as well as the promotion of militarism 'without regard for the needs of foreign policy or military threat' (2000: 108) indicates how the military-industrial complex seems to take on a life of its own. Indeed such an argument has also become the underlying premise for what Chris Hables Gray calls post-modern war. He suggests that the destructive power of nuclear weaponry produced a general deterrence in the formerly bipolar world of the Cold War because it was 'impossible for war and humanity to coexist' (1997: 170). As a consequence 'the old and conservative discourse of war has become wildly experimental and it has institutionalized innovation to an amazing degree. This process has included the colonization of much of Western science and technology as the war system keeps seeking ways to keep war viable' (170). In other words, the military-industrial complex continually seeks the means to ensure its own continuation, or 'protecting the military-industrial complex is as much the armed forces' goal as protecting their countries' (172).

In Gray's analysis the future of war has two paths. The first is the catastrophic continuation of violence as witnessed in the genocide in Rwanda, only with massively destructive weapons and between techno- logically advanced and competing states, or there is the utopian redefinition of war through virtuality, digitization and simulation. It is this latter path that post-modern or cyberwar is seeking to tread. The ideal scenario for the US, as well as for those governments like Britain who see their armed forces as a node to be plugged in and out of the US military matrix when required, is complete control of the global battlespace through attaining absolute dominance over what Paul Virilio has termed 'the logistics of perception' (1989).[6] In this situation where seeing equals killing and being seen equals being killed, complete control of information or what the US military likes to call 'full spectrum dominance' becomes the new deterrence. Wars are then brief sorties into the panoptical field against those who threaten a breach of the peace, thus allowing the military-industrial complex to periodically test and expend its weaponry in a spectacular display of security that further justifies increased defence spending.

According to Gray there are three central elements to cyberwar. The first is the belief that it can be managed scientifically; the second is the belief that war is a matter of information and interpretation; the third is the emphasis on computers as the means by which the first and the second elements will be achieved (1997: 23). While innovations in command technology and the bureaucratization of war can be dated as far back as Lieutenant General Gribeaval's attempts to systematize French artillery between 1763 and 1767 (McNeill: 1982), Gray traces the current obsession with scientific management to F. W. Lanchester's book *Aircraft in Warfare* published in 1916. This, Gray argues, was the first attempt to quantify the laws of combat as one would the laws of nature. War like the natural world was a system, the rules and processes of which were open to rational calculation. This leads to the second element of cyberwar that warfare is a matter of information, or as Manuel De Landa has put it, that each tactical unit within a military force becomes an 'information-processing machine' (1991: 59). War thus becomes the gathering, interpretation and transmission of information through a communications network. The functioning of what has come to be called the C3I network (command, control, communications and intelligence) is the key to the successful prosecution of a military campaign. As was noted earlier, communications technology such as the aerial telegraph were crucial to the development of earlier command structures. Today it is the third and defining element of cyberwar, the computer that is believed to be able to remove the 'friction' in the system. De Landa explains the situation as follows:

The word 'friction' has several military meanings. On the one hand, it refers in transportation and communication networks to the physical friction responsible for delays, bottlenecks and machine breakdowns. But more generally, it is used to refer to any phenomenon (natural or artificial) that interferes with the implementation of a tactical strategic plan. In this extended sense the word 'friction' refers to everything from bad weather to the independent will of the enemy (his active resistance to the advance of one's troops as well as his sabotaging activities). In the case of tactical command networks, friction appears as 'noisy data'. Not only information circulates in the circuits of command networks, but also the uncertainty produced by the fog of war. The most successful command systems in history have been the ones that manage to 'dissipate' uncertainty throughout the hierarchy. (60)

To eradicate 'friction', centralizing systems reduce the core of decision-makers thus reducing error in the communication of commands. However, centralizing systems as De Landa explains actually produces the opposite effect and increases the total amount of uncertainty: 'withdrawing all responsibility from individual soldiers involves defining every command in extreme detail and intensifies the need to check compliance with those commands' (61). Computers, it is believed will become the interface between humans and between humans and machines to form a 'synergistic whole' (80), removing 'friction', and at the outer reaches of military fantasy allow the combined forces to 'swarm' (Dillon, 2002). For De Landa, the utopia of future conflict involves not only 'full spectrum dominance' but also the self-organization of the military force. Here, the vision is for the military to react, not only rapidly, but literally immediately to the emerging threat. Computer processing, satellite communications and digitized networks may hold the secret for producing a kind of military fractal geometry able to calculate the production of singularities, or 'phase transitions' (De Landa, 1991: 18) required for the operation of spontaneously assembling, complex systems. As De Landa explains, for the military to 'swarm' the production of the military equivalent of a machinic phylum is required, this being 'the set of all the singularities at the onset of processes of self-organization – the critical points in the flow of matter and energy, points at which these flows spontaneously acquire a new form or pattern' (132). It is, then, a process whereby distinct elements, previously disconnected, begin to ' "cooperate" to form a higher level entity' (7). As De Landa borrows the term 'machinic phylum' from the work of Gilles Deleuze and Félix Guattari we ought to add that these distinct elements are referred to by them as *assemblages* that 'cut the phylum up into distinct, differentiated lineages, at the same time as the machinic phylum cuts across them all, taking leave of one to pick up again in another, or making them coexist' (Deleuze and Guattari, 1988: 406). In other words the self-organizing war machine comprises distinct assemblages of weapons systems, image systems, communications pathways and human–machine hybrids that can operate independently or collectively, thanks to advances in computer and satellite techno- logy. At Fort Irwin in the Mojave Desert, demonstrations of the latest military assemblages are offered to interested journalists (and academics) permitted to observe the latest digitized war game. During one such game entitled Operation Desert Hammer VI, James Der Derian observed the following:

At the high end of the lethality spectrum there was the improved M1A2 Abrams tank, carrying IVIS (Inter-Vehicular Information System) which could collect real-time battlefield data from overhead JSTAR aircraft (Joint Surveillance and Target Attack Radar System), Pioneer unmanned aerial vehicles equipped with video cameras, and global positioning satellite systems (GPS) to display icons of friendlies and foes on a computer-generated map overlay. At the low end, there was the '21st Century land Warrior' (also called 'warfighter', but never 'soldier' or 'infantryman'), who came equipped with augmented day and night vision scopes mounted on his M-16, a GPS, 8 mm video camera, and one-inch ocular LED screen connected by a flexible arm to his Kevlar, and an already-dated 486 Lightweight Computer Unit in his backpack, all wired for voice or digital-burst communication to a BattleSpace Command Vehicle with an All Source Analysis System that could collate information and coordinate the attack through a customized Windows program. (2001: 5–6)

This vivid account of a weapons-communication assemblage and military cyborg returns us to the central issue concerning the increasing importance of information for the post-modern, post-human (Gray, 2003), self-organizing war machine. For theorists such as Donna Haraway the close connection between the military and techno-science is related to a common belief that the domination of the world becomes 'a problem of coding' (1991: 164), the belief that boundaries are permeable to informa- tion and sufficient information 'allows universal translation, and so unhindered instrumental power' (164). Of course, there is a dual problem here that the military strategists and techno-scientists either choose to ignore or deliberately airbrush out when presenting their vision of cyberwar, namely that the second element of cyberwar, the information/ interpretation element is a question of hermeneutics. While the techni- cians unquestioningly accept the positivist view that war is a matter of rational calculation dependent upon the gathering and transmission of sufficient data, they avoid the problem that the interpretation of that information is a hermeneutic problem qualitatively different from the positivist assumption of transparency. Increasingly cyberwar involves what Don Ihde has called the 'hermeneutic relation' (1990) to technology where a particular piece of technics comes to stand in for the world (imagine a petrol gauge in relation to the petrol). This means that 'the location of the technical problem in hermeneutic relations lies in the *connector* between the instrument and the referent. Perceptually the user's visual (or other) terminus is *upon* the instrumentation itself. To read an instrument is an analogue to reading a text. But if the text does not correctly refer, its reference object or its world cannot be present' (1990: 87). With increased use of screens and video technology in fighter planes, for example, it is not about the instrument itself being faulty, but the possibility of an incorrect reading by the pilot. As the enemy is increasingly de-realized as an avatar on a screen, the operator of the tech- nology is required to make a judgement concerning their status from the digital information available. If we then add the second problem of intentionality, what are the repercussions for soldiers repeatedly trained to see avatars as the enemy? Can intentionality help explain the downing of the Iranian airbus flight 655 in 1988? Did the context of operating amid intelligence that Iran was planning missile attacks on US ships in the Persian Gulf allow the conversion of the airbus's normal descent pattern into an accelerating dive suggestive of an attack? Whatever the conclusions it is impossible for the new war machine to dispel this element of 'friction', but it continues with its dream of full, transparent information nevertheless.

For Paul Virilio the informational element of cyberwar opens up a fourth front amounting to exclusive control of the fourth dimension: 'the *pure* arms of communication and of instantaneous control of oper- ations henceforth prevails over the three other fronts (land, sea and even air), and the orbital front favours [...] the fusion of the global and the local, thanks to the prominent role of satellites. Real time, that is to say the *absolute speed* of electromagnetic exchanges, dominates real space, in other words the *relative speed* of exchanges of position, occasioned until now by offensive and defensive manoeuvres' (2002: 121). Cyberwar thus represents, for Virilio, the overcoming of defensive weapons (fortresses, moats, battlements) as well as offensive weapons (cannons, mortars, rockets) by weapons of control and interdiction (surveillance, imaging, interception) based on a capacity for instantaneous orbital perception and communication.[7] It is not that Virilio downplays or overlooks the destructive force of the new weaponry, he simply wishes to point out what is qualitatively new, namely how, through the precision of navigation, '*intelligent munitions* prevail over the nature of the explosive: the destructive power of the weaponry relying, in the end, on the precision of its guidance system' (118). For Virilio, it was the launch of cruise missiles from the battleships *Wisconsin* and *Missouri* during Gulf War I that was the first application of this new 'vision machine'. Each missile was guided by images obtained from a camera, which were then compared to images stored in its data banks and assisted towards its course by taking further bearings from the Navstar network satellites.

Gulf War I, then, was the actualization of the new military vision that Virilio had been commenting on for many years. His discussion of contemporary war as being dominated by the instantaneity of electronic communications is a development of an interest in speed that has remained one of the abiding themes of his investigations into the tendencies that define our current condition. As John Armitage has noted, the critical question for Virilio is how 'the tyranny of eternally intensifying acceleration' (1999: 6) central to military operations becomes the critical component in the militarization of society, a condition Virilio refers to as the 'trans-political', defined as the contamination of traditional political thought by military thought (Virilio, 1997: 139). In *Speed and Politics* the integral role the military plays in social and political life is summed up in Virilio's statement that 'history progresses at the speed of its weapons systems' (1986: 68). This dromology, or study of movement, offers an alternative evolutionary narrative by emphasizing 'the role of different regimes of dynamic vehicles and the techno-political imposition of differential speeds of social interaction as prime determinants of modern political economy' (McQuire, 1999: 143–4). As the defensive fortress organized urban space as well as social and economic relations, so the Internet, itself originally a system of military communication, now reconfigures the urban, the social and the economic in previously unimagined ways. According to this logic, dromology also suggests that to disarm is to decelerate: 'The essential aim of throwing ancient weapons or of shooting off new ones has never been to kill the enemy [...] but [...] to *force him to interrupt his movement*' (145). In contemporary warfare this interruption of movement is produced through 'full spectrum dominance', or what Virilio refers to as 'ubiquitous orbital vision of enemy territory' (1989: 2).

The central importance of speed for the military is established by Virilio's argument that speed is violence. He asks us to think of his fist, the velocity of its movement determining whether the impact is little more than a touch or has the force of a bruising punch (1997: 37).[8] Speed is crucial to the current tendency in military affairs, that is the shift towards digitization. Writing of the new computerized missiles, Virilio talks of the fusion between communications and weapons: 'the projectile's image and the image's projectile form a single composite. In its tasks of detection and acquisition, pursuit and destruction, the projectile is an image or "signature" on a screen, and the television picture is an ultrasonic projectile propagated at the speed of light (83). Virilio argues that this instantaneity has had a profound effect on the utilization of space as 'the strategic value of the non-place of speed has definitively supplanted that of place' (1986: 133). As was mentioned above, the new military might stems not only from its destructive power but from the omnipresence of the war machine. War as the logistics of perception means the ability to control every space while being absent from any particular place. The current digitized war machine is networked and nomadic commanding the globe by being in all places at once. It is a strategy of global vision, 'an optical, or electro-optical, confrontation' (Virilio, 1989: 2) where the supply of images is equivalent to the supply of ammunition. These logistics of perception generate a new topology in which all the surfaces of the globe are directly present to one another (46). This 'panoply of light-war' (88) works on the premise that what is perceived is already lost. War thus becomes a system of illumination in which infra-red, heat seeking and satellite technology destroy the primitive cover of darkness and expose the enemy at all times. Power thus stems from the ability to see but not to be seen, it is the ability to disappear and illuminate everything to such a degree that the enemy is paralyzed. Power is the ability to give no notice of one's arrival, to create a situation in which the moment of appearance is nothing more than the instant of the enemy's destruction, a capacity integral to the new stealth weapons, in particular the radar-proof B-2 bomber. For Baudrillard such control puts the very status of war at stake. For him, the definition of war includes an uncertainty in relation to the outcome, but Gulf War I was not a war, it was a 'process of electrocution' (1995: 61) and the 'programmed unfolding' (63) of a plan.

In this sense, while attempting to critique Gulf War I, Baudrillard orbits the very ideological terrain that the military wish to promote. Of Gulf War I he wrote: 'Since this war was won in advance, we will never know what it would have been like had it existed. We will never know what an Iraqi taking part with a chance of fighting would have been like. We will never know what an American taking part with a chance of being beaten would have been like' (61). Here Baudrillard reiterates the language of the new deterrence in which the control of information, its gathering as well as the spectacle of its projection through the media are all important. Given that 'full spectrum dominance' dreams of ensuring every enemy move is interrupted before it starts, the difference between victory and defeat are accredited to the military panopticon and its continued refinement. In the utopian vision of the new strategists, total control of information is the capacity to produce a 'machinic perform-ance' (Baudrillard, 1995: 64) able to predetermine the outcome. At the far end of the cyber-scale, war becomes entirely virtual. It is the exchange of digitized war games that prevent the onset of violence in actuality.[9] And while Baudrillard uses the language of the military panopticon to raise important questions about how we use the term 'war', we should also guard against reinforcing the ideology of cyberdeter-rence, for as the insurgency in response to the invasion of Iraq in 2003 has shown, Iraqis have been able to fight and have demonstrated a weakness in the US projection of impermeability. In one sense, the insurgents have shown what happens when the enemy do not play the same game as the strategists in Washington.

However, while Baudrillard slips into the language of deterrence at one level, he is at pains to stress that it was a breakdown of deterrence that actually produced Gulf War I. In 1990 Saddam Hussein operated within a different language game to George Bush Senior. As Baudrillard puts it, 'each plays in his own space and misses the other' (66), a scenario that equally applies to the current war against terror in which martyrdom signals a differend that completely destabilizes the language of deter-rence.[10] In this sense, Baudrillard offers us an important insight into how to challenge this ideology. But such a challenge to the very fabric of deterrence does not seem to undermine the ideology of peace through continual procurement. In 1977 when *Speed and Politics* was first published in France, it was the nuclear deterrent that kept the peace in the bipolar world of the Cold War, now it is the cyberdeterrence of 'full spectrum dominance' that is rhetorically positioned as the peacekeeper. And with this we return to the strange logic, the Orwellian Newspeak that enables weapons development to continue at a pace. Of the nuclear deterrence Virilio wrote: 'the new weapons deter us from interrupting the movement of the arms race, and the "logistical strategy" of their production becomes the inevitable production of destructive means as an obligatory factor of non-war – a vicious circle in which the inevitability of production replaces that of destruction' (1986: 148). Thus the language of peace ensures the anabolic growth of the military-industrial complex and deterrence thus becomes what Virilio calls Pure War where war is no longer a matter of execution, but its 'infinite preparation' (92).

Spectacle

In *War and Cinema* Virilio wrote: 'War can never break free from the magical spectacle because its very purpose is to *produce* that spectacle: to fell the enemy is not so much to capture as to "captivate" him' (1989: 5). This equally applies to the domestic front where TV audiences are captivated by images that help promote the 'peace is procurement' doctrine. However, it is not only the 'hard' media of news bulletins that contribute to this sublime spectacle, but what is perhaps less well documented is how the 'soft', entertainment media are an increasing element in Pure War, diffusing militarism throughout the entirety of contemporary life. In this sense, we ought to remember Guy Debord's contention that the society of the spectacle is not just a collection of images but a social relation and 'the *model* of socially dominant life' (Debord, 1987: 6). To make sense of how this diffusion takes place it will be useful to follow Der Derian on his journeys to numerous nodes of what he calls the Military-Industrial-Media-Entertainment Network, or MIME-NET for short. The MIME-NET, according to Der Derian, 'runs on video-game imagery, twenty-four-hour news cycles, multiple modes of military, corporate, university, and media power, and microchips, embedded in everything but human flesh (so far)' (2001: 126). His aim is 'to study up close the mimetic power that travels along the hyphens' (xx).

Central to Der Derian's analysis of the MIME-NET is the concept of mimesis, which he borrows from Walter Benjamin's essay 'On the Mimetic Faculty', where 'mimesis is understood as a capacity for producing similarities [and a] powerful compulsion [...] to become and behave like something else' (Benjamin, 1979: 160). Der Derian wishes to map the ways in which the various actors in the MIME-NET, which includes film producers and directors, varying levels of military personnel, computer game designers, politicians, diplomats, corporate executives, novelists, script writers, news presenters, journalists, arms dealers, TV producers, advertisers and computer scientists mimic and reproduce the discourse and spectacle of war and thus legitimize its logic. The vectors of mimesis are as numerous as the actors in the sense that mimesis may take the form of the dominant discourse of realism that assumes and asserts a sameness of motivation based on the conception of all human actors and the states with which they identify as 'self-maximizing unit[s]' (Der Derian, 2001: 44). This discourse is, of course, central to the military worldview, but is also common place amongst diplomats, academics, neo-liberal economists, journalists and film-makers.[11] Other vectors include the technologies of simulation and virtuality developed by the military, computer games manufacturers and cinema special effects teams. Similarly, advertisers, TV news editors, security advisers and weapons manufactures all mimic and reproduce the vector of fear that ensures people both arm themselves, especially in America, and consume beyond their needs, a point made exceptionally well by Michael Moore in *Bowling for Columbine*, which can perhaps be taken as an attempt to interrupt this particular mimetic chain. Above all, these actors contribute to the endless circulation of images, the primacy of appearance, the conversion of 'fiction into facticity' (37) and the disappearance of reality into the 'black hole' of spin, desire, illusion, myth, double-talk, deception and show.

Most importantly, for Der Derian, the emerging MIME-NET produces a qualitatively new form of power that can 'seamlessly merge the production, representation, and execution of war [and] represents a convergence of the means by which we distinguish [...] the real from the reproduced' (xx). While the MIME-NET does not have a monopoly over the generation and circulation of information, it is significant that this military-inspired network has an increasing foothold in the varying divisions required for a successful war machine. Its industrial actors develop the weapons, its actors in news and entertainment circulate the requisite representations, while its military and governmental actors execute the warfare itself. The MIME-NET and its multiple vectors is thus akin to what Philip Graham and Allan Luke have called the militarizing of bodies politic. Such bodies are complex structures of technological, intersubjective and corporeal mediations that 'produce specific political forms' (2003: 149). In their view the body politic is a living system that is autopoietic and autodidactic, continually producing and circulating meanings for the purpose of legitimating itself. This autopoiesis is generated via the many vectors of resemblance within the MIME-NET that repeat and reproduce the necessary militarized worldview.

One element of the functioning of the MIME-NET can be seen in the long-standing concern that TV news, for example, privileges war and violence as being especially newsworthy. As Daya Kishan Thussu has put it: 'news is largely about conflict, and conflict is always news' (2003: 117). This is especially the case with 24-hour news services such as CNN and Sky. Because these companies operate in a competitive commercial market they are constantly chasing ratings, and as Thussu notes 'good news does not make compelling television, which instead thrives on violence, death and destruction [...]. In fact it has been argued that the rolling news networks have to be conflict-driven or else they will cease to operate as successful businesses' (123–4). In this scenario, images of conflict, violence and instability are constantly played, securing viewers *and* reproducing the narrative of an infinitely insecure world from which we must protect ourselves at all costs. 'The technical reproducibility of war', Der Derian notes, 'has produced a kind of global swarming' (49); neither new world order nor global village, just 'the angry global hive of real-time TV' (49). And for these issues of foreign policy to remain a ratings-winner, the story must be told with as little deliberation as possible, avoiding historical events that brought us to a particular juncture, and presenting what Richard Nixon called the drama of Good and Evil as personalized stories of individual wickedness and immorality not dissimilar to the narratives of classic Westerns in which Osama bin Laden is wanted 'dead or alive'.[12] And beyond the news services, television schedules more broadly, also tend to mimic the realist discourse that dominates the military mindset. Increasingly, in the wake of the September 2001 and March 2004 attacks, television companies offer a steady diet of documentaries detailing the effects of a 'dirty bomb', or biological weapons attack on London, for example, as well as countless dramas narrating the threat from terrorists, thus contributing to the 'serial murder of the imagination by worst-case scenarios' (Der Derian, 2001: 46). In response to the daily diet of threat and danger, the 'technological exhibitionism' (Mumford, 1964: 342) of American military might acts like Prozac, Der Derian argues, for an American public drip-fed stories of bogey men. It is a 'technopharmacological fix for all the organic anxieties that attend uncertain times and new configurations of power' (2001: 114). Likewise in cinema, films such as *Pearl Harbour* and *Black Hawk Down* exemplify the mimetic functions that Der Derian is trying to trace. For Cynthia Weber, *Pearl Harbour* is of interest because of the place Pearl Harbour has in the American imaginary. Re-releasing it after the events of September 2001 was an attempt to align the newly announced war against terror 'with a time before America questioned its moral purity, i.e. before America dropped the nuclear bomb on Hiroshima' (2003: 192). In turn, *Black Hawk Down* in the context of the war against terror seeks to portray America as both willing saviour and absolute victim.[13]

As these examples of mimesis would suggest, the MIME-NET is not entirely new. These synergies have a long history. What is new, however, is the idea that the actors within the MIME-NET are now losing their relative autonomy and are combining in one cybernetic and autopoietic system. As John Burston argues, it is the 'ubiquity, sophistication and complexity' (2003: 168) of this network that sets new research priorities for media studies. He asks us to consider the recent NBC TV movie *Asteroid*:

> about an end-of-the-world scenario that is averted thanks to the deployment of an airborne laser owned by the US military. This piece of weaponry is actually in development, and a goodly chunk of its funding comes from General Electric (GE). GE is also the parent company of NBC. With properties like *Asteroid*, everybody inside the militainment nexus gets to do a deal and then go home happy. The film's producers agree to certain script recommendations from a Pentagon media liaison and, as reward, are granted full access to air force personnel, bases and aircraft for their shoot. At the same time, both the Pentagon and GE get the right kind of exposure for a new component of the still highly controversial 'Star Wars' weapon system. It is the kind of PR coup the Pentagon's media office, widely regarded as the best in the entire US government, is pulling off with increasing frequency and aplomb. (168)

For Der Derian, the formation of the MIME-NET in the particular synergistic, hybrid and cybernetic form it takes today was first intimated by the appropriation of id Software's *Doom II* for military training purposes. As Rob Riddell (1997) reported for *Wired* magazine, in 1995 following a decision made at the Annual Officers Symposium, the US Army were tasked, according to Lieutenant Colonel Rick Eisiminger, ' "with looking at commercial off-the-shelf computer games that might teach an appreciation of the art and science of war" ' (117). One year later such usage of advances made in modelling and simulation technology by the entertainment industry was to become military doctrine. A US National Research Council report published in 1996 entitled *Modelling and Simulation: Linking Entertainment and Defense* argued that the 'common interests suggest that the entertainment industry and the DOD may be able to more efficiently achieve their individual goals by working together to advance the technology base for modelling and simulation'. The result was the formation of the Institute for Creative Technologies (ICT) at the University of Southern

California 'where technologies of the spectacular are being simultaneously developed as entertainment technology and as cutting edge military technology' (Burston, 2003: 166).[14] As Burston points out, however, the ICT does not only collaborate with Hollywood ('Silliwood') engineers, but also calls on the entertainment industry to expand its rhetorical and storytelling capabilities. At an event at the ICT shortly after 11 September 2001, *Die Hard* screenwriter Steven E. De Souza, television writer David Engelbach (*MacGyver*), and directors Joseph Zito (*Delta Force One*, *Invasion U.S.A* and *Missing in Action*), Spike Jonze (*being John Malkovich*) and David Fincher (*Fight Club, Seven*) were invited to 'brainstorm narrative scenarios in the service of future US-sponsored counter-terrorism efforts' (167). In Der Derian's words, this venture is the first joint avant-garde in film-making and war-making since the Futurists. And if a lot of the cyberwar rhetoric and aspirations of the RMA sounds like something from *Star Trek*, it may be no surprise that the ICT offices were designed by the art director of the original *Star Trek* series, Herbert Zimmerman, and that the ICT's executive director, Richard Lindheim, was vice president of the Paramount Television Group that produced *Star Trek: The Next Generation*, as well as *Deep Space Nine* and *Voyager*. It should, therefore be no surprise when he declares that ICT's Holy Grail is the 'Holodeck'. The technism of the US military has already brought it one calamitous defeat in Vietnam, but this does not seem to have shaken the resolve of the military imagineers.

While Burston calls for the reassessment of research priorities in media studies in relation to this 'militainment nexus', and Der Derian speaks of 'mimetic codes of technoscientific authorities and media elites' (209) that are yet to be mapped, they both fail to address moments of what I would like to call *aberrant mimesis*. If Der Derian is right that the future of war will be a 'contest of signs' (118), and from what has been discussed so far I think there is ample evidence to support this claim, then we need to remember that the sign itself is always already a point of contest. As Roland Barthes wrote, 'all images are polysemous; they imply, underlying their signifiers, a "floating chain" of signifieds, the reader able to choose some and ignore others' (1977: 38–9). It is for these reasons, Barthes notes, that every image today seems to be accompanied by a linguistic message: a title, caption, accompanying article, in order to halt this floating chain and 'anchor' the meaning to that which is preferred. Consequently, while the spectacle may have become the model for socially dominant life, this does not mean that it is 'the sun which never sets over the empire of modern passivity' (Debord, 1987: 13), in fact quite the contrary. The spectacle is also a site of resistance, refusal and subversion. As Stuart Hall demonstrated in his influential essay 'Encoding/decoding', the 'audience is both "source" and "receiver"' of a message (1980: 130). This means that the receiver is active in the process of communication and that if communication is to be successful the receiver, or decoder, must share the encoder's 'frameworks of knowledge' (130). This activity on behalf of the receiver is only hidden because the codes, or frameworks, have been so naturalized. For Hall, three types of reading are possible.[15] Where there is symmetry between encoder and decoder the dominant or preferred reading is taken, but where there is asymmetry, a negotiated, or oppositional reading is taken, dependent upon the degree of this asymmetry. It is these oppositional readings that I am interested in here, preferring instead to call them *aberrant*, so as not to suggest that they operate outside the logic of the spectacle itself.

One example of aberrant mimesis is the use of Hollywood by groups regarded by the dominant as terrorist. One episode of the BBC programme *Real Story*, broadcast on Monday 5 April 2004, reported the activities of the group al' Muhajiroun and its leader Omar Bakri. The reason for the report was the allegation that Bakri was recruiting young British Muslims for suicide missions abroad. In support of his case the reporter Paul Kenyon attended a conference held by the organization at Pride Park, the home of Derby County Football Club. Due to the relaying of the conference throughout the club complex Kenyon was able to record its content, and it is clear that al' Muhajiroun also believe Hollywood can do much to assist them in their war. A recruitment video was being shown in which images from two Hollywood blockbusters were being used to visualize the destruction of America. Amongst other images from these films the video included the famous shot of the Whitehouse being blown up in *Independence Day* and the tidal wave crashing into and destroying New York in *Deep Impact*, a film which amongst many of its promotional tags included the phrase 'Heaven and Earth are about to collide'. Thus, images that originally signified America as the global saviour and epitome of unshrinking human spirit were now used to support fantasies of the ultimate suicide bomb and offer visualizations of the wrath of God. Because the meaning of an image is always actualized in the process of reading, it is certain that future war as a conflict of signs will also be a conflict over the capacity to produce semiotic closure.

The inability to produce such closure is evidenced in the appropriation by the same Islamic group of television footage of '9/11', which as a coded event is 'neither univocal nor uncontested' (Hall, 1980: 134). Al' Muhajiroun have their own interpretation of the attacks on that day. The attempt to present '9/11' as the ultimate crime, never to be repeated, was also starkly undermined by another example of aberrant mimesis in which the attack on the World Trade Center became the inspiration for a copy-cat mission. As Cynthia Weber has noted very few column inches were given to the story of a young boy, aged 15, from Palm Harbour, Florida, who committed suicide by crashing a single-engined plane into the Bank of America building in Tampa, in a salute to Osama bin Laden. This act of 'mimetic identification' (2003: 196) was in part produced by the floating chain of signifieds that hangs under every signifier. Even the commentary that accompanied the pictures of the WTC attacks could not anchor the meaning sufficiently to prevent the boy, whose name was Charles Bishara Bishop, from wishing to create his own piece of '9/11' *homage*. To nullify this act of aberrant mimesis the dominant mimetic grammar was repeated whenever the story was reported. The fact that Bishop's middle name, Bishara, indicated his family's Middle Eastern origin was used to pathologize his actions and thus repeat the mimetic identification whereby his Arabness had become 'a conduit for other evil influences to infiltrate America' (195). In this way the act of aberrant mimesis born of Palm Harbour, Florida, was equated with the unjustifiable evil wrought on America at Pearl Harbour and later New York.

To call the 'attack' on the Bank of America a copy is to forget that the original '9/11' was also an act of aberrant mimesis. In a prescient passage from *Virtuous War* Der Derian writes:

> As superior computing power and networking increase in representational power and global reach, simulation leaves little room to imagine the unpredictable, the unforeseeable, the unknowable *except* as accident. Will God's will, nature's caprice, human error seem puny in effect as simulation becomes more interactive, more complex, more *synergistic*? In the context of industrial accidents, organizational theorists have already identified a 'negative synergism' in complex systems that can produce unpredictable, worst-case failures. In the technological drive to map the future – to deter known threats through their simulation – are we unknowingly constructing new, more catastrophic dangers? (Der Derian, 2001: 96)

The examples of aberrant mimesis outlined above are part of what might only be termed a counter-MIME-NET that shadows the dominant structures of corporate-military power, and whose powers of mutation and subversion are key elements in the 'negative synergism' that announced itself with such surprising force on 11 September 2001.

Baudrillard's analysis of the spirit of terrorism witnessed on that day is framed precisely in these terms. The attacks of 11 September 2001 were all operations of aberrant mimesis within the society of the spectacle. As the dominant maintains itself increasingly through the speed of mass communication and image strategies (Virilio, 2002), so the terrorist functions at the level of the symbolic.[16] For Baudrillard, the collapse of the concrete, glass and steel that rose with such confidence above south Manhattan was 'an additional *frisson*' (2002: 29) added as 'a bonus of terror' (29) to the primary target which was that of the icon, the symbol of American invincibility exposed in that instance as a fiction. In Baudrillard's terms, the negative synergy of this event would be the mutual implication or reciprocity of domination and terror. Terrorism is the 'double agent' (10) of the global 'technocratic machinery' (9), double in the sense that it also deploys and appropriates the weapons of that machinery: 'Money and stock-market speculation, computer technology and aeronautics, spectacle and the media networks – they have assimilated everything of modernity and globalism, without changing their goal, which is to destroy that power' (19). Terrorism appropriates the principle of deregulation at the heart of the contemporary capitalist system and takes advantage of its own nomadic, deterritorializing moments (Van Loon, 2001). The negative synergy thus becomes the act of restoring 'an irreducible singularity to the heart of a system of generalized exchange. All the singularities (species, individuals and cultures) that have paid with their deaths for the installation of a global circulation governed by a single power' (9) thus take their revenge. It is mimetic because it fights 'terror with terror' (9) and deploys the very machinery of globalized modernity that it condemns. It is also mimetic because it adopts 'the banality of American everyday life as its cover and camouflage, sleeping in their suburbs, reading and studying with their families' (19). The unveiling of the terrorist-within functions in the body politic much like the antibody that brings about a life-threatening allergic reation. In this sense, much in keeping with Derrida's notion of auto immunity discussed in the last chapter, the aberrant mimesis of the new global terror sets in play a 'reversibility that is [its] true victory' (31). For Baudrillard, post-9/11 there is no possible distinction between the crime and the response (31). We are continually reminded by Bush and Blair that the terrorists hate our freedom and despise democracy, but the states 'under attack' then proceed to role back democracy to a far greater extent than the terrorists ever could. It is the Bush administration and the Blair government, caught up as they are in the economy of mimesis, that proceed to do the work of those who supposedly hate freedom. Mimesis is thus contagious. The terrorist need only touch us in order to transmit the desire to undermine the Western 'way of life' and set in place semi-autonomous, mimetic acts of war. In response to terror, civil liberties become civil restraints, the open society becomes the surveillance society and freedom becomes regulation.[17]

Applying the concept of mimesis to Baudrillard's reading of the events of 11 September 2001, it is necessary to go beyond the notion of aberrant mimesis and add what I would call negative mimesis to the lexicon of mimetic acts, because what is so compelling about global terrorism is its capacity, according to Baudrillard, to 'defy the system by a gift to which it cannot respond' (17), that is, the gift of death as an absolute, symbolic event. Central to the RMA is the deployment of information, simulation and virtuality to increase lethality and reduce, if not eradicate, mortality. The RMA is the product of a system seeking to eliminate its own death. The counter-RMA, that is global terror, thus deploys death against a system for which death is inconceivable. The counter-RMA deploys death against those that deal death but who, for themselves, can only countenance life. The PSYOPs of the counter-RMA is to declare: 'we want death more than you want life'. It is a negative mimesis that appropriates and inverts the very logic of cyberwar while also removing the possibility of deterrence (cyber or otherwise), as noted above. For every deterrent must assume the universality of a life instinct.

And so this negative mimesis structures the entire metaphysics of the war against terror. Facing each other, George W. Bush and Osama bin Laden deploy all the technologies of the spectacle to play out the drama of Good and Evil. In a symbolic exchange of negative mimesis each casts themselves as the messenger of light and the other as the angel of darkness, a relation of mutuality that is in both their interests and from which both draw their power. A critique of this mimetic structure would therefore require the mapping and exposure of the MIME-NET in all its corporate complexity, the moments of aberrant mimesis that shadow and subvert this network, as well as the negative mimesis that organizes its metaphysics. One might also ask if these examples of aberrant and negative mimesis are equivalent to something like Virilio's 'information accident' (1997: 178). Bearing in mind that 'every technology produces, provokes, programs a specific accident' (38) what will be the communications and information equivalent of Chernobyl? Because information technology involves interactivity, Virilio suggests the new technology will probably introduce the sort of feedback the consequences of which we cannot even begin to fathom (178). In the wake of the events of September 2001, which also triggered an autoimmune response in the victim in the guise of an attack on civil rights and freedoms, perhaps we gained some insight into the nature of the information accident.

In this instance the interpretive confrontation to win a world actually enters into the logistics of warfare itself. When war becomes a conflict of signs, interpretive confrontation becomes the very means of waging war. It was noted that the hermeneutic relation is increasingly taking over from the embodied relation of earlier weapons systems. This means that with each reading of an avatar on a screen an act of world-creation has to take place prior to the act of world-destruction. The operator of the technology has to make an almost instantaneous decision as to the status of this avatar: friend or enemy? Beyond this the counter-MIME-NET also reveals the moment of interpretive confrontation as a weapon. It has been noted how important the spectacle is for captivating both the domestic population and the enemy, but it is increasingly clear that this spectacle and the struggle for semiotic closure means the fourth, information front will never be completely owned by the most militarily and commercially dominant powers. In addition to this, it is by no means a necessity that the new human-machine assemblages must be the sole property of the military. Donna Haraway, for example, has argued that these new technologies present the opportunity for progressive and liberatory couplings. She writes: 'From one perspective, a cyborg world is about the final imposition of a grid of control on the planet, about the final abstraction embodied in a Star Wars apocalypse waged in the name of defence [...]. From another perspective, a cyborg world might be about lived social and bodily realities in which people are not afraid of their joint kinship with animals and machines, not afraid of permanently partial identities and contradictory standpoints' (1991: 154). Here we can begin to see some of the ontological issues that the new technologies open up. Perhaps this is how politics might 'put its hands in the bloody guts of war, and pull out something that could be used – something that is not war' (Virilio, 1997: 107). The interpretive confrontation over the attempt to achieve closure in the future warfare of signs will, as has always been the case with war, be based on strong identities that wish to overcome and eradicate the other. However, in the interpretive confrontation suggested by Haraway we find the partial identities that are possibly the antithesis to war and in this proposed engagement with the technology of cyberwar there might yet be a path beyond it.

8
Economy and Empire

The logic of the sovereign decision and the fantasy of 'full spectrum dominance' explored in the last two chapters have once again put national actors centre stage. This is at a time when the discourse of globalization, while not ignoring the continuing role of nation states has nevertheless understood global governance in increasingly transnational terms. The capacity for transnational economic institutions such as the IMF, World Bank and WTO to undermine local sovereignty by compelling nations to open their borders, resources and services to the movement of capital has lead many commentators to speak of a capitalist empire. Alternatively, the declaration in 2001 of an infinite war against terror and a global state of emergency to be policed by the US has lead others to renew the older discourses of state-centred imperialism formerly thought to be obsolete. For many the policy of 'pre-emptive defence' that emerged as Washington's response to the destruction of the World Trade Center was evidence that the US was prepared to pursue its interests wherever and in whatever form it wished. It also demonstrated a willingness to act unilaterally that raised numerous questions about the logic of sovereignty that had mediated international relations since the Treaty of Westphalia in 1648. It is thus possible to see 11 September 2001 as 'an exemplar of the historical event as disruption and dislocation' (Venn, 2002: 121), given that it seemingly demands a reassessment of sovereignty at the national, international and transnational levels. When Donald Rumsfeld (2001) tells us to 'forget exit strategies, we're looking at a sustained engagement that carries no deadlines', what can the war against terror and the invasions of Afghanistan, Iraq and the anticipated bombing of Iran tell us about this possible tripartite division in sovereignty. Also, how does the state-centred war against terror and the anabolic militarism of the US fit within the broader economic war that is the global implementation of the 'free-market'?

The figure of War

Writing in February 1991 as the ground attack of Gulf War I began, Jean-Luc Nancy commented that 'the return of "war", not as the reality of military operations but as a figure (War) in our symbolic space, is undeniably a new and singular phenomenon, because it produces itself in a world where this symbol seems to have been all but effaced' (2000: 101). At first it is difficult to comprehend this effacement given that conflicts, especially of the ethnic, ideological and liberatory kinds, have persisted without any break from the end of the Second World War, and continue their destructive paths to this day. But this much Nancy concedes, explaining that the effacement of which he speaks has only really affected the nation's who determine 'the planet's core of "law", "order" and "development" ' (102). For these global players, he argues, war, which is not reducible to the logistics of a military operation, but is a conflict between sovereigns, has declined in relation to the growth of 'techno-economics' (104), that is the regulation and administration through which the global dominance of the First World is maintained. What is more, after 1989 and 'the defeat of Communism', the US remained the only hyperpower overseeing this expanding and supposedly pacific realm of techno-economic administration, as capitalism, and in particular the neo-liberal creed of 'free markets', was exported to every corner of the globe. In the wake of this there has been a renewed interest in the concept of empire and debate is currently rife concerning how this new empire might be understood. Given US hegemony, it is easy to assume that over the last fifteen years we have been witnessing the emergence of an American empire that matches the relative might and reach of any previous empire and that the war against terror is a key component in its execution, but is this the case? For Nancy, the empire is not American, despite its lead role in 'the planet's core of "law", "order" and "development" ', but techno-economic, and this is why he spoke of the return of the figure of war. In a manner akin to Baudrillard's (1983) claim that in a simulated world politics becomes the attempt to inject referentiality everywhere, Nancy argues that in an open, borderless, anonymous and endless techno-economic empire there emerges a profound metaphysical impulse for the grounding and finality that is sovereignty; and given that war is the very 'execution or putting to work of sovereignty' (102), this endless techno-economic empire calls forth war and, furthermore, re-legitimates it.

> In war, a brilliant, incandescent, fascinating sovereignty is celebrated (for a split second, in a flash of light). But is this not an essential part of what we think we are deprived of in general: the brilliant flash, the figures of the Sun? Even now, our world does not represent itself lacking in power or intelligence, or even completely lacking in grace. But the lack of Sovereignty surely structures an essential part of our world's representation of itself, and therefore of its desire. (Nancy, 2000: 114)

This desire, then, is motivated by the relativism of global cultural communication; by the equivalence given to all things within the order of money and exchange value; it emerges out of the insecurities borne of delocalized, transnational governance in which every community, including those in the 'planet's core', are opened up to the policies of increasingly distant actors; and it is amplified by the new conflicts for which the destruction of the World Trade Centre is emblematic. Amid this network of faceless agents and enemies, where all things are consumable, the need for sovereign finality has re-emerged, and if Nancy thought the announcement of a new world order prior to Gulf War I prefigured the return of the sovereign, Gulf War II, which saw the usurpation of international law, marks the residency of a politics based on sovereign decision and the attempt by certain leaders to bathe in the vainglory of its incandescent light.

As with Agamben's analysis of sovereign power, of central importance in Nancy's analysis of the re-emergence of war is the structure of the sovereign exception. 'The right to wage war', Nancy writes, 'excepts itself from law at the very point where it belongs to it both as an origin and as an end; this point is a point of foundation, insofar as we are incapable of thinking of foundation without sovereignty, or of sovereignty itself without thinking in terms of exception and excess' (107). A little further on he articulates how this problem is magnified in relation to a law that extends itself beyond the communal and towards the universal, that is, international law. 'This mode of instituting law becomes unacceptable, however, in a world that represents law itself as its own "origin" or its own "foundation", whether this falls under the heading of a "natural right" of humanity or under the heading of an irreversible sedimentation of the experiences of a positive law' (107). In sum this is the recognition of the two poles of modern sovereignty, on the one hand the Hobbesian model of the prince with a monopoly on violence and power over the state of exception, on the other the liberal, or republican model enshrined in the reciprocity of equally rational and, therefore, autonomous citizens with rights enshrined in law that the state is charged with protecting.[1]

It is this model of national sovereignty, with its universalizing of autonomous agents that has become the model used for international law. Here the law is charged with protecting individuals through the Universal Declaration of Human Rights, but is also committed, through a series of treaties, to the recognition of sovereign, territorially bounded states as along as that recognition in turn informs each state's conduct towards the others. The problem for international law, however, is that it has never been able to find a solution to the sovereign moment of the prince. That the model of the prince remains an integral part of republican sovereignty is evidenced, as we have seen, in the state's capacity to decide when to suspend the law and announce a state of emergency. Despite innovations such as the international court, the UN has never had sovereign authority equivalent to the princely exception, or the sovereign's monopoly on violence. It has, therefore, constantly been held hostage by the most powerful individual states that refuse to relinquish their sovereign, national interests. As Nancy notes, there is no supranational law. 'There is only a supposed law that borders nation-states, a law which is only vaguely sure of being founded on universality, and fairly certain of being devoid of sovereignty. So-called international law, where this 'inter', this 'between', causes all the problems is only graspable as that common space devoid of law, devoid of every 'setting in common' (without which there is no law), and is structured *by* the techno-economic network and the supervision of Sovereigns' (105). Thus if it is not seen to be in the interests of the planet's core nations, there can be no intervention in places like Rwanda, for instance, or more recently Darfur, and if Britain and the US decide it *is* in their interests to invade a sovereign country like Iraq, international law is shown to be without sovereignty – an impotent prince without legitimacy. What is more, because international law establishes the model of democracy as the ideal form of states, it has always projected the power of Western states as something to be pursued. In effect, powerful Western states have always paid lip service to the UN and international law because it has never been a threat. In the first instance it endorses their own model of political organization as something that ought to be universalized, and secondly, the UN is unable to challenge those national sovereigns with global reach should they pursue a foreign policy based more in *realpolitik* than international law.

The test for sovereignty, then, is intervention as either suspension (of the law) or force (of will). As was noted above, Nancy believes that 'war is sovereignty's technology *par excellence*' (117). Technology here must not be thought of as a means to an end, but 'the mode of execution, manifestation, and effectuation [...] the mode of [sovereign] accomplishment' (117). One might say that war is the *praxis* of sovereignty, and it is this lack of *praxis* that ultimately undermines the efficacy of international law, for it always relies on some other national or international agent ('the planet's core of "order", "law" and "development"') to set to work its will as was the case in Gulf War I. Without being the end itself, it cannot be thought sovereign, because that which is sovereign is limit, extremity and finality. 'Sovereignty is the power of execution or the power of finishing as such, absolutely so and without any further subordination to something else (to another end). Divine creation and the royal decision compose its double image: to make or unmake a world, to submit to a will, to designate an enemy' (120). The right to wage war is *the* expression of sovereignty because it is the right to challenge the sovereignty of another. 'It is the sovereign's right to confront his *alter ego ad mortem*' (106), and bring about 'a new distribution of sovereignties' (107).[2]

While Nancy saw the re-emergence of sovereignty in 1991, it needs to be said that the exercise of sovereignty as decision and suspension has been most explicitly set to work through the second war in the Gulf. That decisionism rather than consensus has returned was symbolized by George W. Bush's announcement to the UN in 2003 that it could retain its legitimacy only if it supported his decision for war. This was supported by a raft of neo-conservative publications advocating a foreign policy of strong (sovereign) leadership, with Richard Perle's article 'Thank God for the Death of the UN' being particularly representative of the mood. It opens as follows:

> Saddam Hussein's reign of terror is about to end. He will go quickly, but not alone: in a parting irony, he will take the UN down with him. Well, not the whole UN. The 'good works' part will survive, the low-risk peacekeeping bureaucracies will remain, the chatterbox on the Hudson will continue to bleat. What will die is the fantasy of the UN as a foundation of a new world order. As we sift the debris, it will be important to preserve, the better to understand, the intellectual wreckage of the liberal conceit of safety through international law administered by international institutions. (2003)

This is a clear statement that only the national sovereign (specifically the executive) can protect the people. Outside of the US the clearest attempt to justify the new doctrine came from Tony Blair, who, in a speech made in March 2004, set out the model that was now to inform foreign policy. After couching his willingness to go to war in the language of humanitarianism and the 'doctrine of international community', he announced that 'leadership is about deciding'. The nation, indeed the world could only be saved by a decision, his sovereign decision to go to war.[3]

The return of the prince and the figure of war is brought about according to Nancy by a need for sovereignty in a world in which the global administration of 'ecotechnics' undoes the grounding of communities. 'There is no longer any *polis*' he writes, 'since the *oikos* is everywhere: the housekeeping of the world as a single household' (135). The nihilism of consumer culture and the anonymity of marketization open up a void where identity and finality is desired. The space of sovereignty, that is, the space of finishing, is a 'distended space full of holes, where nothing can come to presence' (136). As Nancy puts it the desire for sovereignty and the return of war correspond to 'a time when no one can believe that economics has its own, universally legitimated finality anymore' (110). Unbounded and deterritorialized, committed to infinite obsolescence and planetary administration, transnational capital has no founding event and no finality in sovereign terms. It is replete with 'millions of dollars and yen [...] millions of therms, kilowatts, optical fibres, megabytes' (133), but is without *end*. Given that finishing, that is, providing both origin and end of communal identity is the sovereign event, Nancy suggests there is consequently a metaphysical impulse or need to revive sovereignty. It is so bound up with the Western tradition, that a world without end, even a terrorist-free world, provides its own anxiety and insecurity, and with it the desire for closure and completion. However, in an interesting twist Nancy argues that ecotechnics may call forth sovereignty, but this is always a borrowing of sovereignty because ecotechnics 'damages, weakens, and upsets the functioning of all sovereignties, except for those that in reality coincide with ecotechnical power' (135–6). The summoning of sovereignty in the end only reveals the empty place of sovereignty, it reveals that ecotechnics in fact 'washes out or dissolves sovereignty (137)'. In the administered techno-economic world of globalized capital there can be no sovereignty only the self-interested pursuit of ecotechnical power. At the national level this takes the form of endocolonization, a term used by Paul Virilio (1997) to designate the economic war that strips social welfare programmes of resources to feed the military-industrial complex. At an international level it is the shaping of the globe through the use of client states and the occasional, if regular, deployment of troops. In this situation the borrowed brilliance of sovereignty makes sacred the warrior's sacrifice in a manner that the pursuit of ecotechnical power alone cannot.

In order to think through this paradoxical situation in which ecotechnics is both the lack of and pursuit of sovereignty, it is necessary to consider the possibility that a new paradigm of sovereignty is developing, one where the techno-economic order *is* the sovereign realm, and where for the first time this universal sovereignty is truly able to challenge the sovereignty of nations. Indeed the re-emergence of national sovereigns and the current war against terror can be seen as a direct reaction to this changing order. As was noted above, the sovereignty of the international community never was sovereign, it had no prince, relying on national princes to do its work, but a new networked system has been emerging that might be said to have sovereignty, this is the neo-liberal order of transnational capital. To begin to understand this, it is necessary to address the work of Michael Hardt and Antonio Negri who have offered the most detailed analysis yet of this new paradigm.

Empire

In the opening section of *Empire* entitled 'The Political Constitution of the Present', Hardt and Negri address what they claim to be the paradigm shift in imperial sovereignty by arguing that it is made possible by the bringing together of economic and political power in 'a properly capitalist order' (2000: 9). This, they argue, is accompanied by a shift from conflict between the old, imperialist powers towards a single networked power that covers them all under a new notion of right, 'a new inscription of authority and a new design of the production of norms and legal instruments of coercion that guarantee contracts and resolve conflicts' (9). While this claim that a single power is in command overstates the current situation it nevertheless offers us the means to attempt the necessary reconceptualization of sovereignty that both the return of war and the order of transnational capitalism demands. It might be said that this paradigm shift is not necessarily new but is the realization of a challenge to national sovereignty instigated by the emergence of capitalism in the sixteenth century and epitomized in the writings of Hugo Grotius whose innovation was to theorize sovereign legitimacy for corporations and private trading companies in their attempts to maximally exploit new markets. In this regard, Grotius deployed the concept of just war based on the principle of self-preservation to give legitimacy to wars in pursuit of profit. While the bifurcation of sovereignty between the legal and the extralegal, right and responsibility, does not weaken sovereign authority, but is instead the source of its power, what might be called the bifurcation between the political and the economic, something that marks the shift from feudalism to capitalism, certainly challenges the unity and integrity of sovereign power. There is an antagonism between state and capital whereby the motivations and interests of these respective agents are heterogeneous. For Hardt and Negri these antagonisms are resolved through the dominance of the global market, a solution first set out in the writings of Adam Smith whose political economy articulated the complementarity of private and public interest through the operation of an 'invisible hand' that established the well-being of a society. The primary duty of politicians then becomes the task of enabling the market to do its beneficent work. In this situation, Hardt and Negri argue, the 'political transcendental of the modern state is defined as an economic transcendental' (86), and sovereignty is increasingly tied to this phenomenon. Empire, then, is a new form of rule, a political subject regulating transnational exchanges, supported by national and supranational organisms without any territorial centre or fixed boundaries; it is a *'deterritorializing* apparatus' (xii) managing and commanding a network of hybrid identities and flexible hierarchies, a 'rainbow' (xiii) of flows and scapes. Much like Nancy's vision of ecotechnics, empire is without limit, encompassing the totality of space and suspending, or exhausting history, summoning 'the past and the future within its own ethical order' (11). Although the role of nation-states is limited to the function of nodes within the network, Hardt and Negri nevertheless recognize the privileged position held by the United States. This privileged position, however, is not because it holds (or very nearly holds, or even desires to hold) the princely monopoly on violence, it is rather because the US constitution holds the key to understanding the new formation of imperial sovereignty and the resolution of the politico-economic antagonism. In their preface Hardt and Negri write that by constitution they mean 'both the *formal constitution*, the written document along with its various amendments and legal apparatuses, and the *material constitution*, that is, the continuous formation and re-formation of the composition of social forces' (xiv).

Taking the *material constitution* first, the continuous formation and reformation of social forces is what Hardt and Negri refer to as biopolitics. While the market is transcendent, it operates immanently 'on all registers of the social order [...]. The object of its rule is social life in its entirety, and thus empire presents the paradigmatic form of biopower' (xv) understood as a diffuse network of *dispositifs* (23) and mechanisms of command that evermore 'democratically' produce and re-produce customs, habits and practices. In this sense the imperial market is transcendental in that it is the condition of possibility for social life – with non-marketized life being a non-life, the subject of a sovereign, exclusionary exception – but it is not transcendent, that is, it does not work from a distance but operates upon the very tissue of life itself, organizing and legitimizing desire, controlling and modifying bodies and distilling cultural formations through the minutiae and intimacies of the commodity form. For Hardt and Negri, empire has no outside, but is rather the possibility and potential to include everything within its sphere.

Empire, therefore, unlike older imperialist projects 'is formed not only on the basis of its powers of accumulation and global extension, but also on the basis of its capacity to develop itself more deeply, to be reborn and extend itself throughout the biopolitical latticework of world society' (41). At one level such biopolitics functions through the production of a new proletarian subjectivity. This is an 'ecological struggle [...] over the mode of life' of the proletariat 'expressed in the developments of immaterial labour' (269).[4] However, beyond this productivity biopolitics is not generative but corrupt, constructing, 'black holes and ontological vacuums in the life of the multitude' (389). But in order to understand how biopolitics contributes to the current formation of power a little more needs to be said about this ecological struggle, or what I would prefer to call the economic war that is the technology of this new paradigm of sovereignty. Rather than the lack of an ontological foundation, or the lack of a motor propelling its movement (62) (something that is definitive of empire's corruption), I would like to suggest that it is precisely the *establishment* of an ontological foundation that gives empire its supposed legitimacy, as well as its mode of finishing. To understand the interpretive confrontation that is this economic war, it is necessary to briefly work through the link between economy and polemos.[5]

The primary definition of *oikos* is a house, abode or dwelling. It also refers to the affairs of a household as well as its property and goods. When situated with the word *nomos*, which in its primary definition means enactment, ordinance, rule or law we have *oikonomia*, that is, the management of a household, from which our common understanding of the word economic is derived. *Oikonomia*, however, also has the additional meaning in Greek of the management of the state. Here, we already have a notion that an economic war involves a battle concerning the management of a household, or possibly more importantly for our purposes here, a battle regarding the running of a state. A second level of meaning for the word *oikos* can be found in *oikeo*, which is to inhabit or possess, to dwell or to live, and it is here that the ontological dimension of the *oikos* and the biopolitical dimension of *oikonomia* begins to be revealed. The *oikos* is not only a dwelling but a way of dwelling, a manner of being-in-the-world. *Oikeo* also means to be placed or situated, and in this sense its meaning begins to approach that of *nomos*, which aside from meaning law also means anything assigned or apportioned, stemming from *nemo*, to deal out, or distribute. This complementarity between *oikos* and *nomos*, is even stronger in a third meaning. Here *nomos* means a district, department or province. This definition of the word was of great significance to Hannah Arendt who spoke of the law as a boundary line, a hedge between two allotted pastures, or the wall that indicated where the laws of the city applied, thereby initiating a political community (Arendt, 1958: 63–4).[6] Of course, Arendt's reading of the *nomos* is profoundly influenced by Heidegger who understood the history of Being as varying economies of presence, where the *nomos* of each historical *oikos* governed what was brought into being, be that the actions of politicians, works of art, buildings, institutions, technologies, cosmologies, legislations, rituals and so on; and as was discussed in the opening chapter we have already highlighted this as the site of Dasein's polemos or interpretive confrontation with its world. In 'Letter on "Humanism"' Heidegger writes: 'Νόμος is not only law but more originally the assignment contained in the dispensation of being' (1998: 274). *Nomos* therefore determines how things come into being and how they dwell, and to draw out one final important meaning of *nomos*, the root *nemo* also means to esteem, allowing us to think of the economic war currently being waged in the name of market economics as a conflict over the mode of esteeming or valuing (*nomisis*) that determines the structure of our life (*bios*).

The *nomos* that currently structures our life is the economic doctrine known as neo-liberalism. However, what is most important about neo-liberalism is not its principles of 'free trade', privatization and deregulation, although these principles can hardly be called insignificant, but its ontological underpinnings concerning the nature of human being, for these underpinnings are truly *oikonomical* in the manner I have sought to define the term above. The ontological principles at the heart of neo-liberalism are based in neo-classical economic theory, the three fundamental propositions of which are as follows:

- The 'consumption proposition' states that 'individuals are endowed with the ability to choose rationally from among the sets of opportunities they confront', with rationality signalling that individuals will decide according to the opportunity affording greatest satisfaction or utility. Attached to this assumption is the secondary assumption of 'insatiability', meaning that we always prefer more satisfaction/ 'utility' rather than less.
- The 'production proposition' whereby 'humans are endowed with the ability to transform elements of nature (through work or labour) so as to produce goods that meet human needs, and they do so rationally'. I will come back to this.
- The 'scarcity proposition' which states that all output (in the form of goods and services) requires inputs from nature, and since nature's bounty is finite, output must also be finite. Economics thus becomes the study of rational choice under conditions of insatiability and scarcity (DeMartino, 2000: 38–41).

The importance of the first proposition lies in the belief that choice is exogenous, that is prior to or external to, social activity. In this sense the question of validity does not appear to enter the equation as the expression of choice is the rational expression of an individual's deepest and most authentic personality. In this way, the market, reflecting as it does the aggregate of a multiplicity of rational choices, is the standard of our true desires. Any notion of asymmetrical power and the construction of desire are irrelevant here; and as I have already suggested, this is not just economical but oikonomical defining as it does human nature and the rational means for that nature to be most fully expressed. It is the second proposition, however, that is most important I feel for our analysis of *oikonomia*. The second proposition claims that people produce goods to meet human needs and they do so rationally. Again it is the rider of rationality that is the key, for in this instance it means the most efficient technique for producing maximum yield. Of particular, concern here is the belief that, let us say, land is used only according to the principle of optimal efficiency, but it should be evident that the use of land is irreducible to purely economic pursuits but might also involve a plurality of factors that contribute to the particular character and form of a culture. Neo-liberalism is, therefore, the belief that the unfettered market is the best way for any society to organize itself. Because principles one and two bracket out anything contextual in the way of social or cultural determinants, the market is believed to be universally applicable, only to be resisted by those who are irrational and backward. This in short is the economic, or rather oikonomic, war being waged at present. It is an interpretative confrontation over the nature of human being and the world in which we live, manifesting itself in a profound and deliberate biopolitics.

This issue of interpretation, however, is masked by what John McMurtry calls a 'deist metaphysic' (2002: 21) in which a specific value set is 'reified as the structure of reality itself' (21). This free market totemism, he remarks:

> exceeds in totality stone-age awe before the universal forces demanding the daily sacrifice of human beings to the laws of nature to perpetuate them. Yet, decision-constructed technology and money-demand, not natural laws, drive every moment of every cycle of this system. Economists, not priests, absolutise the order they postulate as independent. Scientific, not religious, superstition reads coerced social uniformities as inviolable laws. The re-engineering of world societies 'cannot be stopped', because they are assumed as written into the order of nature as divine design. (21)

That this is imperial, I think there can be little doubt. Of course, those who are best served by neo-liberalism, the rich North, will continue to argue that they are only pursuing the interests of humanity as a whole; but this has always been integral to justifications of empire. In this regard, the new paradigm of sovereignty sanctifies the violation of cultural life forms as the difficult but just measures of an ultimately benevolent regime. As Agamben has shown, this ambiguity whereby violence is justice is central to the enigma that is sovereignty. He has argued that it is in evidence from the earliest known formulation of sovereign power as set out by Pindar, whose fragment 169 tells how the *nomos*: 'Leads with the strongest hand/Justifying the most violent' (Agamben, 1998: 30). *Nomos*, then, is the unification of these two antithetical principles, violence and justice. It is the harsh necessity of structural adjustments through which the market as sovereign assumes the role of the despot (*despotēs*), the head of the global household, meting out just punishment for those who resist the necessary and rational rule of marketization.

In this regard the third proposition of neo-classical theory, the scarcity proposition, is especially important, because the notion of scarcity lies at the heart of economic and oikonomic organization. From the Roman principle of *res nullius* decreeing that any 'empty thing' such as unoccupied land was common property and therefore available to be put to use, to the work of William Petty who in 1691 calculated the value of an 'improved' Ireland under an English colonial power, the belief that we must do all we can with scarce resources has been the prime mover for justifying imperial expansion. In her study of empire, Ellen Meiskins Wood notes how as early as the sixteenth century the judgement concerning the sufficiently fruitful use of land was made according to the standards of English commercial culture (2003: 75). The most notable seventeenth century exponent of this thinking is John Locke, who not only justified imperialism through arguments concerning the damaging effect of unused land, but proceeded to argue against land that was not used *well enough*, an argument that supported enclosure at home and the appropriation of land abroad. This is most explicitly stated in §37 of *The Second Treatise of Government*. Having already developed Petty's argument concerning the nature of property stemming from the mixing of labour, he now argues that 'he who has appropriated land to himself by his labor does not lessen but increase the common stock of mankind' (1952: 22). This is because, Locke continues, enclosed land is worth ten times more than land lying in waste, as he puts it.[7] The logic of this position means that the person enclosing ten acres is in effect giving ninety back to mankind. The crime according to Locke is not the enclosure of land, but waste. The person who gathers fruit and other materials, kills or tames animals, has through his labour acquired a property in them, but if these perish while belonging to him he has offended against the law of nature. The same applies to land. If the fruit planted, or the grass sown perishes, 'notwithstanding his enclosure', the land is to be looked upon as open to appropriation.

For Wood the key to this justification comes in §40 where Locke stipulates that it is not just labour that produces property but the fact that labour 'put[s] the difference of value on everything' (24). This epitomizes economic war. This argument concerning the value of land, measured according to the method of enclosure, is the means by which Locke justified the theft of land from the American Indians and the devastation of their culture. As Wood points out, the value is not a value intrinsic to the land but the universal equivalence of *exchange* value (2003: 97). This same logic of a universal programme being to the benefit of mankind still drives the supposed legitimacy of current global economic practices. The dereliction of local populations and the attack on local cultural practices is still said to be a good. Remembering that *nomos* signifies allotment, or in Locke's terms enclosure, the new method of imperial enclosure is the rule of privatization and deregulation where public goods, resources and services are appropriated from developing nations through directives set by the WTO, the IMF and the World Bank, a point I will return to in due course. This material constitution of empire is its sovereign capacity to finish. Rhetorically it is a process referred to as 'modernization', a largely meaningless term, regularly deployed by Tony Blair's New Labour to represent resistance to marketization as naïve primitivism,[8] while militarily, as John McMurtry has noted, it results in the 'bombing of non-marketized societies' (2002: 4). Subject to sovereign exclusion within a fully capitalist system, the populations of Afghanistan and Iraq became the bare life that could be killed without being murdered.

With regard to the *formal constitution* of empire, where Nancy only saw a lacuna at the heart of international law because it has no common setting, Hardt and Negri argue that empire does in fact work through a common notion of right. With the establishment of the market as the sovereign protector of and provider for the multitude, empire pushes 'the coincidence and universality of the ethical and the juridical to the extreme' (10). The market is the Good and it is right that all people should be given access to its supreme beneficence. The rulings of the IMF, World Bank and the WTO can be nothing other than just given their purpose is the extension of the free market and that access to a free market together with the satisfaction of free choice is the foundation of the new morality.

In this regard, this new paradigm of sovereignty that is coterminous with the commodification of freedom through which it supposedly secures consent thus claims to have resolved the tension between liberty and subjection, which marks the modern path of sovereignty and is articulated around three moments. First, there is the revolutionary discovery of the plane of immanence where humans claim their autonomy and declare themselves masters of their own lives, a process often referred to as secularization or humanism. Secondly, there is the counter-revolution, a reaction against immanence and the crisis of authority; the crackdown on heretics and dissenters. This is then resolved in a third moment with the formation of the modern state and the universal recognition of the equality of all free persons. In this process the constitutive power of the multitude is 'made safe' in the constituted power of the reformed state. Immanence is reified and the singular, corporeal, affective and active desire of the multitude becomes the abstract, disembodied, reasonable and represented work of the citizen.

The sovereignty of empire, however, marks a break with this triple articulation as it refuses the limiting function of the third reforming moment; the immanence of marketization supposedly representing a 'rolling back' of the state and greater autonomy for the individual, but also providing the means for immediate social control at the biopolitical level. Formally sovereignty is constituted via 'a whole series of powers that regulate themselves and arrange themselves in networks [. . .] exercised within a vast horizon of activities that subdivide [sovereignty] without negating its unity' (162) – an arrangement of checks and balances, limits and equilibria that constitute a central yet dispersed 'democratic' power. The constitution of the United States thus 'represents a moment of great innovation and rupture in the genealogy of modern sovereignty' (160), not by making a clean break with the past but by once again recovering the past for itself. 'It is striking', they comment, 'how strongly this American experiment resembles the ancient constitutional experience, and specifically the political theory inspired by imperial Rome!' (166). The connection with the Roman imperial tradition lies in the tripartite organization of power between monarchy, aristocracy and democracy, or Emperor, Senate and popular *comitia*, as described by Polybius,[9] and which translates into the division of republican state functions between the executive, the judiciary and the representative. But empire takes further inspiration from imperial Rome, namely its principle of expansion, which is analyzable as the three characteristics of the US Constitution. The first, as has already been noted, is the immanence of power. The second arises out of the plane of immanence and the plural, conflictual nature of the multitude. At this point there is a tendency to revert to transcendence as a form of control, as Hardt and Negri argue was the case in England and France, but instead the third characteristic of the US Constitution is to preserve the project by releasing tension outwards in limitless expansion in a renewed declaration of democratic foundation. Empire can therefore be thought of as a 'universal republic, a network of powers and counterpowers structured in a boundless and inclusive architecture' (166), and yet it must be thought otherwise to older imperialist forms for 'when it expands, this new sovereignty does not annex or destroy the other powers it faces but on the contrary opens itself to them, including them in the network' (166).[10]

Of course, the tripartite republican division of power does require some reconceptualization to bring it fully in line with the new imperial order, thus the *bomb* replaces the monarchic/executive branch, *money* the aristocratic/legislative branch, and *ether* the popular/representative branch. The bomb represents 'an operation of absolute violence' (345) and the monopoly of legitimate force; money becomes the arbiter of justice and the financial centres the regulators of value; while the ether manages communication, education and culture. We have, then, in this analysis of the material and formal constitution of empire a highly innovative and provocative analysis that permits us to continue to think sovereignty in the age of ecotechnics. But does the reduction of war to a form of police action within this empire allow us to understand what is at stake in the return of war in a world where, after 1989, it was thought to have been effaced? There is a temptation, Hardt and Negri note, to assume that the US is in charge of these mechanisms: bomb, money and ether. 'It might appear as if the United States were the new Rome, or a cluster of new Romes: Washington (the bomb), New York (money), and Los Angeles (ether). Any such territorial conception of imperial space, however, is continually destabilized by the fundamental flexibility, mobility, and deterritorialization at the core of the imperial apparatus' (347). Yet while this is no doubt a correct analysis of the fluidity and even the virtuality of global power it remains partial precisely because this focus on the transnational loses sight of the lingering realism in *international* relations, that is, it fails to adequately note the resistance the nation state has to its supposed dissolution. If the ecotechnical realm has become sovereign, and if power is now fully networked and nodal how are we to understand the re-emergence of national sovereignty that Nancy believed he was witnessing in 1991? How might this new paradigm of sovereignty explain the unilateralism, protectionism, isolationism and pre-emption of the most militarily, financially and technically powerful global agent? The question that needs to be addressed, therefore, is how does the economic war that is the technology of the new paradigm of sovereignty relate to, or stand alongside, the figure of war as the technology of traditional sovereignty.

Civil war

Despite Hardt and Negri's analysis, empire is anything but smooth, in fact, as a properly capitalist order it is riven with competition, which is at its most intense amongst those actors who most dogmatically adhere to the imperial doctrine of marketization. While the identities and binaries of older imperial orders may be dispersing beneath a logic of power that actively deploys differences and hybridities in its favour, there nevertheless remains a structure of dominance and irregularities of distribution and organization that prevent us from portraying empire as a fully fluid system. In the process model offered by Hardt and Negri in which empire is akin to a self-regulating monad, a vital (eco)system of relations and operating principles, the concept of 'just war' is deployed to sacralize its own authority. Empire can thus practice war while continually speaking of peace, or rather it speaks of war in terms of 'security' thereby making war and peace *absolutely contemporary with one another* (Alliez and Negri, 2003: 110). And yet the re-emergence of the figure of war, as Nancy calls it, suggests that something in excess of global policing is actually taking place.

As was discussed earlier, sovereignty has always been split between its particular, princely mode and its universal, republican mode. Up until now the universal pretensions of the international order have never achieved sovereignty as the international model lacked any capacity to finish, always in the end sub-contracting the princely monopoly of force and will to national sovereigns. However, within the properly capitalist order a universal sovereignty has emerged with the capacity to finish (ontologically and juridically). To return to Carl Schmitt's analysis of sovereignty, this new paradigm, because it makes absolute the coincidence of the ethical and the juridical in the *nomos* of the market, has the capacity to 'decide on the extreme possibility' (1996: 39) and distinguish between friend and enemy. Schmitt argued that if the globe was to become a unified economic entity, without the distinction between friend and enemy 'it still would not be more of a social entity than a social entity of tenants in a tenement house, customers purchasing gas from the same utility company, or passengers travelling on the same bus' (57). However, should economics be able to decide on the extreme possibility, then it 'in actuality has become the new substance of the political entity' (39), and in placing non-marketized societies under a sovereign ban, allowing the people of these societies to be killed without being murdered, it is thus possible to speak of capital or the market as a sovereign entity. This also permits us to see why Nancy would argue that sovereignty is dissolved apart from where it coincides with ecotechnical power. Possibly for the first time in the history of the concept the universal mode is truly wresting authority away from nations, and it is here, in the competition between these sovereigns to maximize their coincidence with ecotechnical power and maximize material benefits from the new imperial order that we need to place the figure of war. In their more recent work, Hardt and Negri have placed a little more emphasis on the notion of civil war that found a muted articulation in *Empire*. In *Multitude*, for example, while still understanding war as an element of biopolitics[11] and therefore as a police activity, they define current conflicts as 'imperial civil wars' (2005: 4); struggles 'for relative dominance within the hierarchies at the highest and lowest levels of the global system' (4). In this situation the declaration of an infinite war against terror only announces a condition that had already come to maturity, a condition in which the relationship between politics and war has been inverted: 'War is no longer an instrument at the disposal of political powers to be used in limited instances, but rather war itself tends to define the foundation of the political system' (341). In the global state of emergency it is war (the exception) that has become the rule. In this sense we appear to have plunged back into an indistinct state of war that gave birth to the Hobbesian account of sovereignty. Then as now the war/security couplet serves conventional needs of sovereignty in controlling the violence that threatens it while also imposing order on the multitude. This, they argue, is the purpose of Huntington's civilizational thesis: 'civilizations will make global conflict coherent and divide nation-states into stable groups of friend and enemy. [...] The so-called alliance of the willing and the axis of evil designate strategies for grouping nation-states into blocs and thus making their violence coherent' (239–40). However, this revised position fails as an account for the lingering realism that defines traditional sovereignty and the return of the princes. Because they argue the new paradigm of sovereignty, as the realm of transnational capital, is a decentred power, networked and distributed through the minutiae of discursive regimes and biopolitical procedures, Hardt and Negri cannot consider civil war as competition between competing capitalist agents in an attempt to gain proximity to ecotechnical power, which while diffuse still has a centring effect in the sense that it is not an organic, self-organizing system, but the product of innumerable decisions made by the men and women who gather in the buildings of transnational economic institutions and the web of affiliated corporations. The appointment of Paul Wolfowitz as head of the World Bank would support the claim that the empire of capital still does have a centre effect and that proximity to this locus of ecotechnical power remains a high priority.

Two theories that are helpful for thinking this persistent competition and the antagonism between the national and transnational realms are Leslie Sklair's analysis of the transnational capitalist class (TCC) and David Harvey's adaptation of the theory of primitive accumulation. For

Sklair, the members of the TCC are the actors who have the greatest proximity to ecotechnical power. The TCC is deterritorialized because '[w]here a capitalist class starts to shake itself free from unwelcome state involvement in its affairs, or starts to shape this state involvement, new opportunities to forge transnational connections will arise' (Sklair, 2001: 53). The TCC comprises corporate executives, media bosses and what Sklair calls 'technopols', the politicians, bureaucrats, technical (and one should add military, professionals 'who accept and propagate the necessity for the permanent expansion of the global capitalist system' (137); and who 'partake differentially in recognizable global patterns of capital accumulation, consuming and thinking' (12). The Bush and Blair administrations, together with other partners such as Berlosconi in Italy, clearly fit into this definition of the technopol who perceive the interests of a democratic nation to be comparable with the interests of a business, and therefore run a country according to the principles of corporate performance. This means that globalization, or empire, does not diminish the state's capacity to regulate, it is now a question of 'whose interests it serves when it regulates' (90).[12]

Although the TCC is a class in the sense that it shares a set of interests and a set of operational rules, it is important to remember that as a capitalist class its fraternity does not decrease but actually increases competition between different actors. In this sense, the TCC (and therefore empire) may be deterritorialized, but it cannot be smooth. Instead, I would suggest, the TCC itself is organized, as is any class, through a structure of dominance. As an aristocracy differentiates between 'old' and 'new' money, and yet still has a class identity, so the TCC is stratified by different levels of influence and control within empire. New neo-liberal elites such as the one being constituted in Iraq will join the TCC and play an important role in relation to the advance of the global market and yet this actor will clearly not have the influence or control of the US.[13] That the US is hegemonic is not in question, and the belligerence of the neo-conservatives in Washington clearly indicates that realism, or what I call transnational realism, still has a place in the international order. However, the question remains for how long the US will maintain its dominance and to what scale it is prepared to defend its interests as the dominant agent in the TCC. At present the US can manage the economic war in its own interests. The rule of marketization favours many in the rich North, in particular the US, but Harvey has recently argued that US hegemony is about to be challenged by China. The opening up of China means that the Chinese elite are also set to join the TCC, indeed are set to become the lead nation, as a rapidly growing China becomes what Harvey calls a 'spatio-temporal fix' for overaccumulated capital (2003: 122). If there is to be a massive redirection of investment from the US to China, as Harvey's analysis suggests, it would bring about the kind of structural adjustment in the US currently enforced on lesser nations in the economic war of marketization and would bring about the sort of austerity not seen in the US since the Great Depression (208).

For Harvey, one of the key elements in the current global situation is the predatory nature of capitalism itself, the fact that capitalism constantly seeks something outside itself that it can feed off. He refers to Rosa Luzembourg's analysis that capitalism always needs an outside to trade with because the structure of wage-labour under capitalism produces underconsumption (the wage not being equivalent to the productivity of the worker) leading to overproduction and the crises in which idle capital has to find a 'spatio-temporal fix' in order to once again be profitable. In the current order in which the entire globe comes under the logic of capitalist production it would appear that Luxembourg's thesis is proved wrong as there is little left outside the capitalist system to stabilize overproduction. In this situation, however, Harvey explains how capitalism must manufacture this outside through new methods of primitive accumulation which he refers to as 'accumulation by dispossession'.[14] One such method is the manufacture and management of crises within the capitalist system itself. Crises can be created to produce devalued stock that can be reappropriated by other capitalists in order to provide solutions to their own problems of overproduction.

> Regional crises and highly localized place-based devaluations emerge as a primary means by which capitalism perpetually creates its own 'other' in order to feed upon it. The financial crises of East and South-East Asia in 1997–8 were a classic case of this. The analogy with the creation of an industrial reserve army by throwing people out of work is exact. Valuable assets are thrown out of circulation and devalued. They lie fallow and dormant until surplus capital seizes upon them to breath new life into capital accumulation. The danger, however, is that such crises might spin out of control and become generalized, or that the 'othering' will provoke a revolt against the system that creates it. One of the prime functions of state intervention and of international institutions is to orchestrate devaluations in ways that permit accumulation by dispossession to occur without sparking a general collapse. (Harvey, 2003: 151)

In this analysis, it becomes immediately apparent why it is imperative for the US to remain hegemonic within the TCC in order that such crises, as well as other means of primitive accumulation such as the management of debt through the IMF and World Bank, intellectual property rights and the enclosure of commons are managed in a way most amenable to them, and why the threat from China is so significant.[15] The question then becomes whether or not the US will quietly relinquish its position as leading agent in the TCC and chief beneficiary of the economic war.

The full emergence of the neo-conservatives from the shadows of the Reagan administration perfectly encapsulates the duality of sovereignty within empire. In Hobbesian terms, it is assumed that the market has become the protector and commonwealth of the multitude. It is at once the realization of desire through the universalizing of the commodity form, and the figure of authority through the implementation of trade regulations, economic restructuring and the management of debt. This globalized sovereignty is supranational in the sense that it is 'on the model or schema of "that which has nothing above itself", of the unsurpassable, the unconditional, or the nonsubordinable' (Nancy, 2000: 131), and in many respects the neo-conservative project is a reaction to this shift. While neo-liberalism is a cornerstone of neo-conservative ideology they will only pursue the free market as long as it is in their interests. Once those interests are threatened, the transnational institutions of this new sovereignty are as much open to attack as the older institutions that represented the universal sovereignty of the international political community, so despised by Richard Perle. At a political level, then, what Nancy perceives to be the return of national sovereignty is the manoeuvring of national agents in response to the sovereign power of empire, and in this respect war *does* remain at the disposal of political powers. The invasions of Afghanistan and Iraq were attempts by the US to maintain its position of privilege within the empire of capital, and secure an economic *lebensraum* (Smith, 2003). If one reads through the set of publications linked to the *Project for a New American Century*, it becomes clear that the belligerence of the Bush administration is entirely directed to the undermining of trading blocks that may become genuine competitors to US ascendancy. In this regard the invasion of Iraq in particular did a number of things in relation to the undermining of regional hegemons. It created a split within Europe (delivered primarily by Tony Blair), it constituted a physical bridgehead in the Eurasian land mass, while also contributing to the political and military containment of China (Harvey, 2003: 81–5).[16] As Schmitt claimed, even when economics becomes destiny 'it cannot escape the logic of the political (1996: 79). Nancy is thus correct to argue that in the ecotechnical realm there is no sovereignty unless it coincides with ecotechnical power; and what is most intriguing about the Bush administration is the overt way in which it is prepared to preserve this coincidence.

Finally, while this competition between the existing and newly emergent actors within the TCC prevents us from thinking of the deterritorialized empire of capital as smooth, there are *cultural* elements to the re-emergence of national sovereignty that also question Hardt and Negri's analysis. In that analysis, difference is the prime mover of imperial expansion at a cultural level. Difference no longer has transformative, liberatory or progressive potential as all cultural differences now become marketing opportunities. While this is no doubt a key element of Post-Fordism, it is inadequate as an analysis of culture. For, while the vast majority of those people who most benefit from the new networked empire might be defined as cosmopolitan, this does not mean they have lost all ties with the specificity of place. Culture certainly undergoes the kind of deterritorialization one experiences with the opening up of borders and the networking of space, but this is also met by a strong re-territorialization of identity that is a key contributor to the re-emergence of the figure of national sovereignty and of war. We must not lose sight of the fact that it was the perceived loss of territorial sovereignty on 11 September 2001 that gave legitimacy to an open-ended war in which any country not 'with us' could be targeted for reprisals. The current war was born of an anxiety in relation to deterritorialized, transnational forces *and* a concern for national identity. The current war, therefore, is not just a system-wide police action designed to re-stabilize empire it is also the expression of a cultural politics that is profoundly tied to the sovereignty, that is, identity of community. This recognition of culture in the current formation of war is not to concur with Huntington's thesis of a clash of civilizations, for the identity within the TCC puts pay to the absurdity of civilizational identities. It suggests something closer to the war of princes supposedly superseded by centuries of European history.

Nancy is correct, of course, to claim this sovereignty of community is borrowed. In relation to the realities of transnational capital and transnational terror, the national sovereign is profoundly undermined, and yet these challenges to national integrity, in an environment hypersensitive to risk, do indeed re-legitimate war in the eyes of the threatened community. Thus the pursuit of ecotechnical power can easily borrow and successfully deploy the incandescent light of sovereignty. In an endless state of emergency in which the exception has become the rule, it is this conflictual dialectic between the transnational and the national, this play between deterritorialized and re-territorializing sovereignty that gives contemporary war, and the war against terror in particular, one of its most defining features.

Epilogue

The events of 11 September 2001 brought the announcement of a permanent state of emergency in an infinite war against a ubiquitous enemy. It represents the ascendancy of pure war, as well as the colonization of government by an increasingly powerful military-industrial complex. Thirty years ago Senator J. William Fulbright warned that: 'We cannot, without doing ourselves the very injury that we seek to secure ourselves against from foreign adversaries, pursue policies which rely primarily on the threat of the use of force, because policies of force and pre-eminence given to the wielders of force – the military – are inevitably disruptive of democratic values' (1971: 14). While the suspension of the law, evidenced in the rolling back of civil liberties and the introduction of draconian counterterrorist measures in the US, Britain and Europe, can be understood in terms of the constitutional dictatorship believed necessary to protect democracy, we must also remember that the slippage from the logic of constitutional dictatorship to the practice of unconstitutional dictatorship is very hard to prevent, and that as the mentality of militarism increasingly pervades our everyday lives our willingness to resist these inroads into democratic government by profoundly illiberal forces may be significantly reduced. Our susceptibility to the discourse of 'war as security' is no doubt encouraged by a phenomenon that Ulrich Beck has called 'risk society' (1992). For Beck, risk society is not determined by a quantitative increase in the insecurities of life but by 'a *de-bounding* of uncontrollable risks' (Beck, 2002: 40) that include, for example, the threat of global warming, the implications of revolutionary technologies such as cloning and nanotechnology, as well as the unpredictability of global markets, and now the threat of transnational terror.[1] This experience of non-quantifiable insecurities is also heightened by the fact that previously stable coordinates such as the social welfare that concluded the 'first modernity' are dissolved in a 'second modernity' (Beck *et al.*, 2003) dominated by deregulation and marketization. As Zygmunt Bauman has insightfully argued, if the early modern socio-political experience was determined by the quest for freedom, in a society where the rules of the game are becoming increasingly uncertain late modern experience becomes a quest for security (1998: 117). As a result of this perceived vulnerability the populations of the developed world become increasingly susceptible to a popular media that profits from the fear of others and politicians that seek 'to feign control over the uncontrollable' (Beck, 2002: 41).[2]

We are accustomed to having wars of all kinds: wars against drugs and against crime that are all part of the 'emergent apocalypse' (Van Loon, 2002: 170) of urban experience. We are, at all levels of society, on a permanent war footing. And in this instance both Bush and Blair know, like the great philosopher of social apocalypse Thomas Hobbes that 'the passion to be reckoned upon is fear' (1994: 88), for nothing drives people to greater dependency on a leader that projects himself as strong. The greatest weapon of the terrorist, therefore, is the deployment of our already existing fears.[1] What is more, the enemy is no longer marked by any uniform. Nor, in the age of multicultural nations and cosmopolitan religions, are there any absolute physical markers. John Walker Lindh is the perfect expression of de-bounded risk, exposing as he did, the possibility that every single person was a potential terrorist, even kids with basketball hoops in their drive. This is indicative of another feature of risk society, namely the shift from active trust, whereby individual members of society recognize implicit dependencies on fellow citizens, to active mistrust, where social and filiative networks are drawn increasingly tighter in ever-decreasing circles, an operation which itself heightens the perception of risk. Active mistrust, because it tends to reduce both the quantity and quality of social relations, feeds off the dissolution it breeds, thereby heightening tensions, anxieties and prejudices. All in all a central feature of risk society is a deepening culture of suspicion.[2] This is the social environment in which the global state of emergency finds its popular support.

As was noted in Chapter 6, consciousness of debounded risk largely represents fear of specific threats, even if these threats are hard to quantify, but accompanying this fear is the anxiety that Heidegger argued stemmed from the 'nothingness' of the world, something that is revealed in an especially powerful way during a time of war when, as

Scarry proposed, the survival of our world is at stake. This world, of course, is not just the physical infrastructure of buildings and communications networks, more importantly it is our sense of worldhood; the values to which we might attribute the highest cause, and the commitment to those values that are essential for our sense of identity. This suggests that if we are to develop a critique of war that might contribute to a lessening of violence and the sharing of a globally, heterogeneous world, it is necessary to reflect upon the motivations for both our fear of specific threats and the ontological insecurity that is manifested in the anxiety we experience regarding the fragility of our world. It also means that we need to differentiate between strategic and ontological warfare, where strategic warfare represents violent competition for resources and ontological warfare represents the confrontation to preserve and expand fragile worlds. This distinction does not mean the two are separate, for in practice there is never any pure strategic warfare. Ontological warfare is always deployed to legitimize practices at the level of strategic warfare as we saw in the two Gulf Wars when it was unlikely that either Bush Senior or Bush Junior would have been able to secure popular support for their actions without the demonizing of Saddam Hussein and his representation as a threat to the its way of life. While the two are distinct in the sense that the invasion to marketize Iraq's economy requires an analysis of political economy quite distinct from the hermeneutic analysis that seeks to understand the way in which America views itself and the hallowed nature of its values, it is also important to recognize that strategic and ontological warfare are connected in that these values will also include notions of competition and possessive individualism that serve to naturalize the strategic war over the ownership of resources. While the specific historical, political and economic motivations of strategic war must continue to be analyzed in an attempt to reveal the actual workings of global power, an ontological analysis can complement these studies because it too seeks to address and question the values that are naturalized, given legitimacy, and indeed universalized in the construction of our world. What is important to understand is how our sense of the world becomes a worldview able to judge others as friend or enemy, good or evil.

While an ontological analysis of war can help in understanding the nature of the economic war that is currently being waged in the name of neo-liberalism and facilitates the study of the ways in which wars in pursuit of ecotechnical power are given legitimacy and accrue popular support, an ontological analysis of war most importantly enables a deconstruction of the belligerence of military logic and the subjectivism on which it is premised. We have seen how psychology, sociology and philosophy have explained war, aggression and hostility in terms of a desire for unity and communion, that is, the desire to be part of the continuity linking each individual through his or her community to the highest cause, be that God, people or nation. We have also seen how the subject of this desire is split in a manner that privileges the search for completion in and as an ideal subject, a subject that secures a substance and a ground for identity. Here, however, we begin to approach the tragedy of being human, epitomized by the search for a ground and a foundation that arises precisely out of the fact that human being is actually groundless, or open. Our freedom, in some peculiar twist of fate, predisposes us to the infinite, and infinitely vain search for a foundation that will put an end to the radical nature of that freedom and secure the world not as a fiction we have created but as the revelation of a fundamental truth, and it is in the name of these foundations that we go to war. Some wars will scarcely reveal this confrontation between founding, substantiating values, for when war becomes a police action, or as Baudrillard describes it, the programmed unfolding of a plan, the ontological stakes of war hardly surface given the inevitability of the process. What is important about the war against terror, however, is that in the space of a few hours the certainty of the New World Order's police force was exposed and experienced as fragile. Being American did not equate to being human, and being human no longer equated to being or wanting to be American. America's 'manifest destiny', its sense of universality and truth was for a brief time interrupted and deposed, even if it was quickly reaffirmed as the agent of justice doing battle with the forces of iniquity as the full scope of ontological warfare was brought centre stage in the clash of civilized versus barbarous worlds.

With regard to the tragedy of human freedom, we are indebted to Nietzsche as possibly the first modern philosopher to understand its implications. He informed us that our will to determine what is true and thereby secure a ground for our freedom was little more than the will to power. There is nothing more fundamental to humans than the capacity to esteem and attribute value. Wherever we have secured certainty we have in a more primary way already attributed value to the concept of certainty, and unless we recognize that we are first and foremost valuers involved in a perpetual transvaluation of values, we will never adequately understand ourselves and will remain condemned to the fruitless search for a foundation that endures. For a philosopher that could see so far into the human condition his one moment of myopia was to privilege the will of the subject who values, thereby becoming unable to fully overcome the metaphysics of the subject and the violently wilful struggles for which his thought was recruited. In response, Heidegger was able to overcome this last vestige of subjectivism and talk of human being as a hermeneutic project involving the confrontation (polemos) between world and earth, that is, between that which is given and that which is yet to come, a future in which Being is never fully disclosed and thus cannot guarantee any world. Once his work had divested itself of the existential struggle and the need for the resolute decision, it opened the way to an ethics that refuses all grounds, or posits, in his words only an abyssal ground, an *Abgrund*, in which human being is understood as open and undetermined both in origin and in aim.

Let us indeed say that the highest cause is human freedom, but let us also say this means that human beings are open and infinitely creative. Let us recognize that our worlds are fictions, beautiful fictions, and that no world can ever be taken as the end or conclusion of that openness, that no world should ever render others illegitimate, invalid, backward, perverse or evil. We are now embroiled in a clash of fundamentalisms seeking to do precisely that. To substantiate the absolute truth of American values and the absolute truth of Islam, two worlds (that significantly neither represent the openness of America nor the openness of Islam) are colliding in which thousands of people are sacrificed in order to make material, or realize these beliefs. In this confrontation, mass murder is the wager laid down in the bid to substantiate a world. This call to respect the pluriverse of human freedom, then, might appear to be a rather fancy way of repeating the liberal ideals of respect and tolerance for individual belief systems, but this is not the case. Clearly tolerance is not the sole property of liberalism given its earlier manifestation in the Islamic recognition of different forms of worship, but it is not liberalism because liberalism remains tied to a subjectivist metaphysics and a privileging of autonomy that too often succumbs to the promotion and pursuit of self-interest. The ontology of war thus demands the historicizing of the reality principle that privileges the competitive individual. It also requires challenging our desire for completion. It therefore demands the recognition of our constitution in and through others, as well as the deconstruction of genealogies of friendship and enmity. Most importantly, however, what the ontology of war can show us is that being human, in a way that is essential to our freedom, is an interpretive confrontation to win a world, but that this confrontation is anarchic (*an-archē*) in the sense that it cannot be derived from, legitimated by or secured with a founding principle that destines any particular world to be *the* world at the end of history. Human freedom is anarchic not in the sense that it is without rules, for no such world is possible, it rather means that humans are not determined by a governing first principle that in a final way brings to an end our questions concerning world, value and identity.

Notes

Introduction

1. See Richard Johnson, 'Defending Ways of Life: The (Anti-) Terrorist Rhetorics of Bush and Blair', *Theory, Culture & Society*, 19/4 (2002), 211–31.
2. Agnes Heller (2002) has also used this argument to counter the claim that Al'Qaeda represent 'the wretched of the Earth'.
3. Robin Blackburn's article 'The Imperial Presidency, the War on Terrorism, and the Revolutions of Modernity' (2002) is a very useful commentary on these issues.
4. www.darpa.mil/iao/FutureMap.htm, accessed 30 July 2003.

1 Power and polemos

1. These are as numbered in the standard Diels and Kranz edition of Herclitus's fragments.
2. Given the set of lectures quoted above are infamous for Heidegger speaking of the 'inner truth and greatness' of National Socialism, I do not believe his philosophy is reducible to it. What is more, the (polemical) task of reducing Heidegger's thought to Nazism holds all future readers of his work to an interpretation of the author's life, and this is something to which I cannot subscribe. All thought, all writing exceeds the intention of the author. There is something akin to what Umberto Eco (1992) referred to as the intention of the text, which certainly sets limits to interpretation, but these limitations still allow a philosopher's thoughts to work afresh, in a different time and a new context.
3. This rhetorical model takes centre stage in *Thus Spoke Zarathustra*. Zarathustra announces the absence of a supersensory binding power and the presence of an immanent will to power. He *goes down* from his mountain to preach the path the spirit is to take if it is to attain complete nihilism and affirm life. This task is set out in the first of Zarathustra's discourses entitled 'Of the Three Metamorphoses'. The metamorphoses from camel to lion and finally to the child represent the journey from the weight-bearing spirit of the ought, through the sacred 'no' of the lion who defeats the dragon, on whose scales a thousand years of values glitter and is called 'Thou Shalt', to the child who utters the sacred 'yes'. While the lion creates the freedom for new creation it is the child that is a new beginning, wills its own will and wins its own world. The child is the new dispensation of values achieved for the first time knowingly.
4. Considering human becoming Nietzsche writes: 'There is a lake that one day ceased to permit itself to flow off; it formed a dam where it had hitherto flown off; and ever since this lake is rising higher and higher [...] perhaps man will rise ever higher as soon as he ceases to *flow out* into a god' (1974: 230).

5. In *The Ethics* Spinoza presents the *conatus essendi* in Part III, Proposition VI: 'Everything, in so far as it is in itself, endeavours to persist in its own being' (1955: 136).

6. Aside from Fried, two very good engagements with Heidegger's Nazim are Jean-François Lyotard (1988a) and Phillipe Lacoue-Labarthe (1990).

7. Part of this battle is the deployment of everyday, factical life as the ground of philosophy. 'Turning Husserl's own word against the master, Heidegger excludes what Husserl would include – the neutrality of the *epochē*, the tranquillity of pure intuition – and includes what the master would exclude – the facticity of life' (Caputo, 1993: 49).

8. Fried points out that Heidegger does mention fragment 53 for the first time in 1933 in a private letter to Carl Schmitt that responds to the gift of a copy of *The Concept of the Political* that Schmitt had given to Heidegger. Heidegger remarks that he had an interpretation similar to Schmitt's set down for years and that he appreciated Schmitt's analysis of war in its relation to sovereignty (polemos as king).

9. Another translation by Heidegger of fragment 53 reveals the close link between *polemos* and clearing, or *Lichtung*. In *Early Greek Thinking* the translation is as follows: 'πόλεμος, the setting-apart-from-each-other (the lighting [clearing]), manifests some of those present as gods, others as men, and brings some forward into appearance as slaves and others as free' (1984: 119).

10. This robbery and wresting truth from entities is radically revised in Heidegger's later work where he prefers the interpretation of unconcealment as *Gelassenheit*, translated as releasement or letting-be.

11. If we are to avoid this falling away of principles, it is necessary to think Being an-archically, that is without *archē*, or principle. A schematic working out of this problem can be found in my book *Against Autonomy: Lyotard, judgement and action*, see Chapter 5 'An-archy: Principles and Foundations'.

12. The eight major civilizations include Western, Confucian, Japanese, Islamic, Hindu, Slavic-Orthodox, Latin American and African.

13. Plato's conception of the being of beings as εἶδος marks the closing of the great age of Greece and 'predestined the world's having to become a picture' (Heidegger, 2002: 69).

2   Life and death

1. In the light of this, Marcuse opens his 1966 'Political Preface', written on the tenth anniversary of the publication of *Eros and Civilization*, with the following: '*Eros and Civilization*: the title expressed an optimistic, euphemistic, even positive thought, namely that the achievements of advanced industrial society would enable man to reverse the direction of progress, to break the fatal union of productivity and destruction, liberty and repression – in other words, to learn the gay science (*gaya sciencia*) of how to use the social wealth for shaping man's world in accordance with his Life instincts, in the concerted struggle against the purveyors of Death' (2001: 97).

2. The 'economic' is one of the three components in the metapsychology that includes the 'topographic' and the 'dynamic'.

3. See, in particular, 'Group Psychology and the Analysis of the Ego' (Freud, 1991c).
4. The metaphor Freud uses is of 'mills that grind so slowly that people may starve before they get their flour' (1991c: 360).
5. 'The revolt against Christian civilization appears in various forms: anti-semitism, terrorism, social Darwinism, anti-intellectualism, naturalism. Common to all of them is the rebellion against the restraining and transcendental principle of Christian morality' (Marcuse 1998b: 144).
6. Marcuse defines the function of the *Führer* as follows: 'Ideologically, he is the embodiment of the German race, its infallible will and knowledge, and the seat of supreme sovereignty. In reality, however, he is the agency through which the diverging interests of the three ruling hierarchies are coordinated and asserted as national interests. He mediates between the competing forces; he is the locus of final compromise rather than sovereignty. His decision might be autonomous, particularly in minor matters, but it is still not free, not his own, but that of others. For it originates and is bound to the philosophy and policy of the governing imperialist groups which he has served from the beginning' (1998b: 76).
7. Hitler's analysis of the world situation in 1932 is summed up as follows: 'The essential thing is to realize that, at the present moment, we find ourselves in a condition which has occurred several times before in the history of the world: already there have been times when the volume of certain products in the world exceeded the demand... there has arisen such an increase in productive capacity that the present possible consumption market stands in no relation to this increased capacity' (Marcuse, 1998b: 73).
8. In this late essay, Benjamin's critique of aestheticized politics (1992) is never far away. Marcuse writes: 'In its emphasis on the sensuous "image", on the "sex appeal" of the political leader, the American system has mastered in a terribly efficient way, the depth dimension of satisfactory submission beneath the political dimension. The real issues recede before the instinctual affirmation of the image: the people find themselves in their leader' (2001: 170).
9. For a reading that problematizes this area of Marcuse's work, see Christopher Lasch *The Minimal Self* especially Chapter VII, 'The Ideological Assault on the Ego'.
10. In *An Essay on Liberation* Marcuse writes: 'Art would recapture some of its more primitive "technical" connotations: as the art of preparing (cooking!), cultivating, growing things, giving them a form that neither violates their matter nor their sensitivity – ascent of Form as one of the necessities of being, universal beyond all subjective varieties of taste, affinity, etc.' (1969: 32).

3 Master and slave

1. This thesis of Fukuyama's has since been amended, not least because of the continuing challenge that technological, especially biotechnological, innovation (Fukuyama, 2003) poses for humanity.
2. This equation, of course, takes place along an axis of historical progression where the notion of the *Aufhebung* is crucial to any temporal realization.

Often translated as 'sublation', *aufheben* means to overcome while at the same time raising up and preserving in the new entity that which was negated.

3. Kojève writes: 'Napoleon himself is the wholly "satisfied" Man, who, in and by his definitive Satisfaction, completes the course of the historical evolution of humanity. He is the human *Individual* in the proper and full sense of the word; because it is through *him*, through *this* particular man, that the "common cause", the truly universal cause, is realized; and because this particular man is recognized, in his very particularity, by all men universally' (1980: 69).

4. In addition to Williams, Axel Honneth (1995) challenges Kojève's position by thinking the struggle for recognition in relation to Hegel's earlier commitment, prior to the *Phenomenology*, to the normativity of communicative relations and the potential for a deeply social understanding of recognition that he argues is lost in the later work.

5. Williams has clearly failed to consider other works by Kojève where reciprocity is given a much more significant role (see in particular Bryan-Paul Frost, 1999).

6. While speaking of specters, it should also be noted that the Real, the third moment in Lacan's analysis leaves its own ghosts. Slavoj Žižek speaks of a passion for the Real: 'The authentic passion for penetrating the Real thing (ultimately the destructive Void) through the cobweb of semblances that constitute our reality' (2002: 12). In the postmodern world of semblance and simulation this experience of virtuality is endemic throughout the social body and prompts a violent passion for the return of the Real even if the production of an effect is all that is possible. For Žižek the attack on World Trade Centre was an attempt to inject the effect of the Real into the life of the West, to force the one and only hyperpower to touch the Void.

7. It is interesting to note at this point that Kojève likened the Wise Man, in his complete knowledge, to a perfectly flat and indefinitely extended mirror on which the reality of humanity reflects itself: the 'Wise Man' as 'Gestalt'.

8. For Žižek (2004) the three moments that are part of subjective formation for Lacan can all be read in the reasons for invading Iraq in 2003. The rationalized discourse claiming the invasion was about freedom, and democracy represents the Imaginary projection of an 'ideal-I' on behalf of the US. The symbolic proper, that is the maintenance of the law, is revealed in the realist admission that the invasion is about preserving US global hegemony. Finally, the Real, which Žižek understands as an excess interrupting both Imaginary and Symbolic realms, appears as the economic desire to secure oil fields. For Žižek this eruption of the Real represents an identification with the 'obscene underside of Power' (2002: 30)

9. In a recent set of published essays, Said condemns contemporary Orientalism, especially as it is practiced by Samuel Huntington, as 'the purest invidious racism' (2004: 293).

10. Nowhere are the current workings of the master and slave dialectic more in evidence than in the idea that the only good Arab is the Arab who appears on the Western media to decry Arab culture; 'academics whose very language reeks of subservience, inauthenticity, and a hopelessly stilted mimicry' (Said, 2004: 246). Here we are reminded of Franz Fanon's formulation of

colonial consciousness, itself profoundly influenced by Kojève's lectures on Hegel. In *The Wretched of the Earth*, Fanon claims that this ventriloquism completes the work of breaking in the native. In Fanon's earlier work entitled *Black Skin, White Masks* he shows how the articulation of his blackness by the colonial masters positions him as 'an object in the midst of other objects' (1986: 109). He is not recognized for what he is or what he wants to be, but is only given an identity relative to the colonial master. Very much in keeping with Said's analysis of colonialist discursive practices, Fanon laments how the elements of his identity were provided by the white man, 'who had woven [him] out of a thousand details, anecdotes, stories' (111).

11. Socrates uses the story of Leontion as an example of these differing parts of the soul. It is Leontion who, coming across some corpses covered by sheets, and with the executioner standing over them, is filled with a macabre desire to look at the dead bodies. Unable to resist, he pulls back the sheets and immediately reproaches himself for having done so. This story is used as proof that *thymos*, as anger, is different from desire and sometimes opposes desire.

12. See Socrates' story whereby God created a differentiated community of rulers fashioned from gold, auxiliaries from silver and farmers fashioned from iron and bronze, while also allowing for the occasion where a silver child is born to gold parents, and a gold child to silver parents and so on (Plato, 1955: 182).

13. For an informed discussion of Fukuyama's use of thymos, see Victor Gourevitch (1993).

14. While Socrates and Hegel were both committed to the universal and the general, it is important to note that the positivity of the Socratic subject would have made the negating, transforming subject of Hegel appear both imperfect and weak, if not perverse, and hence morally unsound.

4 Community and sacrifice

1. As in all wars the combatants fought with God on their side, but one story, or legend rather, recounted by Paul Fussell beautifully illustrates the protective purpose of national destiny at play in the Great War. This particular legend concerns the angels of Mons, spirits of bowmen from Agincourt, that appeared in the sky to protect the British retreat from Mons in August 1914 (1977: 116).

2. Interestingly, Stromberg notes the autobiography of Ludwig Marcuse who 'tells of a friend who continued to think in the trenches that Kant's third antinomy was more important than the war' (1982: 157).

3. This is a claim adequately proved by the case of Uzbekistan who received aid in return for permission to maintain military bases from which attacks on Afghanistan and the Taliban could be made in the first wave of reprisals in the war against terror. Interestingly enough, while Bush and Blair prosecute their wars in the name of freedom and liberty they turned a blind eye to the catalogue of human rights abuses in the country and the record of President Kamirov who infamously boiled alive a member of the opposition. These abuses having been aired by the British ambassador to Tashkent, Craig Murray, and the decreasing importance of Uzbekistan to US strategic concerns has meant that at the time of writing, the provision of aid was being questioned.

4. In gift-giving the article of exchange 'was not a *thing*' (1988: 65).
5. Importantly, however, and something that contributes to the intensity of the ritual practice, the transgression does not dismiss the taboo as invalid, it rather repeats the absolute power of the interdiction producing an anxiety amongst the practitioners without which the taboo would have no meaning. Transgression, then, suspends the taboo without suppressing it. 'Anguish is what makes humankind, it seems; not anguish alone, but anguish transcended and the act of transcending it' (Bataille, 2001: 86).
6. Richardson summarizes Bataille's position as one that called for the development of a sacred of the left. 'More than half a century later', Richardson concludes, 'this is a question that has barely even been delineated and there seems little denying that Bataille's perception was acute: we can see that only fascism has ever managed to overthrow a capitalist government and no socialist movement has come close to doing so since 1922' (1994: 93).
7. In a very revealing passage from *Eroticism*, Bataille speaks of war in terms of satisfaction: 'Organised war with its efficient military operations based on discipline, which when all said and done excludes the mass of the combatants from the pleasure of transgressing the limits, has been caught up in a mechanism foreign to the impulsions which set it off in the first place; war today has only the remotest connection with war as I have described it; it is a dismal aberration geared to political ends. Primitive war itself can hardly be defended: from the outset it bore the seeds of modern warfare, but the organised form we are familiar with today, that has travelled such a long way from the original organised transgression of the taboo, is the only one that would leave humanity unsatisfied' (2001: 80).

5   Injuring and mourning

1. While this chapter engages with the issue of gender its focus is not war and gender as such. For a very broad account of these issues, see Joshua S. Goldstein (2003). For discussions of women and the military, see Cynthia Enloe (1988 and 1989), Betty A. Reardon (1985) and Jeanne Vickers (1993).
2. Some of the problems involved with a privileging of autonomy I have set out in *Against Autonomy: Lyotard, judgement and action* (2001).
3. In considering what she calls the 'symbolic equivalence between childbirth and war' (1986: 127), Nancy Huston has argued that because women are 'marked' by their capacity to reproduce men are compelled to find something that similarly distinguishes and confirms their masculinity. She notes that women have not been totally excluded from war and military combat, drawing on numerous narrative sources to demonstrate that female virgins have always had some proximity to the violence of combat, epitomized by the Maid of Orleans, Joan of Arc. 'Virginity', she argues, 'is seen as an invisible armour, and the hymen as a shield designed to protect both the body and the soul of the young girl. Once it has been pierced, once she has succumbed to this first paradigmatic wound, all other wounds become possible. The deflowered female body is irremediably permeable, irreversibly vulnerable' (129).

4. This practice contains the four ideals of renunciation, resistance, reconciliation and peacemaking (Ruddick, 1989: 161).

5. For further material on the recovery of masculine identity after the Vietnam War, see Susan Jeffords excellent book *The Remasculinization of America* (1989).

6. As Jean-François Lyotard (1988a) has argued, in relation to Freud's concept of the protective shield (see Chapter 2) a central function of memory is forgetting; forgetting the trauma that threatens the political body with dissolution. Through the sublimation of sacrifice the threatened dissolution of the subject becomes its affirmation. For a very interesting discussion of sublimation and sacrifice in war memorials, see Michael Rowlands (1999).

7. See her book *Just War Against Terror* (2003).

8. For further information visit www.countthecasualties.org.uk and www. iraqbodycount.net

9. In response to this dehumanization and de-realization, and writing in response to the deployment of women's rights as a reason for justifying the invasion of Afghanistan, Butler writes: 'That this foreclosure of alterity is taking place in the name of feminism is surely something to worry about' (41).

10. A very good study of this form of disappearance can be found in John Taylor's book *Body Horror: Photojournalism, Catastrophe and War*.

11. An infamous example of this was Madeleine Albright's comments on *60 Minutes*. As Secretary of State in the Clinton Administration, she was asked to comment on reports that the sanctions against Iraq had killed over half a million children. 'I think this is a very hard choice', she replied, 'but the price – we think the price is worth it'.

6   Friend and enemy

1. Mixed with a good dose of heroic virtue, a good example is Robert D. Kaplan's book *Warrior Politics*, which argues that a life without struggle is a life of decadence (2002: 26). Struggle, however, ought to be limited to military campaigns against identifiable enemies rather than socio-political struggles that are more often than not without solution, and that 'the wise employment of force [is] the surest guide to progress' (2002: 154). That the problems facing us are not modern 'but a continuation of "the ancient"' (15) and that in order to respond to these issues we should learn from the ancients, will not surprise those who are familiar with the Straussian underpinnings of neo-conservatism.

2. Another useful study of Strauss's influence on neo-conservativism is Shadia B. Drury (1997).

3. The metaphysics of the friend–enemy distinction is made clear in Chapter 8 when Schmitt complains that the triple structure of Comte (theological, metaphysical, scientific) and Hegel (family, civil society, state) weakens the polemical punch of the double-structured antithesis. He goes on to note that in a time of crisis, Germany reverted to double structure of Tönnies (*Gemeinschaft* and *Gesellschaft*).

4. Schmitt argues that Hobbes's *protego ergo obligo* is the *cogito ergo sum* of the state (1996: 52).

5. 'A domination of men based upon pure economics must appear a terrible deception if, by remaining non-political, it thereby evades political responsibility and visibility' (Schmitt, 1996: 77).

6. A war in the name of humanity 'is necessarily unusually intense and inhuman because, by transcending the limits of the political framework, it simultaneously degrades the enemy into moral and other categories and is forced to make him a monster that must be not only defeated but also utterly destroyed. In other words, he is an enemy who no longer must be compelled to retreat into his borders only' (1996: 36).

7. This also takes place within the context of what Ulrich Beck has called the de-bounding of risk (1992, 2002).

8. For analyses of the Uniting and Strengthening America by Providing Appropriate Tools Required to Intercept and Obstruct Terrorism Act (USA PATRIOT Act) see CCR publications, in particular those by Jeff Fogel and Nancy Chang (www.ccr-ny.org/v2/home.asp).

9. The CCR report notes that 'Section 802 of the Act defines domestic terrorism as 'acts dangerous to human life that are a violation of criminal laws' that 'appear to be intended to influence the policy of a government by intimidation or coercion'. This definition is so vague that acts of civil disobedience may be construed to violate the law. Civil disobedience typically seeks to influence government policy, and therefore may be construed as an attempt to coerce that change. Furthermore, the portion of the definition stating that acts must be 'dangerous to human life' is extremely broad: it does not distinguish between intentional acts and those that might cause inadvertent harm. Thus a spontaneous demonstration that blocks the path of an ambulance might invite charges of domestic terrorism under the new law' (www.ccr-ny.org/reports/).

10. This position was reinforced by the British Law Lords who in December 2004 condemned the Blair government's anti-terrorist legislation as undemocratic. Lord Hoffman declared: ' "The real threat to the life of the nation, in the sense of a people living in accordance with its traditional laws and political values, comes not from terrorism but from laws such as these" ' (Verkaik and Grice, 2004).

11. For an excellent account of the conditions at Guantánamo Bay and its relation to International Law and the US Constitution, see Ratner and Ray (2004).

12. It may seem strange that Schmitt the Catholic should take Cromwell the Protestant as exemplary with regard to what is at stake in the political decision to name the enemy, but as Meier (1998) explains this only confirms that Schmitt does not think in a purely doctrinal way but thinks existentially, that is, how to decide at a specific concrete and historical moment the nature of the enemy.

13. With regard to the social role of premillennialism, Northcott writes: 'Dispensationalism is a classic instance of religion as the "opiate of the people". It acts as an ideology, a smoke-screen, which mystifies and shrouds the roots of the extreme social division and growing violence on the streets of America in the deregulatory mania of extreme capitalism from Reagan to Bush junior. Behind the walls and security guards of corporate gated communities, or in the ghettos and deracinated working-class neighbourhoods of post-industrial American cities, rich and poor alike take refuge in

the dream that they might be included in the rapture to compensate for the failed dream of a commonwealth of liberty and democracy' (2004: 72).

14. It should be pointed out that the tension between the logic of neo-liberalism and the millennialist attack on global corporatism offers the chance of an immanent critique of the neo-conservative worldview.

15. In opposition to this imperial cult, Northcott's central thesis is that the true apocalypse – apocaplypse meaning unveiling or revelation – is the coming of Jesus as a challenge to imperial rule. The forgiveness of sins, or more literally debts, frees the Jews from both the obligations to the Roman occupiers and collaboration of the Jewish authorities. 'Instead of the Temple system Jesus offers the free grace of God [. . .] in effect challenging the monopoly on religious and economic power that the Temple authorities claimed for themselves' (117). 'Peasants who were released from the requirement to submit tribute to the Temple were to use their new freedom [. . .] to develop a new kind of society in which love for God and neighbour, even for enemies, became the rule. [. . .] Instead of mimicking their rulers, and "using debt to control others" they are to enact a new ethic and practice of forgiveness' (120). The apocalypse of Jesus as revealed through the crucifixion was also pacific and the end to sacrificial cults (129, 130, 138). The reading of the forgiveness of sins as the forgiveness of debts can also be found in Alain Joxe (2002: 115).

7 Media and machine

1. In line with Jürgen Habermas's (1989) assessment of a public sphere increasingly losing its antagonistic and critical relation to government, and in an age when politics is becoming increasingly mediatized, when politicians are increasingly obsessed with their image, and policy invariably becomes a public relations exercise, the legendary and perhaps singular influence of Hirst is becoming far more endemic and prosaic. How, for example, should we respond to Rupert Murdoch's declaration that the best thing to come out of the invasion of Iraq would be oil at $20 per barrel (Greenslade, 2003)?

2. One other key communications technology in the Crimean War was the railway. It also proved its worth for the maintenance of an empire. Mattelart quotes Cecil Rhodes who described the train as ' "an instrument of pacification which costs less than the cannon and carries farther" ' (20). Likewise, when German superiority in the large-scale movement of troops proved decisive in the Franco-Prussian war, Mattelart records the words of the Prussian general Von Moltke who confessed he ' "preferred the building of railroads to that of fortifications" ' (22).

3. On hearing that the OSI was to shut down, Donald Rumsfeld is alleged to have remarked; 'if you want to savage this thing, fine, I'll give you the corpse. There's the name. You can have the name, but I'm gonna keep doing every single thing that needs to be done and I have' (FAIR, 2002).

4. This belief, however, has by no means achieved consensus. Paul Hirst, for example, believes that up to this point there have been two weapons revolutions that will still determine the future of military operations and shape the conflicts to come (2001: 78). These two earlier RMAs were the deployment

of gunpowder in the sixteenth century and the application of industrialization in the nineteenth century that delivered the total war of 1914–18.

5. For Virilio the military-industrial complex emerged out of the creation of the wartime economy demanded by total war (1997: 16).

6. This logistics of perception is also a complex including military, media and civilian components (see Armitage, 2001: 186–7).

7. In *Pure War*, Virilio differentiates between weapons of obstruction, destruction and communication (1997: 175).

8. During the arms race between France and Burgundy in the second half of the fifteenth century one innovation is a good example of the relationship between speed and violence. The 'forming of gunpowder into small grains or "corns" [...] allowed a more rapid ignition, since the exposed surfaces of the separate corns could all burn at once. The explosion became correspondingly more powerful, for rapidly generated gases had less time to leak out around the cannonball while it accelerated along the barrel' (McNeill: 1982: 88).

9. This is suggested by the fact that a plan to liberate Kuwait had been played out in a war game by General Schwarzkopf two years before Saddam Hussein invaded (Gray, 1997: 42).

10. I am borrowing the concept of the differend form the work of Jean-François Lyotard who defines a differend as 'a case of conflict, between (at least) two parties, that cannot be equitably resolved for lack of a rule of judgement applicable to both arguments' (1988b: xi). Deterrence operates according to the rule of life, martyrdom according to the rule of death, or after-life.

11. With regard to the role of the print media in this MIME-NET, Ignacio Ramonet's (2005) report for *Le Monde Diplomatique* reveals that two French arms manufacturers, Serge Dassault and Arnaud Lagardère, now control a large part of the French print media.

12. Although Manuel Castells (1997) is right to have argued that despite these corporate synergies, news services must retain some element of distance from corporate interests to retain credibility, the emergence and success of Fox News does question this axiom of media theory.

13. See George Monbiot (2002).

14. Details of ICT projects and publications can be found at www.ict.usc.edu/disp.php

15. The number of different types of readings has been expanded in recent cultural studies literature. See, for example, Kim Christian Schrøder (2000).

16. In *Pure War*, Virilio notes that the original attack on the WTC in 1993 was scheduled to catch the early evening news (1997: 174). This communicative function of terrorism is also explained in Joseph S. Tuman (2003).

17. As Downey and Murdock have argued, the campaign of global terrorism brings about a process requiring 'information to be gathered from every available location [dismantling] the protective walls that have separated the military from civil society' (2003: 79).

8   Economy and empire

1. This latter model clearly has a significant limiting effect on the sovereign given that the sovereign has to recognize the rights of citizens and therefore

cannot simply exercise arbitrary will. But even in the princely model the sovereign was consented to on the basis that he would provide protection and would at least guarantee property rights, for example. This, then, is the double problematic of sovereignty, the exception that is also the foundation of the law, and a power that is absolute yet limited.

2. It should be noted that sovereignty is also the power to announce when this new distribution has occurred. Sovereign pronouncement is always performative and inconstestable, it relies on nothing beyond its own appropriative utterance to bring something into being. See Susan Watkins (2004) for an interesting account of the 'hand-over' in Iraq and the establishment of formal sovereignty.

3. The case for the illegality of Gulf War II from the perspective of international law is very well set out by Nehal Bhuta (2003).

4. It ought to be noted that Hardt and Negri's analysis of labour in *Empire* does not pay sufficient attention to the widespread proletarianization of people, and gives too much attention to the skilled and semi-skilled (immaterial) workers that in turn become a rather romanticized revolutionary subject. For a useful discussion of this deficiency, see Andreas Kalyvas (2003).

5. Corruption might, then, be said to stem from the positivism of this ontological foundation and the accompanying perversion and privation of the hermeneutics of human freedom.

6. Arendt draws one further important interpretation from this understanding of law and distribution commenting that the Greeks did not count legislating as a political activity, 'the lawmaker was like a builder who had to do and finish his work before political activity could begin' (1958: 195).

7. Locke actually goes on to say that he has 'rated the improved land very low in making its product but as ten to one, when it is much nearer a hundred to one; for I ask whether in the wild woods and uncultivated waste of America, left to nature, without any improvement, tillage, or husbandry, a thousand acres yield the needy and the wretched inhabitants as many conveniences of life as ten acres of equally fertile land do in Devonshire, where they are cultivated well' (1952: 23).

8. For a sustained discussion of this use of 'modernization', see Frederic Jameson *A Singular Modernity* (2002).

9. For Polybius, monarchy represented continuity, aristocracy virtue, and democracy the satisfaction of the People (Hardt and Negri, 2000: 314).

10. Peter Gowan differentiates between the power to command and the power to shape: 'The emergent global system is geared to shaping the environments of sovereign states so that developments within them broadly match the interests of the Pacific Union – while responsibility for tackling these developments falls squarely on the governments of the sovereign states concerned' (2001: 90).

11. Of biopower and war, Hardt and Negri write: 'War really became absolute only with the technological development of weapons that made possible for the first time mass and even global destruction. Weapons of global destruction break the modern dialectic of war. War has always involved the destruction of life, but in the twentieth century this destructive power reached the limits of the pure production of death, represented by Ausch-

witz and Hiroshima. [...] When genocide and atomic weapons put life itself on center stage, then *war becomes properly ontological*' (2005: 19).

12. For Hardt and Negri because the nation-state is always a limiting function in that it converts the immanence of the multitude into the transcendent concept of a People, class struggle pushes, or ought to push, beyond the nation-state and reveal empire itself as the site of conflict. However, just a brief look at Sklair's analysis would suggest that analysis based on nation-states is not necessarily reactionary, but reveals the important workings of states in relation to empire in their juridical and executive capacity and therefore offers the opportunity for theorizing resistance and alternatives within a national framework.

13. Naomi Klein's (2004) concept of 'Appointocracy' is useful for thinking about these political and economic processes.

14. Hardt and Negri also deploy Luxemburg arguing the primitive accumulation as a relation is exported in order to produce 'a social form that will breed or replicate itself' (2000: 226), and in this manner primitive accumulation contributes to the totalizing of the system.

15. For an opposing view of the threat of China, see Paul Hirst (2001).

16. This view is supported by Simon Bromley. He writes: 'China (and India) have a growing dependence on Middle East oil, and the largest expansion of oil consumption over the next several decades will be in Asia. On current trends, an increasing proportion of world oil exports will be accounted for by the Persian Gulf region, over one-half and perhaps as much as two-thirds by 2020. Maintaining influence in the Middle East, and countering the influence of Russia, China and Iran in Central Asia are thus becoming increasingly important elements in US thinking' (2003: 49).

Epilogue

1. Susan Willis (2003) notes how such risks are countered by state and corporate preparedness in the guise of massive information 'back up' systems. 'The field leader', Willis writes, 'is Iron Mountain, which operates 600 facilities worldwide, eight of them hundreds of feet underground. Like those of the shadow government, the company's facilities originated in the Cold War; the authorities apparently envisaged a need to save documents as well as people from Soviet attack' (65–6). Iron Mountain stores all major media including, paper, computer discs, microfiche, audio and video tapes.

2. The BBC, for example, have commissioned a new reality game show called 'Crisis management: Could you run the Country?' in which contestants take on the role of ministers. They are faced with a dramatization of a crisis and are asked to make decisions aimed at preventing a human and economic disaster. Their judgement is tested against that of crisis-management experts. The BBC notes that the programme is not intended 'to shock or frighten you. The intention is to provoke thought and awareness in a changing world' (www.bbc.co.uk/crisiscommand/).

Bibliography

Adorno, T. 'The Schema of Mass Culture', *The Culture Industry: Selected Essays in Mass Culture* (London: Routledge, 1991).

Adorno, T. and Horkheimer, M. *Dialectic of Enlightenment* (London: Verso, 1986).

Agamben, G. *Homo Sacer: Sovereign Power and Bare Life* (Stanford: Stanford University Press, 1998).

Agamben, G. *The Open: Man and Animal* (Stanford: Stanford University Press, 2004).

Agamben, G. *The State of Exception* (Chicago: The University of Chicago Press, 2005).

Ahmed, A. S. 'America and the Challenge of Islam', *The Hedgehog Review*, vol. 5, no. 1, Spring 2003, pp. 19–31.

Ali, T. *The Clash of Fundamentalisms* (London: Verso, 2002).

Alliez, É. and Negri, A. 'Peace and War', *Theory, Culture & Society*, vol. 20, no. 2, April 2003, pp. 107–18.

Arato, A. '*Minima Politica* after September 11', *Constellations* vol. 9, no. 1, 2002, pp. 46–52.

Arendt, H. *The Human Condition* (Chicago: The University of Chicago Press, 1958).

Arendt, H. 'Labour, Work, Action', in *Amour Mundi*, J. W. Bernauer (ed.) (Dordrecht: Martinus Nijhoff Publishers, 1987).

Arendt, H. *On Revolution* (London: Penguin, 1990).

Armitage, J. 'Paul Virilio: an Introduction', *Theory, Culture & Society*, vol. 16, nos 5–6, October–December 1999, pp.1–23.

Armitage, J. (ed.) *Virilio Live: Selected Interviews* (London: Sage Publications, 2001).

Arquilla, J. 'The Great Cyberwar of 2002', *Wired*, 6.02, February 1998.

Balakrishnan, G. *The Enemy: An Intellectual Portrait of Carl Schmitt* (London: Verso, 2000).

Barthes, R. *Image, Music, Text* (London: Fontana Press, 1977).

Bataille, G. *Visions of Excess: Selected Writings, 1927–1939* (Minneapolis, University of Minnesots Press, 1985).

Bataille, G. *The Accursed Share, Volume 1* (New York: Zone Books, 1988).

Bataille, G. *Theory of Religion* (New York: Zone Books, 1989).

Bataille, G. *The Accursed Share, Volumes 2 and 3* (New York: Zone Books, 1991).

Bataille, G. *Eroticism* (London: Penguin, 2001).

Baudrillard, J. *Simulations* (New York: Semiotext(e), 1983).

Baudrillard, J. *The Gulf War did not Take Place* (Sydney: Power Publications, 1995)

Baudrillard, J. *The Spirit of Terrorism* (London, Verso: 2002).

Bauman, Z. *Modernity and the Holocaust* (Cambridge: Polity Press, 1989).

Bauman, Z. *Modernity and Ambivalence* (Cambridge: Polity Press, 1991).

Bauman, Z. *Globalization and the Human Consequences* (Cambridge: Polity Press, 1998).

Beck, U. *Risk Society: Towards a New Modernity* (London: Sage Publications, 1992).

Beck, U. 'The Terrorist Threat: World Risk Society Revisited', *Theory, Culture & Society*, vol. 19, no. 4, August 2002, pp. 39–55.

Beck, U., Bonss, W. and Lan, C. 'The Theory of Reflexive Modernization: Problematic, Hypotheses and Research Programme', *Theory, Culture & Society*, vol. 20, no. 2, April 2003, pp. 1–34.

Benhabib, S. 'Unholy Wars', *Constellations*, vol. 9, no. 1, 2002, pp. 34–45.

Benjamin, W. 'The Work of Art in the Age of Mechanical Reproduction', *Illuminations* (London: Fontana Press, 1992).

Benjamin, W. *One-Way Street* (London: Verso, 1979).

Berkowitz, P. *Nietzsche: The Ethics of an Immoralist* (Cambridge, MA.: Harvard University Press, 1995).

Berman, P. *Liberalism and Terror* (New York: W. W. Norton, 2003).

Bhuta, N. 'A Global State of Exception? The United States and World Order', *Constellations*, vol. 10, no. 3, 2003, pp. 371–91.

Blackburn, R. 'The Imperial Presidency, the War on Terrorism, and the Revolutions of Modernity', *Constellations*, vol. 9, no. 1, 2002, pp. 3–33.

Boose, L. E. 'Techno-Muscularity and the "Boy Eternal": From the Quagmire to the Gulf', in *Gendering War Talk*, M. Cooke and A. Woollacott (eds) (Princeton: Princeton University Press, 1993).

Borradori, G. *Philosophy in a Time of Terror* (Chicago: Chicago University Press, 2003).

Bromley, S. 'Reflections on *Empire*, Imperialism and United States Hegemony', *Historical Materialism*, vol. 11, no. 3, 2003, pp. 17–68.

Brown, R. 'Spinning the War: Political Communications, Information Operations and Public Diplomacy in the War on Terrorism', in *War and the Media* D. K. Thussu and D. Freedman (eds) (London: Sage Publications, 2003).

Burston, J. 'War and the Entertainment Industries: New Research Priorities in an Era of Cyber-Patriotism', in *War and the Media*, D. K. Thussu and D. Freedman (eds) (London: Sage Publications, 2003).

Butler, J. *Precarious Life: The Powers of Mourning and Violence* (London: Verso, 2004).

Caillois, R. *Man and the Sacred* (Urbana: University of Illinois Press, 2001).

Caputo, J. D. *Demythologizing Heidegger* (Bloomington: Indiana University Press, 1993).

Casey, E. S. and Woody, M. J. 'Hegel, Heidegger, Lacan: The Dialectic of Desire' in *Interpreting Lacan: Psychiatry and the Humanities* vol. 6, J. H. Smith and W. Kerrigan (eds) (Minneapolis: University of Minnesota Press, 1983).

Castells, M. *The Power of Identity: The Information Age – Economy, Society and Culture: Vol. 2* (Oxford: Blackwell Publishers, 1997).

Center for Constitutional Rights. 'The State of Civil Liberties: One Year Later' (www.ccr-ny.org/reports/, 2002).

Cohn, C. 'Wars, Wimps, and Women: Talking Gender and Thinking War', in *Gendering War Talk*, M. Cooke and A. Woollacott (eds) (Princeton: Princeton University Press, 1993).

Cohn, C. 'Nuclear Language and How We Learned to Pat the Bomb', in *Feminism and Science*, E. F. Keller and H. E. Longino (eds) (Oxford: Oxford University Press, 1996).

Creel, G. *How We Advertised America: the First Telling of the Amazing Story of the Committee on Public Information that Carried the Gospel of Americanism to Every Corner of the Globe* (New York: Ayer Co. Publishers, 1972).

Curtis, N. *Against Autonomy: Lyotard, judgement and action* (Aldershot: Ashgate Publishing, 2001).

Debord, G. *Society of the Spectacle* (Rebel Press, 1987).

De Landa, M. *War in the Age of Intelligent Machines* (New York: Zone Books, 1991).

Deleuze, G. *Nietzsche and Philosophy* (London: Athlone Press, 1983).

Deleuze, G. and Guattari, F. *A Thousand Plateaus* (London: Athlone Press, 1988).

DeMartino, G. F. *Global Economy, Global Justice* (London: Routledge, 2000).

Der Derian, J. *Antidiplomacy: Spies, Terror, Speed and War* (Oxford: Blackwell Publishers, 1992).

Der Derian, J. *Virtuous War: Mapping the Military-Industrial-Media-Entertainment Network* (Boulder: Westview Press, 2001).

Derrida, J. *Politics of Friendship* (London: Verso, 1997).

Derrida, J. 'Hospitality, Justice and Responsibility: A Dialogue', *Questioning Ethics: Contemporary Debates in Philosophy*, R. Kearney and M. Dooley (eds) (London: Routledge, 1999).

Dillon, M. 'Network Society, Network-Centric Warfare and the State of Emergency', *Theory, Culture & Society*, vol. 19, no. 4, August 2002, pp. 71–9.

Dorfman, A. 'Open Letter to America', *The Observer*, 8 September 2002.

Downey, J. and Murdock, G. 'The Counter-Revolution in Military Affairs: The Globalization of Guerrilla Warfare', in *War and the Media*, D. K. Thussu and D. Freedman (eds) (London: Sage Publications, 2003).

Drury, S. B. *Leo Strauss and the American Right* (New York: St. Martin's Press, 1997).

Durkheim, E. *The Elementary Forms of Religious Life* (London: Simon and Schuster, 1995).

Eco, U. *Interpretation and Overinterpretation* (Cambridge: Cambridge University Press, 1992).

Elshtain, J. B. *Women and War* (Brighton: The Harvester Press, 1987).

Elshtain, J. B. 'Freud's Discourse of War/Politics', in *International/Intertextual Relations*, James Der Derian and Michael Shapiro (eds) (New York: Lexington Books, 1989).

Elshtain, J. B. *Just War Against Terror: The Burden of American Power in a Violent World* (New York: Basic Books, 2003).

Enloe, C. *Does Khaki Become You? The Militarization of Women's Lives* (London: Pandora Press, 1988).

Enloe, C. *Bananas, Beaches and Bases: Making Feminist Sense of International Politics* (Berkeley: University of California Press, 1989).

FAIR 'The Office of Strategic Influence is Gone, But are its Programs in Place?' www.fair.org/press-releases 27 November 2002.

Fanon, F. *Black Skin, White Masks* (London: Pluto Press, 1986).

Fanon, F. *The Wretched of the Earth* (London: Penguin Books, 1990).

Flahault, F. *Malice* (London: Verso, 2003).

Fogarty, B. E. *War, Peace and the Social Order* (Boulder: Westview Press, 2000).

Foucault, M. *The History of Sexuality: Volume 1* (London: Penguin Books, 1990).

Franco, P. *Hegel's Philosophy of Freedom* (New Haven: Yale University Press, 1999).

Freud, S. *New Introductory Lectures on Psychoanalysis, The Penguin Freud Library Volume 2* (London: Penguin, 1991a).

Freud, S. *On Metapsychology, The Penguin Freud Library Volume 11* (London: Penguin, 1991b).

Freud, S. *Civilization, Society and Religion, The Penguin Freud Library volume 12* (London: Penguin, 1991c).

Fried, G. *Heidegger's Polemos: From Being to Politics* (New Haven: Yale University Press, 2000).

Frost, B-P. 'A Critical Introduction to Alexandre Kojève's *Esquisse D'une Phénomenologie du droit*', *The Review of Metaphysics* 52, 1999, pp. 595–640.

Fukuyama, F. *The End of History and the Last Man* (London: Penguin, 1992).

Fukuyama, F. *Our Posthuman Future: Consequences of the Biotechnology Revolution* (London: Profile Books, 2003).

Fulbright, J. W. *The Pentagon Propaganda Machine* (New York: Vintage Books, 1971).

Fussell, P. *The Great War and Modern Memory* (Oxford: Oxford University Press, 1975).

Goldstein, J. S. *War and Gender* (Cambridge: Cambridge University Press, 2003).

Gourevitch, V. 'The End of History?', *Interpretation*, vol. 21, no. 2, pp. 293–306.

Gowan, P. 'Neoliberal Cosmoplitanism', *New Left Review*, 11, September 2001, pp. 79–93.

Graham, P. and Luke, A. 'Militarizing the Body Politic: New Mediations as Weapons of Mass Instruction', *Body & Society*, vol. 9, no. 4, 2003, pp. 149–68.

Gray, C. H. *Postmodern War: The New Politics of Conflict* (London: Routledge, 1997).

Gray, C. H. 'Posthuman Soldiers in Postmodern War', *Body & Society*, vol. 9, no. 4, 2003, pp. 215–26.

Gray, J. *Al Qaeda and What it Means to be Modern* (London: Faber and Faber, 2003).

Greenslade, R. 'Their Master's Voice', *The Guardian*, 17 February 2003.

Gupta, S. *The Replication of Violence: Thoughts on International Terrorism after September 11th 2001* (London: Pluto, 2002).

Habermas, J. *The Structural Transformation of the Public Sphere* (Cambridge: Polity Press, 1989).

Hall, S. 'Encoding/decoding', *Culture, Media, Language*, S. Hall, D. Hobson, A. Lowe, and P. Willis (eds) (London: Hutchinson, 1980).

Haraway, D. J. *Simians, Cyborgs and Women: The Reinvention of Nature* (London: Free Association Books, 1991).

Hardt, M. and Negri, A. *Empire* (Cambridge, MA: Harvard University Press, 2000).

Hardt, M. and Negri, A. *Multitude* (London: Hamish Hamilton, 2005).

Harvey, D. *The New Imperialism* (Oxford: Oxford University Press, 2003).

Hegel, G. W. F. *Philosophy of Right* (Oxford: Oxford University Press, 1967).

Hegel, G. W. F. *Phenomenology of Spirit* (Oxford: Oxford University Press, 1977).

Heidegger, M. *Being and Time* (Oxford: Basil Blackwell Ltd, 1962).

Heidegger, M. *Early Greek Thinking* (New York: Harper Collins, 1984).

Heidegger, M. *An Introduction to Metaphysics* (New Haven and London: Yale University Press, 1959).

Heidegger, M. *Phenomenological Interpretations of Aristotle* (Bloomington: Indiana University Press, 2001).

Heidegger, M. *Off the Beaten Track* (Cambridge: Cambridge University Press, 2002).

Heller, A. '9/11, or Modernity and Terror', *Constellations*, vol. 9, no. 1, 2002, pp. 53–65.

Heraclitus *Fragments*, trans. T. M. Robinson (Toronto: University of Toronto Press, 1987).

Hirst, P. *War and Power in the 21st Century* (Cambridge: Polity Press, 2001).

Hiltermann, J. R. 'America Didn't See to Mind Poison Gas', *International Herald Tribune*, 17 January 2003.

Hobbes, T. *Leviathan* (Indianapolis: Hackett Publishing, 1994).

Honderich, T. *After the Terror* (Edinburgh: Edinburgh University Press, 2002).

Honneth, A. *The Struggle for Recognition: The Moral Grammar of Social Conflicts* (Cambridge, Polity Press, 1995).

Howard. M. *War and the Liberal Conscience* (New Brunswick: Rutgers Universtiy Press, 1986).

Huntington, S. P. 'The Clash of Civilizations?', *Foreign Affairs*, vol. 72, no. 3, Summer 1993, pp. 22–49.

Huston, N. 'The Matrix of War: Mothers and Heroes', *The Female Body in Western Culture*, S. R. Suleiman (ed.) (Cambridge, MA: Harvard University Press, 1986).

Ihde, D. *Technology and the Lifeworld: From Garden to Earth* (Bloomington: Indiana University Press, 1990).

Irigaray, L. *Speculum of the Other Woman* (Ithaca: Cornell University Press, 1985).

Jameson, F. *A Singular Modernity* (London: Verso, 2002).

Jardine, A. A. *Gynesis: Configurations of Woman and Modernity* (Ithaca: Cornell University Press, 1985).

Jeffords, S. *The Remasculinization of America: Gender and the Vietnam War* (Bloomington: Indiana Univeristy Press, 1989).

Joas, H. *War and Modernity* (Cambridge: Polity Press, 2003).

Johnson, Richard 'Defending Ways of Life: The (Anti-) Terrorist Rhetorics of Bush and Blair', *Theory, Culture & Society*, vol. 19, no. 4, 2002, pp. 211–31.

Joxe, A. *Empire of Disorder* (New York and Los Angeles: Semiotext(e), 2002).

Kagan, R. 'Multilateralism, American Style', *The Washington Post*, 13 September 2002.

Kalyvas, A. 'Feet of Clay? Reflections on Hardt and Negri's *Empire*', *Constellations*, vol. 10, no. 2, 2003, pp. 264–79.

Kant, I. *Perpetual Peace and Other Essays* (Indianapolis, IA: Hackett Publishing Company, 1983).

Kaplan, R. D. *Warrior Politics: Why Leadership Demands a Pagan Ethos* (New York: Vintage Books, 2002).

Kaufman, W. *Nietzsche, Heidegger and Buber: Discovering the Mind vol. 2* (New Brunswick: Transaction, 1992).

Klein, N. 'Of Course the Whitehouse Fears Free Elections in Iraq', *The Guardian*, 24 January 2004.

Kojève, A. *Introduction to the Reading of Hegel* (Ithaca: Cornell University Press, 1980).

Lacan J. *Écrtis: A Selection* (London: Routledge, 1977a).

Lacan, J. *The Four Fundamental Concepts of Psychoanalysis* (London: Penguin, 1977b).

Lacoue-Labarthe, P. *Heidegger, Art and Politics: The Fiction of the Political* (Oxford: Blackwells, 1990).

Lala, M-C. 'The Hatred of Poetry in Georges Bataille's Writing and Thought', *Bataille: Writing the Sacred* (London: Routledge, 1995).

Laplanche, J. *Life and Death in Psychoanalysis* (Baltimore: Johns Hopkins University Press, 1976).

Lasch, C. *The Minimal Self: Psychic Survival in Troubled Times* (New York: W. W. Norton, 1985).

Laswell, H. D. *Propaganda Techniques in the World War* (New York: Alfred Knopf, 1927).

Losurdo, D. *Heidegger and the Ideology of War: Community, Death and the West* (New York: Humanities Press, 2001).

Locke, J. *The Second Treatise of Government* (Indianapolis: Bobbs-Merrill, 1952).

Löwith, K. *Martin Heidegger and European Nihilism* (New York: Columbia University Press, 1995).

Lyon, D. *Surveillance after September 11* (Cambridge: Polity Press, 2003).

Lyotard, J.-F. *Heidegger and 'the jews'* (Minneapolis: University of Minnesota Press, 1988a).

Lyotard, J.-F. *The Differend: Phrases in Dispute* (Minneapolis: University of Minnesota Press, 1988b).

MacIntyre, A. *After Virtue: A study in Moral Theory* (London: Duckworth, 1985).

Mann, M. *Incoherent Empire* (London: Verso, 2003).

Marcuse, H. *An Essay on Liberation* (Boston: Beacon Press, 1969).

Marcuse, H. *Eros and Civilization: A Philosophical Inquiry into Freud* (London: Routledge, 1998a).

Marcuse, H. *Technology, War and Fascism: The Collected Papers of Herbert Marcuse Volume 1* (London: Routledge, 1998b).

Marcuse, H. *Towards a Critical Theory of Society: The Collected Papers of Herbert Marcuse Volume 2* (London: Routledge, 2001).

Mattelart, A. *Mapping World Communication: War, Progress, Culture* (Minneapolis: University of Minnesota Press, 1994).

McMurtry, J. *Value Wars: The Global Economy versus the Life Economy* (London: Pluto Press, 2002).

McNeill, W. H. *The Pursuit of Power* (Chicago: University of Chicago Press, 1982).

McQuire, S. 'Blinded by the (Speed of) Light', *Theory, Culture & Society*, vol. 16, nos 5–6, October–December 1999, pp. 141–59.

Meier, H. *Carl Schmitt and Leo Straus: The Hidden Dialogue* (Chicago: Chicago University Press, 1995).

Meier, H. *The Lesson of Carl Schmitt: Four Chapters on the Distinction Between Political Theology and Political Philosophy* (Chicago: University of Chicago Press, 1998).

Melling, P. *Fundamentalism in America: Millennialism, Identity and Militant Religion* (Edinburgh: Edinburgh University Press, 1999).

Miladi, N. 'Mapping the Al-Jazeera Phenomenon', *War and the Media* D. K. Thussu and D. Freedman (eds) (London: Sage Publications, 2003).

Miles, H. *Al'Jazeera: How Arab TV Challenged the World* (London: Abacus, 2005).

Monbiot, G. 'Both Saviour and Victim', *The Guardian*, 29 January 2002.

Morris, R. 'A Tyrant Forty Years in the Making', *New York Times*, 14 March 2003.

Mumford, L. *The Pentagon of Power: The Myth of the Machine* (New York: Harcourt Press, 1964).

Nancy, J.-L. 'War, Right, Sovereignty – Technē', *Being Singular Plural* (Stanford: Stanford University Press, 2000).

Nietzsche, F. *The Will to Power* (New York: Vintage Books, 1968).

Nietzsche, F. *Thus Spoke Zarathustra* (London: Penguin, 1969).

Nietzsche, F. *The Gay Science* (New York: Vintage Books, 1974).

Nietzsche, F. *Ecce Homo* (London: Penguin, 1979).

Nietzsche, F. *Beyond Good and Evil* (London: Penguin, 1990).

Northcott, M. *An Angel Directs the Storm: Apocalyptic Religion and American Empire* (London: I. B. Tauris, 2004).

Norton, A. *Leo Strauss and the Politics of American Empire* (New Haven: Yale University Press, 2004).

Nye, J. S. *Soft Power: The Means to Success in World Politics* (New York: Public Affairs, 2004).

Palast, G. *The Best Democracy Money Can Buy* (London: Constable and Robinson, 2003).

Perle, R. 'Thank God for the Death of the UN', *The Guardian*, 21 March 2003.

Plato *The Symposium* (London: Penguin, 1951).

Plato *The Republic* (London: Penguin, 1955).

Ramonet, I. 'Final Edition for the Press', *Le Monde Diplomatique*, January 2005.

Ratner, M. and Ray, E. *Guantánamo: What the World Should Know* (White River Junction, VT: Chelsea Green Publishing, 2004).

Reardon, B. A. *Sexism and the War System* (New York: Teachers College Press, 1985).

Reid, T. 'How US Helped Iraq Build Deadly Arsenal', *The Times*, 31 December 2002.

Richardson, M. *Georges Bataille* (London: Routledge, 1994).

Riddell, R. 'Doom Goes to War', *Wired*, 5.04, April 1997.

Rose, G. *Mourning Becomes the Law: Philosophy and Representation* (Cambridge: Cambridge University Press, 1996).

Rose, J. *Why War? – Psychoanalysis, Politics and the Return to Melanie Klein* (Oxford: Blackwells, 1993).

Roth, M. S. 'A Problem of Recognition: Alexandre Kojève and the End of History', *History and Theory*, vol. 24, no. 3, 1985, pp. 293–306.

Rousseau, J-J. *The Social Contract* (London: Penguin Books, 2004).

Rowlands, M. 'Remembering to Forget: Sublimation as Sacrifice in War Memorials', in *The Art of Forgetting*, Forty, A. and Küchler, S. (eds) (Oxford: Berg, 1999).

Roy, A. *The Algebra of Infinite Justice* (London: Flamingo, 2002).

Ruddick, S. *Maternal Thinking: Towards a Politics of Peace* (London: The Women's Press, 1989).

Ruddick, S. 'Notes Towards a Feminist Peace Politics', in *Gendering War Talk*, M. Cooke and A. Woollacott (eds) (Princeton: Princeton University Press, 1993).

Rumsfeld, D. 'A New Kind of War', *New York Times*, 27 September 2001.

Said, E. *Orientalism* (London: Penguin, 2003).

Said, E. *From Oslo to Iraq and the Roadmap* (London: Bloomsbury, 2004).

Scarry, E. *The Body in Pain: The Making and Unmaking of the World* (Oxford: Oxford University Press, 1985).

Schmitt, C. *Political Theology: Four Chapters on the Concept of Sovereignty* (Cambridge, MA: MIT Press, 1985).

Schmitt, C. *The Concept of the Political* (Chicago: The University of Chicago Press, 1996).

Schrøder, K. C. 'Making Sense of Audience Discourses: Towards a Multidimensional Model of Mass Media Reception', *European Journal of Cultural Studies*, vol. 3, no. 2, May 2000, pp. 233–58.

Shapiro, M. 'Warring Bodies and Bodies Politic: Tribal versus State Societies', *Body & Society*, vol. 1, no. 1, 1995, pp.107–23.

Shaw, M. *War and Genocide* (Cambridge: Polity Press, 2003).

Simmel, G. 'The Meaning of Culture', in *George Simmel: Sociologist and European*, Peter Lawrence (ed.) (Sudbury-on-Thames: Nelson, 1976).

Simmel, G. 'The Crisis of Culture', in *Simmel on Culture*, David Frisby and Mike Featherstone (eds) (London: Sage Publications, 1997a).

Simmel. G. 'The Future of Culture', in *Simmel on Culture*, David Frisby and Mike Featherstone (eds) (London: Sage Publications, 1997b).

Sklair, L. *The Transnational Capitalist Class* (Oxford: Blackwells, 2001).

Smith, N. *American Empire: Roosevelt's Geographer and the Prelude to Globalization* (Berkeley: University of California Press, 2003).

Snow, N. *Information War: American Propaganda, Free Speech and Opinion Control since 9–11* (New York: Seven Stories Press, 2003).

Spinoza, B. *The Ethics* (New York: Dover Books, 1955).

Stromberg, R. N. *Redemption by War: The Intellectuals and 1914* (Lawrence: The Regents Press of Kansas, 1982).

Taylor, J. *Body Horror: Photojournalism, Catastrophe and War* (Manchester: Manchester University Press, 1998).

Taylor, P. M. *War and the Media: Propaganda and Persuasion in the Gulf War* (Manchester: Manchester University Press, 1992).

Taylor, P. M. *Munitions of the Mind* (Manchester: Manchester University Press, 1995).

Thussu, D. K. 'Live TV and Bloodless Deaths: War, Infotainment and 24/7 News', in *War and the Media*, D. K. Thussu and D. Freedman (eds) (London: Sage Publications, 2003).

Toulmin, S. *Cosmopolis: The Hidden Agenda of Modernity* (Chicago: The University of Chicago Press, 1990).

Tuman, J. S. *Communicating Terror: The Rhetorical Dimensions of Terrorism* (London: Sage Publications, 2003).

Tumber, H. and Palmer, J. *Media at War: The Iraq Crisis* (London: Sage Publications, 2004).

Van Loon, J. 'International Terrorism as a Nomadic War Machine: Reflections on the Collapse of the World Trade Centre and its Aftermath', *Space and Culture*, issue 11/12, December 2001, pp. 173–6.

Van Loon, J. *Risk and Technological Culture: Towards a Sociology of Virulence* (London: Routledge, 2002).

Vattimo, G. *The End of Modernity* (Cambridge: Polity Press, 1988).

Venn, C. 'World Dis/Order: On Some Fundamental Questions', *Theory, Culture & Society*, vol. 19, no. 4, August 2002, pp. 121–36.

Verkaik, R. and Grice, A. 'Law Lords Condemn Blunkett's Terror Measures', *The Guardian*, 17 December 2004.

Vickers, J. *Women and War* (London: Zed Books, 1993).

Virilio, P. *Speed and Politics* (New York: Semiotext(e), 1986).

Virilio, P. *War and Cinema: The Logistics of Perception* (London: Verso, 1989).

Virilio, P. *Desert Screen: War at the Speed of Light* (London: Athlone Press, 2002).

Virilio, P. *Ground Zero* (London: Verso, 2002).

Virilio, P. and Lotringer, S. *Pure War* (New York: Semiotext(e), 1997).

Virno, P. *A Grammar of the Multitude* (New York: Semiotext(e), 2004).

Watier, P. 'The War Writings of Georg Simmel', *Theory, Culture & Society*, vol. 8, no. 3, 1991, pp. 219–33.

Watkins, S. 'Vichy on the Tigris', *New Left Review*, vol. 28, July–August 2004, pp. 5–17.

Weber, C. 'The Media, the "War on Terrorism", and the Circulation of Non-Knowledge', in *War and the Media*, D. K. Thussu and D. Freedman (eds) (London: Sage Publications, 2003).

Webster, F. 'Information Warfare in an Age of Globalization', in *War and the Media* D. K. Thussu and D. Freedman (eds) (London: Sage Publications, 2003).

Williams, R. *Hegel's Ethics of Recognition* (Berkeley and Los Angeles: University of California Press, 1997).

Willis, S. 'Empire's Shadow', *New Left Review*, 22, July 2003, pp. 59–70.

Wood, E. M. *Empire of Captial* (London: Verso, 2003).

Žižek, S. *Welcome to the Desert of the Real* (London: Verso, 2002).

Žižek, S. *Iraq: The Borrowed Kettle* (London: Verso, 2004).

Index